Morgan Odell

Lewis and Clark College
1954

The Republic

and

The Person

A Discussion of

Necessities in Modern American Education

The Republic

and

The Person

A Discussion of

Necessities in Modern American Education

GORDON KEITH CHALMERS

HENRY REGNERY COMPANY

CHICAGO • 1952

HENRY REGNERY COMPANY

Chicago 4, Illinois

Manufactured in the United States of America

For Robert Frost

Acknowledgments

CHAPTER 2 has appeared substantially in its present form in *School and Society;* Chapter 17, in the *American Scholar;* and shorter passages of this book, in the *Virginia Quarterly*, the *Association of American Colleges Bulletin*, and bulletins of Kenyon College, the College English Association, the Social Science Foundation of the University of Denver, and the Newcomen Society; and in a volume, *Liberal Education after the War*, published by the Princeton University Press.

Grateful acknowledgment is made to the authors and publishers for permission to reprint certain passages from the following publications:

Broomsticks by Walter de la Mare, copyrighted in 1925 by Alfred A. Knopf, Inc., *Education for* All *American Youth*, copyrighted by The Educational Policies Commission; "General Education in a Free Society," Report of the Harvard Committee, Harvard University Press, copyrighted in 1945 by the President and Fellows of Harvard College; "The Left: End and Beginning" by Max Lerner, February 10, 1940, copyrighted by *The Nation;* "The Irresponsibles" by Archibald MacLeish, May 18, 1940, copyrighted by *The Nation; John of Barneveld* by John Lothrop Motley, copyrighted in 1900 by Harper & Brothers; "The Corruption of Liberalism" by Lewis Mumford, April 29, 1940, *New Republic*, copyrighted by Westbury Publications, Inc.; *The Sixteenth Century* by Sir Charles Oman, copyrighted in 1937 by E. P. Dutton and Company, Inc.; "A Reply to Mr. Evans," July 2, 1949, copyrighted by *The Saturday Review of Literature;* "A Definition of the Humanities" by Ralph Barton Perry, in *The Meaning of the Humanities*, copyrighted in 1938 by Princeton University Press; *Report on Prelegal Education* by the Hon. Arthur T. Vanderbilt, American Bar Association; *Liberal Education* by Mark Van Doren, copyrighted in 1943 by Henry Holt & Company, Inc.

Table of Contents

The Republic

and

The Person

I

Introduction

THE LATE William Allan Neilson, speaking at the 1940 commencement at Kenyon College, told the graduates that his generation of university professors and presidents had been guilty of wrapping the young in romantic cotton wool. Much school and university teaching in the 1950's continues to do the same. Years ago it hardly seemed to matter that American thinking was sentimental. Now, it is clear that such thinking will throw in jeopardy the world, our self-respect, and our safety. We can no longer afford leaders, thinkers, and voters in any large number who delude themselves or think irresponsibly.

The leadership of American education in the period between the world wars has generally been regarded as "liberal," and brief examination will reveal that not only the temper and vocabulary, but the announced aim of schools, colleges, and universities in the 1920's and 1930's endeavored to promote the "liberal" view of national life and policy. In many quarters American thought has toughened and matured since 1940, but not in the statement of the aims of education. If the more influential of such current statements continue to preside over general instruction in this country, we shall continue to promote, in the decade of integrated Russian despotism, the same sentimentalism which bedeviled and confused us in 1940 and which in 1942 and 1943 cost us dearly.

Speaking of the aim and temper of college education, President Neilson quoted from *The City of Man*, a book on which he had collaborated, the opinion of numerous intellectual leaders that the liberalism which they had taught and promoted in the Twenties and Thirties was in important particulars established not on ethical fact but on sentiment. It was, said the authors of that volume, a "disintegrated liberalism." They stated that the illusions of the Thirties had produced a timidity and lack of conviction in many Americans concerning the true character of the Nazis and their threat to democracy. One may add that they also produced a romanticized notion of the true nature of the Communists. This sentimentalism was directly traceable to the ethical ignorance of persons thought to be learned. Many of these later admitted that the university world had persuaded the young that evil itself, extensive and malignant, does not exist; that various explanations and terminologies can lead us to utopias both public and private; that statistics and organizations will set up the alabaster cities "undimmed by human tears." This book will endeavor to state what is required to reorient the aims of American teaching and learning if it is to promote responsible American liberalism of a kind adequate to meet our obligations abroad and at home.

Much is connoted by the phrase *responsible American liberalism*—taste, belief, affection, opinion, a whole standard of life, a whole conception of humanity. It is first of all a political principle, most simply stated by saying that all provision for order and common welfare must not only avoid violating the rights of the individual but must positively serve the maximum opportunity for the individual to exercise his civil rights. Such liberalism is responsible not only to the people but to justice and right. It can be so only if based on a reliable account of human nature. This ethical basis of responsible American liberalism is now emphasized by a political issue—our dispute with the Kremlin. Observing the terms of that dispute we can readily see what lies at the center of the American idea of freedom.

At the center will always be found a philosophical proposition about the individual: that he is valuable and subject to law within himself. This basic idea has been challenged in every century. The challenge today is peculiar only in the potential military weight which lies behind it; for if we are to believe what we read of Russian philosophy, avowals of Russian policy, and recent Russian performance, the Soviets officially hold that the individual is not valuable except as a servant of the state and that there is no law within, only expediency. Philosophically, America now stands in much the same relation to our enemy as in 1940. It is not the nature but the nationality of the enemy which has changed—from German to Russian; and our national life is still organized to prevent, if possible, the destruction of the opportunity for the liberal idea of the individual to operate.

The individual is important and subject within himself to law. We know this proposition in two ways: by dogma, and by critical judgment of the facts. Our dogmatic knowledge is not to be taken lightly. The Christian Church teaches the proposition as a delivered doctrine; so does Judaism. Americans once stated it in secular terms: "We hold these truths to be self-evident, that all men . . . are endowed by their Creator with certain unalienable Rights, that among these are Life, Liberty, and the pursuit of Happiness." In a religious spirit we repeat that affirmation of faith, and here the slogan of the Independence Day orator and the dogma of the church agree.

Dogmas and slogans have their proper place, deserve respect, and are usually effective. They share, however, a common weakness: that with changing times and shifts of language our understanding of them will change. "O Liberty! how many crimes are committed in thy name!" It was of dogmas and slogans that the popular semanticists were thinking when they proposed that all language is notably ambiguous. If as a nation we should become so ignorant that we lacked the information on which a critical estimate of the nature of the individual is based, we should, of course, hold the conception of his value and his responsibility only in dogmatic terms. By that time we should have lost the live idea altogether, for dogmas and slogans have proved themselves for centuries too unsteady, too variable in their connotations, decade to decade, when not corrected, analyzed, and interpreted—in other words, kept alive—by critical thought. Thus, valuable and useful as are the Christian and the Jewish doctrines about the individual, and cherished as our patriotic slogans may be, their meanings would change on our lips if left unexamined for twenty years by critical knowledge and intelligence.

Human nature is such that, except by a few rare persons, the examination of operative beliefs in politics, morals, and religion is put off until they are not only challenged but threatened. For vast numbers of highly educated Americans the only source of the ethical basis of democracy today is a dogmatic one. One entitled by his studies and observations to know whereof he speaks recently remarked, apropos of the increasing complacency toward crime, that the dignity of man is an idea to which in general he has observed nothing more impressive than lip service.

To make sure that the "self-evident" truths will be understood as well as reiterated dogmatically is the necessary national task of education. The question is not only, Will these truths be understood? Their truth has been more precious to many Americans than life itself. They are present virtues, active and alive, not holy relics. How may the minds of young men and women find them really alive, now, and for themselves? The pragmatic, inductive, and positive methods of dealing with experience for the classroom learning of most American young people must refrain from reliance on religious dogma. But the belief involved here is not only the dogmatic belief with which churches deal, it is pre-eminently a critical belief, of the kind proper to schools.

The mystery of education eludes all description, but one fact is revealed by comparisons: given an alert young person, it will make a world of difference who teaches him. Anyone who is responsible for choosing teachers, and who perhaps in a small way influences their work, senses how effective are his own ideas about the end of the whole endeavor of teaching and learning. You cannot be party to fixing a school budget or selecting college trustees or outlining legislative appropriations without observing all down the line—through the decisions of college president, school superintendent, dean, chairman of department, and instructor—the direct bearing of a single guiding idea upon what school or college will do to the student. What should that single guiding idea be? What does the subtle and complex enterprise called education really intend to achieve? The child starts off with his new red book on a strap, and formal learning has begun. To what end?

This book is written in the belief that for American teaching and learning in the middle of the twentieth century the question, "to what end?" has not been adequately assessed either for the country or for the individual. At the outset it will consider the following circumstances: In the thinking of those who have announced the aims of the educational system, preoccupation with immediate social problems has obscured and neglected the teaching and learning necessary to an understanding of individual man. The general object of education has become more and more to condition the mass attitude toward specific social improvements, and enthusiasm for these reforms has diverted energy from the ancient and central task of converting the reason—of converting it from the knowledge and love of what is mean to the knowledge and love of what is worthy. While the second war taught political and literary thinkers something of the importance of a critical and responsible view of the individual, educational thinking has not, on the whole, benefited by this lesson, and the statements of the aims of school and college now in favor continue in the illusions about human nature so prevalent in the pre-war period.

To meet the present challenge not simply to democracy, but to its ethical basis, it is necessary for education to execute a reversal of thinking analogous to the changes in literary and political thinking occasioned by the war. In sum, these changes amount to an abandonment of the disintegrated or sentimental liberalism of the pacifist and appeasement era, and the adoption of an ethical liberalism based on critical knowledge of the nature of individual man. Only if taught with such ends in view may young Americans achieve a reasoned, as distinguished from a dogmatic, affirmation of the value of the individual and his responsibility. The knowledge which makes possible this affirmation should stand at the center of common education in order that we may maintain our conception of what free government truly is and in order to equip us for the greatness, both personal and national, which is demanded of us by the times.

The proper study of Americans is liberty. The first four chapters of this book show why in school and college the center of this study is the understanding of persons. Chapters 5 through 15 suggest what this proposition requires in the curriculum and manner of studies; Chapters 15 through 18 deal with some eminent statements of the aim of education now influential, and show the practical and working difference between the application of such statements and the view proposed by this book—that our central aim ought to be the understanding of man, his nature, and place.

> There are two laws discrete
> Not reconciled,—
> Law for man, and law for thing;
> The last builds town and fleet,
> But it runs wild,
> And doth the man unking.

The presiding educational theories to be discussed in this book have a human sound. They are kindly, peaceable, and humanitarian, but in fact all but one are conceived and applied as parts of the law for thing. This book sets out to show why education, though preoccupied with both laws, should be directed at its center to ends indicated by the law for man and to suggest what is necessary if such direction is to become effective.

2

Disintegrated and Responsible Liberalism

WAR, which sifts out the hearts of men and brings many to their finest hour by leading them to deeds magnanimous beyond imagining, refines men's thinking as well. Its ferocity shocks them into moments of clarity and perception above their ordinary powers. American thinking in the 1930's had been dominated by wishes which were taken for facts. War made us drop them in a hurry. The illusions we deserted had blinded us to the simple issue between freedom and the lack of it. What were the illusions, and in what way was education involved with them?

In general, the movement of which President Wilson was the exponent progressed a long way from 1915 to 1935. It brought us from a wilful ignorance of world affairs to a widespread study of them and a growing belief that our own prosperity is bound up with the peace of the world. But much of our internationalism was romantic. Temporary reliance upon military strength in the first war was quickly displaced by a hope that agreements alone would suffice. It was thought that the Parliament of Man could be achieved by committees. In the 1920's the favored agencies of peace were the League of Nations, the Disarmament Conferences, and the World Court. While America slowly and painfully renounced isolationism, American writers and other leaders fell victim of the sentimental view that all nations would listen to reason, and that reasonableness, represented by protocols, treaties, conferences, and courts with "moral" power only, would prevail if only sufficiently reasonable.

As the second war approached, our sentimentality produced two errors: a mistaken idea of the totalitarian states; and an erroneous belief that however tyrannical they were, they would not seriously threaten us. The sentimentalism in America was shared by many "conservatives" and many "liberals." Some isolationists were simply living in the pre-air, pre-schnorkel age; some "liberals" were living in the golden and impossible future. Many American noninterventionists held with Prime Minister Chamberlain that the interest of the United States as well as Britain would be served if Hitler could be turned against Stalin, in the hope that they would exhaust each other. The reference to "liberal" thinking about the war in these pages involves neither the isolationists nor the noninterventionists; these enter the discussion only at the point where the opinion of some led them to praise and recommend the Fascists and the Nazis. What follows deals almost entirely with the self-styled "liberals," because the leading theories proposed to guide the educational system belonged in their territory of thought and feeling.

Many an American "liberal" failed in the 1930's to analyze correctly the tyrannies in Germany, Italy, and Russia. In general, also, they failed to look closely enough at the lust for conquest in these governments, and to weigh probable results. As early as the 1920's, one independent American philosopher had said that our chief concern with Russia should lie in the fact that she was potentially a great military power. His was a lone voice, derided and abused. Unlike his, much American "liberal" thought in those days was not thought at all but a system of hopes. So strong were its hopes for communism that it believed Utopia would soon arrive in Moscow.

To a degree the second war has corrected these errors, for leading liberal thought now acknowledges the real character of

Russian communism and holds with the United Nations that behind the open discussion of international questions and the effort to make reason prevail there must be sanctions, not only economic but military. The sentimental pacifism of the first postwar period may have been echoed for a brief and hopeful time when One World appeared to some a possibility. But the One-World dream for the immediate future has vanished and with it the idea that liberties may be won or maintained without the willingness and ability to take up arms. The United Nations has already served many mighty purposes, one of the most important of which has been to bring into the open rather swiftly the fundamental dispute of the world and to show forth the ideas as well as the armies and the censorships which truly divide it. The survival of the U.N. will depend, of course, upon its ability to meet the common condition of survival on this planet, which may be described as the ability to treat realistically at one and the same time both ideas and physical force. In the 1920's there was talk about an international police force, but how remote from reality the talk then sounded! Few dared imagine at San Francisco in 1945 that such talk, there revived, would result by 1950 in the flying of the United Nations flag over armies fighting to defend half the world from totalitarian aggression.

War is always a prideful thing, and undoubtedly we were guilty of pride in fighting this last one, but of less pride, I believe, than heretofore. Our purposes were much more humble than those announced in our slogans of 1917–18. There was no expectation that we were going to end wars. We did not imagine that we were going to establish democracy. True, President Wilson had merely said, "to make the world safe for democracy," but in reiterating his ringing words we imagined for ourselves that distant lands would be made so safe for it that democracy would shortly spring up as in a protected garden. A few years after that, when the League of Nations appeared less and less effectual, H. G. Wells announced that his disappointment in the peace was so profound that he had decided that the war had been fought in vain. G. K. Chesterton replied that the trouble was not with the war but with Mr. Wells. The British fought the war, said Chesterton, for one simple purpose: to stop the Germans. To make a peace and construct a free Europe was the task of the postwar governments and peoples. Mr. Wells was, in effect, overvaulting in his expectation of results from the first war; and so were we.

During the second war we set humbler goals for ourselves: to stop the spread of totalitarianism and break its power at Rome, Berlin, and Tokyo. Here our expectations of the fighting itself came to an end. Our slogans, songs, and wartime speeches, on the whole, avoided romantic idealism. Mr. Roosevelt and Mr. Churchill have been bitterly accused of pretending in the Atlantic Charter that we could grasp the moon, and it is undoubtedly true that the charter inspired false hope in the breasts of many peoples. However, I question whether the effect of the charter on American editors, clergymen, and other popular leaders was so extensive as was that of the World War I slogan, war to end war.

What we said in the Broadway plays of World War II and the films that followed them, what we said in the editorials and from the pulpits, was that the evils of dictatorship are everywhere implicit in men's thoughts; that they have blazed forth time and again to consume the urbane and the civilized; that because of them fascism and nazism were putting out the lights in the capitals of Europe. No mammoth searching of the soul is performed to perfection, but this confession and self-review was well supported in this country. We need not boast of it, except to remark that it was better expressed and better received than might have been thought possible.

How sentimental had we been between the wars? One could observe refusal to face the moral facts at all levels, from the man in the street to the scholar and the specialist. In 1938 some American students were talking about the coming war. "When the war comes, they won't find me." "Where'll you be?" "I'm going to get a sailboat and hide in the South Pacific."

As late as 1942 one heard generally the view that the war was another round in the contest of competing imperialisms. At the Harvard commencement of 1941 the twenty-five-year class met at one side of the Yard to make speeches urging us to get into the fight; at the other side a large meeting sponsored by undergraduates reiterated that the struggle was really a contest between the fascists and the capitalists and no concern of the people. At about the same time a symposium of students from many colleges contained the opinion of an undergraduate editor that he would rather "deal with Hitler in his own economic terms" than "rot in some far-off battlefield, or return home maimed and neurotic."

This was the period of *The Wave of the Future*, written by a brilliant young graduate of one of the foremost liberal colleges. In 1941 that dangerous little book was voted by a poll of schoolteachers to be the book of the year. Its theme was that fascism is the wave of the future; Hitler and Mussolini have leapt upon it; and if we are smart we Americans will do the same. As if to illustrate the proposition of *The City of Man*, *The Wave of the Future* appeared a few months after the confession that the university world had been promoting a "disintegrated liberalism."

The naïveté of American thinking which persisted into 1942 had had a lively interbellum history. In 1931 the British Government, mindful of the pacifism of the British and the American voters, declined to follow Secretary Stimson's suggestion that jointly they and we stop the Japanese occupation of Manchuria, then just beginning. In 1935 Congress refused to fortify Guam lest we offend the Japanese. In the same period that students at Oxford, Cambridge, and other British universities solemnly resolved never to fight for king and country, ten thousand clergymen, editors, and other American leaders solemnly swore they would never support our taking up arms.

How most of these editors, clergymen, Congressmen, and students reversed themselves in the late 1930's! Yet many retained their promiscuous and uncritical good will to the end of the decade. Consider, for example, the following passage from Robert A. Dahl's *Congress and Foreign Policy*, published in 1950 by the Yale Institute of International Studies:

> In a poll taken before war broke out in Europe in 1939, the Society for the Psychological Study of Social Issues found that only half the social scientists in the United States thought an increase in the size of the armed forces was desirable—whereas 75 per cent of the public gave its approval. In retrospect it seems clear that the social scientists were making a policy choice less rationally adapted to achieving their preferences than was the general public. Accelerated rearmament was, as it turned out, a necessary means to securing preferences that were probably shared widely by social scientists and the public at large. But it seems evident that social scientists permitted their interpretations and forecasts of international politics, their pictures of reality, to be seriously influenced by their inner wishes for peace.[1]

The present chapter is not directly concerned with the political wisdom or unwisdom of American decisions at the beginning of World War II, but rather with the sentimental thinking which confused the issues and stayed our hand as with a palsy. The chapter is not even concerned with the whole source of this confusion, but with one important part of it, our sentimental liberalism. Consideration of it enters into this book on the aims of education today because the temper and purpose of much school and college teaching then, and of much institutional development, contributed to our dangerous illusions. No one illustration of that fact will prove it, and it is possible to quarrel with each example proposed in this chapter. Those, however, who have been in close touch with the academic world for the three decades following 1920 are aware of the immense and complicated involvement of the liberalism of the higher learning with some of the sentimental assumptions concerning human nature which went a long way toward producing the confused thought about political issues here noticed.

In 1940, Lewis Mumford called the liberal thinking of the period "pragmatic liberalism." The pacifism of the time was related to this. It was pragmatic pacifism. When it proved unlikely to work it was abandoned for a principle brought forth by the pressure that demands action instead of philosophy. The pragmatic pacifism which was displaced is to be distinguished from the ethical pacifism of the Quakers. No ethical pacifist will abandon his principles because of any ten- or twenty-year failure to get results.

American and British popular pacifism and our friendly interest in dictatorship for other peoples ("Mussolini made the trains run on time") were related in some fashion to the critical discussions of the intellectuals. Some of the relationship was doubtless coincidental, but much of it was causal. The historical fact is that during the Twenties and Thirties when popular thought was so weakened by sentimentality about the enemies of peace and freedom, men of letters, philosophers, and others interested primarily in ideas were announcing principles which countenanced and even supported the pacifism and complacency of popular thought.

The underlying sanction of pacifism lay in the widespread conviction among thoughtful Americans that evil does not really exist in individuals, but arises only because of bad arrangements among them. Jean Jacques Rousseau was recollected and quoted in his numerous avowals that all souls are beautiful and, if let alone by society, good. The almost unanimous affection for bolshevism among advanced thinkers of the period arose from this opinion about morals rather than from economic principles. The natural goodness of the Russian worker was to be given its chance by the social arrangements outlined by Karl Marx. The idealism in the *Communist Manifesto* appeared to Christians a practical way to express the commandment to love one's neighbor as one's self; affection for the Russians became with some a religious faith.

Although some liberals of the Twenties and Thirties understood the true position of democracy during this period when the two totalitarianisms were crowding it from the right and the left, most of the weight of liberal thought was on the left, and promoted the idea that there are not three major principles of government in the modern world, but only two—fascism and communism. The old-fashioned and thriving American democracy was little mentioned in the discussions of the time.

The gathering war is nothing but a rivalry of competing imperialisms—so went one line of liberal reasoning. Suppose you did not object to imperialism. It was only natural to conclude in 1940 that Hitler, with his superior air force and highly organized country, was the man with whom to do business, even on his own terms. Fascism was the wave of the future. On the other side of the dispute, those who hated American capitalism called it fascism and debated whether to love Trotsky or Stalin.

In 1940 there occurred a dramatic renunciation. Assisted no doubt by the Hitler-Stalin pact, it was concentrated in the seventy-fifth anniversary number of the New York *Nation*, in which some of the brilliant essayists, publicists, and men of letters who had been writing for that able journal for many years announced that they had been wrong about Russia. Russia—that is, the ethical theories for which Russian bolshevism and communism had stood in the world for two decades—had been for these men and women a major preoccupation. But they had been wrong, they said. Moscow was not on the way to Utopia as they had thought. It was, or soon became when the revolution was consummated, a dictatorship not unlike, except in its professions, the dictatorship of that young socialist, Mussolini.

Besides its lack of confidence in itself, its unwillingness openly to oppose the Nazis, its adherence to the united front and to Stalin, and its diffidence about American and British democracy, the liberalism of the 1930's had the following characteristics: It held that men are rational, that the passions can be ignored, that progress will immediately follow if people are shown the reasonable thing to do. Many a liberal believed that Voltaire and Rousseau were correct in assigning the evils of the world entirely to priests and bad social arrangements and that the utilitarian thinkers of the industrial revolution were correct in assigning them to failure of production and distribution. Most liberals believed that, to be effective, reasoning should be "scientific." "The defects of liberalism," said Lewis Mumford in 1940, "are not due to isolated mistakes of judgment that individual liberals have made; they are due to fatal deficiencies that go to the very roots of liberal philosophy."[2] These deficiencies he named: chiefly the lack of "any true insight into these stubborn facts of human experience–corruption, evil, irrational desire." Max Lerner at about the same time wrote:

> The concepts and stereotypes on the left have too long clung to the eighteenth- and nineteenth-century belief in an ordered universe where men have only to discover the principles of order and then call upon their fellows to enact them. . . . Our efforts toward the reconstruction of the societies in which men live will have to take account of the whole person and not just half of him; of the fact that he is governed by passions, fears, and myths as well as by interests and ideals.[3]

The liberalism of the Thirties, which of all movements of thought in our country was the one most concerned with the meaning of free government and free opinion, frequently boasted that it was "confused." The confusion, the diffidence, and notably the embarrassment at any spiritual association with the old-fashioned American freedom arose out of severe determination to be rational about something sentimental; that is, to apply with utter logic a romantic version of brotherly love. Small wonder the "liberals" were confused. The air was rancid with the smoke of unexamined feelings. A few weeks before the bombing of Rotterdam, Mr. Mumford wrote:

> That there are modes of insight into man and into the cosmos which science does not possess, the liberal did not suspect; he took for granted that the emotional and spiritual life of man needs no other foundation than the rational, utilitarian activities associated with getting a living. Hence, finally, liberalism's progressive neglect of the fields of esthetics, ethics, and religion.[4]

American intellectual history for 1940–42 should be called "The Ordeal of the Confused." What brought a degree of clarity was war.

Besides the sentimental liberalism of the eighteenth and nineteenth centuries responsible for the errors mentioned above, there is an older tradition of freedom implicit in our own instruments of government which is based upon an ethical conception of the individual. Its chief characteristics are a critically derived belief in the dignity of a person and a conception of impersonal law designed to guarantee him justice. As the Constitution, the Bill of Rights, and the early decisions of the Supreme Court notably record, this responsible American liberalism is concerned with restraints as well as independence, and it sets above all social values—above wealth, security, and comfort of the creature—civil rights. This old spirit of liberty, which has brought forth every constitutional democracy, has never lost its understanding of individual failure. It trusts not the wild, undisciplined, "emancipated" man, but the man aware of his own failings and dependent on something more abiding and higher than himself. This responsible liberalism understands that community cannot be produced by natural human gregariousness; indeed, that the inevitable consequence of human association at the animal level is murder and rapine. Community, it knows, arises from holding communion—common respect and admiration for that abiding and higher something with which each man may communicate.

This being true, responsible American liberalism is no mere negative, no mere absence of restraint; it is rightly said to "have a pattern of its own." This pattern requires it to respect all men but to understand that they are men, not heavenly angels: that is, not utterly rational creatures universally endowed with utterly good will. Understanding the beast in us as well as the angel, responsible American liberalism understands that when it faces organized bestiality it must be strong not only in will and mind but also in armor. One of its notable qualities is acumen, and it judges among proposed associations, friendships, and enmities, distinguishing between economic, military, and other marriages of convenience on the one hand, and alliances of the spirit on the other. It may at times and temporarily find it necessary to make use of the former, but it never confuses them with the latter. To this old liberalism which made the constitutional democracies, tyranny is the ultimate abasement; aggressive, expanding tyranny within its own shores or abroad, the primary menace.

In 1940, Mr. Mumford addressed a large and important group of American thinkers and writers who were victims of an intellectual illusion. They were friendly in spirit, humanitarian, and convinced of the natural goodness and innocence of all men not deflected from their primitive rightness by convention and social machinery. From this romantic sentimentalism of systematic thinking, he recalled American thought to the central liberalism which relies entirely upon men's ability to know themselves and to find in manhood at its best that paradox of freedom and restraint which makes possible the guarantee of political liberties. He spoke to the political and social thinkers of the time and demanded a reversal of opinion.

While France was falling in 1940, men of letters were being asked to execute a similar reversal of opinion. The American poet, Archibald MacLeish, demanded the change in an eloquent piece of writing entitled "The Irresponsibles." He noticed that "Intellectuals in America and elsewhere—writers, scientists, the men of learning . . . have pretended to themselves that the burning of books, the exiling of artists, the invention of mythologies were merely incidents, afterthoughts, decorations: that the true crisis was the crisis of food, the crisis of arms, the crisis created by political forces, by economic collapse; that they had, and needed to have no truck with it."[5] "The scholar in letters has made himself as indifferent to values, as careless of significance, as bored with meanings as the chemist. He is a refugee from consequences, an exile from the responsibilities of moral choice.

His words of praise are the laboratory words—objectivity, detachment, dispassion. His pride is to be scientific, neuter, sceptical, detached—superior to final judgment or absolute belief."[6]

Mr. MacLeish described a similar romanticism in the writers of his generation:

> The writer's irresponsibility is no less. Where the modern scholar escapes from the adult judgments of the mind by taking the disinterested man of science as his model, the modern writer escapes by imitation of the artist. . . . His devotion, as with every honest painter, is devotion to the thing observed, the actual thing, the thing without its consequences or its antecedents, naked of judgment, stripped of causes and effects. The invisible world, the intellectual world, the world of relation of ideas, the world of judgments, of values, the world in which truth is good and lies are evil—this world has no existence for the honest artist or the honest writer who takes the artist for his model.[7]

The fault which Mr. MacLeish found with the writers of his generation is really the fault of naturalism, the assumption that the human nature with which most writing deals is essentially the physical nature appropriately observed by the ear, eye, nose, and the other organs of sensation. Of the typically contemporary writer who thinks of himself as one thinks of a painter, Mr. MacLeish says: "If he concerns himself with motive at all he concerns himself with the 'real' motive, meaning the discreditable motive which the actor conceals from himself. His most searching purpose is to find, not the truth of human action, but the low-down, the discreditable explanation which excuses him from care."[8]

It is true that America has been blessed with poets and novelists of great accomplishment, who consistently, from their earliest books, have been preoccupied with the war in the cave, the private warfare in a man's own breast between the fair and the foul. Robert Frost's name leads all the rest. Willa Cather's; Thornton Wilder's: in some of his stories and in *For Whom the Bell Tolls,* Ernest Hemingway's; in his criticism and poems,

Mark Van Doren's, to name a few, belong in the procession. Some of these before the first war and consistently for three decades have expressed the delicate and subtle nature of responsibility in letters.

"The disputes of the flute players" are usually more elaborate than those of the political philosophers. Never is the question of morals and letters raised without the implication or the statement that moral poetry means nothing else than poetry with a moral or precept. It seems difficult for the disputants to observe that a poem is moral if it tells the truth about men, whatever it may be, the purest examples being the tragedies of the ancients or of Shakespeare.

During the 1930's the dispute among poets, novelists, and playwrights was deflected from its literary and ethical terms by the political thinking of the time. A moral writer was thought to be a writer with a social cause, and the phrase "moral writer" became equated in some circles with "party-line writer." Communists were called moral because they wrote their stories in order to turn the world to communism. In reaction, a group who tried to assert literary value as distinguished from party propaganda began reviving the old slogan of Oscar Wilde: "Art for art's sake." If one should name but two camps among the literary faddists of the 1930's, they would be the so-called "moralists" who followed the party line, and the aestheticists, who held that form is everything, that content is nil, and that a work of art is responsible to nothing but its own shape.

An allied fad showed itself in philosophy. For some years after the first war American and British thought had entangled its feet in epistemology, the science of how and in what terms we may know. In the Thirties, thanks to the vogue of Professor I. A. Richards, there was great talk about meaning. At the popular fringe, Korzybski and Hayakawa became famous for the so-called science of semantics. Semantics is, of course, an old and honorable study, revealing, if thoroughly and deeply mastered, a surprising constancy of meaning through many centuries and languages, a science essential to any who would read and understand. But the semantics of the 1930's was designed to prove something—that the so-called ideas behind words are so varying and inconstant that all we really have left at any time is names. It proposed that words change so fast and so often that you can never trust an immediate meaning. In short, the new semantics was nominalism. How ironic that this fad should have been popular here on the eve of the war years when the meaning behind the names *America*, *honor*, *courage*, *democracy*, *freedom* became clear enough to many men to cause them to defend it with their lives. The fad had something to do, surely, with the popular hesitancy, as the war approached, about which side would be ours.

That the influence of this fad was really of some moment we may observe in the following obiter dictum of the Supreme Court of the United States. In the opinion upholding the conviction of the eleven Communist leaders in 1951, Chief Justice Vinson, writing for the majority, said: "Nothing is more certain in modern society than the principle that there are no absolutes, that a name, a phrase, a standard has meaning only when associated with the considerations which gave birth to nomenclature. To those who would paralyze Government in the face of impending threat by encasing it in a semantic straitjacket we must reply that all concepts are relative." In criticism of this statement Felix Morley pointed out that it was not necessary to sustain the opinion of the court. He called the statement not only irrelevant but irreverent, since it denies the absolutes on which our basic instruments of government establish the authority of law and courts.

All men being fallible, it is, of course, in a literal sense true that all *concepts* are relative. Preoccupied with the apparent shiftiness of human whim and taste, the Heracliteans of the world have long contended that it is not only the *concepts* that are in flux; what the concepts refer to is in flux also. There is nothing fixed whatever. They applaud the condition described in *The Green Pastures:* "Everything dat's fastened down is comin' loose." For example, a learned bishop recently said that a hymn like "O God our help in ages past" must be constantly revised, perhaps at some time abolished; God Himself changes with our changing conception of Him. But truly, both Christianity and courts of justice depend upon the existence of a fixed and absolute God, no matter what our changing ideas of Him may be, and of a definite and abiding truth, no matter how liable to error may be the man-made concepts by which from generation to generation we try more nearly perfectly to express it. Concepts are relative; and thinking earnestly about their unsteadiness, men in our generation, as in previous ages of uncertainty, have pathetically told each other that whatever we may seek to understand is unsteady, too.

For the law, politics, morals, taste, and religion, a lower level of this problem also is important. Are our best concepts really so shifty? If one follows the accepted judgment of the best minds since ancient times concerning what is understood by justice, good, virtue, integrity, compassion, and magnanimity, the surprising thing is not the disagreement over these concepts, but the extent of agreement. Men in widely different circumstances, living centuries and continents apart, speaking tongues of diverse linguistic families, have come to amazingly similar conclusions in their effort to describe human nature and to distinguish between right and wrong. Excessive preoccupation with minor disagreements has led fashionable semanticists to imagine that the terms richly meditated upon, which for ages have formed the hard core of language applied to men, are unreliable. Deeper study, on the contrary, and attention to the central meaning of the great critical opinions, lead to the opposite conclusions: that in judgments of first importance discerning and sensitive men have shown remarkable constancy. But to say that there exists a true convention or coming together of critical judgment and that there is something durable about the great ethical opinions is not to say that concepts are absolute.

They are steady, and we trust them, but we cannot prove them, Q.E.D. Those who hold that matters of opinion are absolute are authoritarians. The nominalists and followers of Heraclitus, on the other hand, who hold that there is no steadiness in men's ethical understanding, also lay, however unwittingly, the ground for tyranny; for their own logic drives them ultimately to say that there exists no sanction of truth and right above and beyond us. It leads them to add that what we call right in the last analysis is merely the proposition polling the largest vote.

The Chief Justice and the bishop spoke directly out of the lecture halls of the higher learning. They might have been quoting. For the era of John Dewey and Justice Holmes, the most influential scholarship has consistently endeavored to prove that there are no absolutes and to stress the relativity of all concepts. In that period of roughly half a century, an effort was made to correct the illusion that human knowledge itself may be absolute and that we can therefore be dogmatic about morals. In this effort, modern semanticists have stressed the inconstancy of taste and understanding. But what has really made possible the liberty of the individual has been not only its root in truth but the constancy of human agreement about the relation of men to God, right and wrong, good and evil. Stress in letters, philosophy, and law upon the inconstancy and, indeed, uncertainty of the essentials of this relation has contributed to the disintegration of liberalism.

While there were many writers who with the approach of war intensified their meditations upon the nature of freedom and democracy and the nature of man, observing as they did that beneath the economic and political forces bringing on the conflict were some old-fashioned human qualities such as pride and lust for power—while there were notable examples of men who, brought face to face with unremitting facts, changed the direction of their thinking, it cannot be said that these literary and philosophical fads to which I have referred were abandoned. There was nothing in letters comparable in extent to the abandonment among political thinkers of the sentimental and "pragmatic" pacifism of the Thirties. The new semantics and "art for art's sake" persist, both divorcing themselves from value and responsibility in the world of action.

The reasoning associated with "art for art's sake" was responsible for the award by the Fellows in American Letters of the Library of Congress of the one-thousand-dollar prize early in 1949 to Ezra Pound for his *Pisan Cantos*. In the dispute which followed, two distinct and unrelated issues emerged: First, are poetry and the other arts to be judged on their own merits, or in terms of the morals of the artist? Second, if judged on its own merits is a work of art to be considered only technically, in terms of form and artistic dexterity, or is it necessary also to consider what the poem or other work of art says? The contest was sharpened by the fact that Pound, under indictment for treason, had been declared insane and had not been tried, and by the fact that though the prize was supported by a private foundation, the judges had been appointed by the Library of Congress.

In the clamor against the award the strongest argument was the affirmation that the *Pisan Cantos* are not good poetry because, though at times they are witty, there is question whether what they say is worth saying. The Librarian of Congress announced that he, too, thought them inadequate as poetry, but he defended the award by avowing the irresponsibility of the arts. He said in effect that poetry may be judged by specialists but not by men of general intelligence. He accused the editors of the *Saturday Review of Literature* of holding the view, in their denunciation of the award, "that poetic quality must somehow pass a political test." In reply the editors stated that they do not hold this opinion and added:

> But while one must divorce politics from art, it is quite another matter to use the word "politics" as a substitute for values. We do not believe, in short, that art has nothing to do with values. We do not believe that what a poet says is necessarily of lesser importance

than the way he says it. We do not believe that a poet can shatter ethics and values and still be a good poet. We do not believe that poetry can convert words into maggots that eat at human dignity and still be good poetry.[9]

If it is true that the second war had a hand in revealing to even a few of the younger writers and critics that poetry is pre-eminently occupied with values, it may be said to have taught us something in the literary field as well as in the political one.

The examples cited above to illustrate a change which came over American thinking in 1938–42 and after are drawn from families of ideas and groups of thinkers somewhat remote from each other, and one may be accused of undue optimism in imagining that the changes are either widespread or thorough. For example, it would be too much to expect that the realities of totalitarianism when brought home to men of action would promptly dethrone the sentimental philosophy which for a long time has persuaded the American academic world that the evils of our life are primarily social and not individual. But in popular thinking one important step appears to have been taken during the past decade. It is illustrated by a discovery about this country. The important step was to discover, as Professor Raymond English has said, that America and its constitutional democracy exist on a plane utterly different from that on which the crude and related ideologies of fascism and communism operate—"as a debate is on a different plane from a street fight, or a court of law from a lynching mob, or a sane person from a maniac, or a family from an experiment in free love—which is not to say that it is impossible to descend from the higher plane to the lower."

The error of the "liberals" arose in part from their habit of crusading for a cause. They tended to think in one direction only, like an evangelist seeking converts and constantly counting them up when he has made them. One wartime discovery of American popular thought was this: that ideas about humanity are not usually achieved in a kind of monologue, a single statement leading by logical progression to a conclusion. Instead, they are known in a dialogue—in the soul's conversation with itself; and the right or the truth, so far as we may discover it, turns out to be a kind of mediation between extremes. In political terms this fact remains fairly clear to us as the cold war becomes warmer. American freedom is not all privileges; there are checks and balances. In literary and philosophical terms the underlying ethics of that political fact emerges in the popular mind. The evils which scare us when administered by the Gestapo or the Ogpu are the evils always incipient or rampaging in our own peculiar breasts. There is no immunity from them, not in the child, not in the artist. To understand life is to understand these evils and think responsibly about them. To understand art involves, along with other obligations, the necessity to see how, although it does not "moralize," it is constantly accountable to values other than the technique of the art.

The advent of the second war produced the following corrections in the disintegrated liberalism which had characterized American political thinking: *a*) the world cannot be governed by agreements, treaties, and reasonableness unsupported by sanctions; *b*) "pragmatic pacifism" will not work; *c*) the division of societies exclusively into fascist and communist is false; *d*) fascism is not the wave of the future; *e*) no dictatorship, even that of the proletariat, is likely to produce free government.

These corrections occurred at the level of action. They led to our defending political liberty by fighting the war. They led also to hard thought about the following philosophical assumptions on which the disintegrated liberalism of the Thirties had been based: *a*) men are so rational that the passions may be ignored; *b*) the reasoning most appropriate to human affairs is scientific reasoning; *c*) men being naturally good, the evils of the world arise primarily from bad social arrangements, whence it follows that the problems of the world may be treated exclusively as group problems—economic and social; *d*) in treating these problems one may ignore both the virtues and the vices of the individual; *e*) scholarship is best when "objective," and as irresponsible as science; *f*) letters are not concerned with adult judgment; *g*) a moral writer is one with a "party line," who will submit himself to the demand for propaganda; *h*) excellence in letters is to be found altogether in how you say it, not in what you say.

3

The Two Kinds of Liberalism in Education

Education has everything to do with the responsible liberalism that protects the freedom and rights of the individual, in which we profess to believe. Between the wars education at once reflected the tenets of the literati and social liberals and carried us so far in the wrong direction that we have not even partially found our way back. The presiding ideas in school and university were of a piece with the sentimentalism described above.

A few parallels between educational and other kinds of thinking come quickly to mind. In the 1920's poets and story writers became more and more absorbed in their own sensations and moods. The heroes of James Farrell and Thomas Wolfe in the 1930's were forever consulting their own feelings and taking their own emotions with incredibly adolescent seriousness. After scores of stream-of-consciousness novels had appeared, Hugh Walpole exclaimed that the twenty-four-hour classical period of dramatic action had been displaced by a fifteen-minute period (which could, nevertheless, take up four to six hundred pages) during which the hero simply sat on the edge of his bed in striped pajamas and decided whether he would or would not take an aspirin. The marvel is that millions of readers stood for this sort of thing by the volume. They stood for it because everything taught them, school included, that one's own desires and whims are of prime importance. This was the period of Progressive Education and the pupil-centered school, two useful correctives of the aridness which in some quarters they displaced, but soon themselves to be carried to extremes.

The depression of the Thirties occasioned a new account of the social task of education. For generations schools had thought of the world into which boys and girls would graduate in terms of either the missionary society or Horatio Alger. Christian missions lost favor in the Twenties; the depression proved that the path to affluence was closed to millions. Intense concern for the satisfaction of the individual led to the idea that the proper task of school was to adjust the pupil to society. It is ironic that adjustment became the aim of the institutions built upon the ideas and labors of such forceful individualists as Horace Mann, William Rainey Harper, Mary Lyon, Eleazar Wheelock, Philander Chase, and Francis Wayland. Our greatest schools had been founded precisely in order that the young would not be content to adjust themselves to society, but would set about with vigor and courage to adjust society where they saw it in need of change. The new "Education for Adjustment" was still the cry when in 1940 *The Wave of the Future* was published, advising us all to adjust ourselves to what soon became the hellish New Order for Europe. Adjustment was the accepted aim of schools small and large, the idea to be translated into speeches and M.A. theses by the teachers who wanted to get ahead, the idea inculcated by many an educationist's lecture and committee report read by the teachers who voted *The Wave of the Future* the best book of 1941.

The evident success of the New Deal, the Christian socialism which had been growing since the first war, and the religious conviction of many that the Communists were building Utopia in Russia had their effect upon the development of the aims of education. About the middle of the Thirties the slogan, "Education for the Future," referred largely to the development, by means of the "social attitudes" of the young, of more and more public provision for welfare. In New Orleans in the winter of 1937 those who passed the word expressed alarm and called a halt. The reversal was announced in the convention of the Department of Superintendence of the National Education Association, which met ten thousand strong early in the year. The deans of teachers' colleges and other speakers on the aims of the school system had vacationed in Europe the previous summer, and there they found Hitler taken seriously and saw the French Communists on the march. These ominous signs of the times led them to do some hard thinking about America, and they announced to the superintendents and principals of the country's schools that for the coming year the slogan would be "Education for Citizenship."

The early years of progressive education had been the heyday of psychology. Critical judgment and the will were already in eclipse; the desires and feelings of the individual, in the ascendant. The beautiful soul of the child unspoiled by convention was cherished in its sweet and true childlikeness. No one called the child a "noble savage," but the sentimentality about his native goodness revived the age of Rousseau and Chateaubriand. Soon the *New York Times* sensed a change. In reporting a Christmas meeting of psychologists it observed the disagreement by some of the scientists with the wholesale substitution of conditioning for critical decision, and carried a headline: "Soul Stages Comeback." In the last of the Thirties the word *discipline* returned into favor among the educationists, and lecturers reminded each other that soon the young then at school might be asked to shoulder great responsibilities, for which they would be unprepared. A group of educators, in a meeting also reported by the *Times*, confessed that the instruction over which they had been presiding had permitted the young to become morally soft.

The aim of teaching the young has always been regarded as a common concern of the city or nation. It was so in Sparta and the *Republic* of Plato. The charters of the early New England colleges speak of posterity and the leadership their graduates will give the community. The common weal is still the end of education, and those who stress the teaching peculiar to individuals will argue that the prosperity of the nation rests upon the fullness of the lives of its members. Concern for the national security in the late Thirties led to a notion of the social responsibility of schools, if not new in America, at least new in the way in which it was understood. The new conception was twofold: first, that school and college students should be treated in the mass, and second, that for the sake of national well-being the chief concern of teachers should be the group "attitude" on specific questions.

The double proposition may not sound new or surprising until set beside the excellent principle really at work in schools and colleges of genuinely liberal practice. The liberal aim is, of course, to increase the number of individuals who are competent to think and act on their own. To many an educationist this aim means mere skill in thinking. But it involves as well the ability to establish for one's self a standard by which to determine what is most worth thinking about and doing.

The statement of the aim of teaching and learning under consideration in these chapters is no mere academic debate among theorists. It is the effort to lay down a working policy which can be applied. So it is always a compromise between the desirable and the achievable. The practical restrictions upon the aims of American schools are immense, and in general those who have proposed the ends in the development of the school system have dealt faithfully and realistically with the practical limitations. The inadequacy of the purposes which are announced and do in fact motivate the great energies of the educational system arises from a poor conception of what is desirable. Here be it said that the failures have been committed not so much by the educational leaders themselves as by the professional philosophers who have been their teachers. If there is any fault of the educational leaders it would lie in their inability to find better philosophers to follow.

For decades the most limiting practical consideration in the debate about the aims of school and university has been their size. Some deplore the fact that the American student body is enormous and aver that we made a mistake to legislate for every young person as early in history as we did, not only the right, but, to a certain age, the obligation to go to school. These objectors point to European countries and the unquestioned superior advancement of the few young people permitted to progress to the university. By eliminating the ill-equipped, the European systems undoubtedly outstrip us in the quality of the average student's performance.

That their ablest students are not one whit abler than ours, nor more numerous in proportion to the population, has been common knowledge among scholars for generations. And in spite of our own failure to reckon fairly the cost of legislating for all the opportunity and obligation to go to school, despite our failure adequately to pay the school bill, and other disappointments, the American school system has demonstrated in thousands of ways that it is appropriate for America.

To increase the facilities and enlarge the opportunity for all young people remains the first administrative obligation of the system. To this end, an eminent committee of the National Education Association sponsored early in the war an extensive study culminating in the report, *Education for* All *American Youth* (1944). The solution of the problem, according to the report, lies in regarding schools as a "social service." Like other "social services," this one should study the immediate needs of the group it is designed to serve, and these needs, according to the report, are the sociological ones of job, family life, and practice in democratic living.

In America the aims of teaching and learning must be applicable to great school systems and enormous universities and groups of state colleges. As a democratic nation we have been notably successful in handling size. So far in history no country has done better. We manage millions in politics, hundreds of thousands in labor, in industry, the Army, Navy, and Air Force. The principles which apply to these seem readily adaptable to education. That Congress, the public, and the editors should think of schools in pretty much the same terms as they think of other large national institutions is no fault of theirs, but of the educators who have failed to demonstrate the difference between a social service agency and a school.

Sad to say, the educators in stating their aims have adopted with enthusiasm the mass ideas which have proved so effective in the organization and management of other enterprises. All modern life is characterized by increasing collectivism, from corporations to consumers' unions. Educational thinking exhibits the same temper of thought, and collectivism is the new conception which has grown in influence since the Thirties and Forties.

This idea was well established among public school leaders in the days of "Education for the Future." The purpose of school was then thought to be to prepare the New Society. It was admitted that many pupils were unpromising intellectually, and, in the spirit of progressive education, "activities" were sought which would be within the compass of the unpromising. What fraction of the so-called unpromising had been the victims of poor teaching because of crowding and underpay in the elementary schools was hardly introduced into the argument. Since the pressing consideration for the common good appeared to be to build the New Society, it was reasoned that this could be done if only the young people coming out of the schools had the right "attitude" toward certain social questions. These were the very real problems of intolerance, isolationism, unemployment, relation of labor to management, and public health. The social purpose of school became to condition the young to favor an enlightened and advanced settlement of these issues.

The belief that schools and colleges are useful to the commonwealth primarily as instruments for the influence of public social attitude was not confined to writers about the public schools. For a generation this idea has been echoed at university and college convocations. The reasoning usually goes as follows: mankind has progressed in its mastery of matter more rapidly than in the invention of means of social control; therefore the task of school and college is to improve the means of social control. The fallacy comes in the *therefore;* and in the pages of many of the commencement speakers the *therefore* undoubtedly constitutes a slip. The speaker may have been concerned with support of the League of Nations or the World Court or a fair deal for the sharecroppers or, recently, the control of the atom bomb. He was thinking largely of public opinion with which, perhaps as an editor or politician or in some other leading position in the community, he was directly concerned. He was not thinking of the whole task of the instruction of the reason which preoccupied Socrates and engages the thousands of able teachers in our generation who take him for a model. What fully half of the speakers meant to say was simply: we must all put more thought and energy into the improvement of the United Nations, the school board, the Parent-Teachers Association, and the Better Government League, or we shall not be able to manage the marvels of mechanics and they will manage us.

But nearly half the orators meant what they said. One of them, a Nobel Prize winner of some years ago, and for a generation the head of a powerful scientific institution, stated in such a speech: "Individual morality has little to do with social morality, for this latter depends not at all upon what I in my ignorance think is right, but rather upon what sort of procedures do actually best promote social well-being, or 'the good of the whole.' " If this statement is true, it follows not only that social procedures are the prime need of the hour but also that schools meet this need only when they study these first and subordinate or reinterpret all other studies accordingly. That is the idea which gained prominence in the Thirties and increasingly colored the statement of aims of school and college. Good was thought to be pre-eminently a social matter, not an individual one. To promote the good by means of school and college meant to treat the problem only as a social one. What would be important would not be independent critical judgment, but the attitude of the mass. Make sure that the mass attitude is right and (in the mid-1930's) you will build the society of the future; (in the late 1930's) you will defend America.

Many thoughtful persons demurred or raised revealing questions; but it is not surprising, with the gathering war, and the real danger that the American public would miss its issues so thoroughly that they would fail to see which side was ours, that any means would be taken to influence the mass attitude. In 1942, I heard a magazine editor and novelist tell an assembly of college boys that we must make America worth fighting for by raising wages in the shipyards! We were in a hurry in those days and understandably frantic. We did a lot of silly things, but most of them worked, and in retrospect they do not appear as absurd as some of the things we said in 1917. In schools and colleges, with whatever help we could get, we were concerned with the "attitude" of American youth. Student discussion at the Harvard commencement of 1942 was far different from that of 1941.

As the war came to a close and peacetime educational plans were published, the idea that the chief national concern of schools is the "attitude" of the young toward specific social problems persisted. It was abetted by the increasing confidence of those responsible for government and other American institutions that the answer to the world's ills lay in social techniques. This conviction appears to have been responsible for the increasing search by staffs of the great foundations for limited solvable social problems toward the solution of which they may spend their funds. It appears, also, to be implicit in the extension by some of the engineering schools of instruction and research into social techniques, paralleling the same concern with applied physics, chemistry, and mathematics.

At the level of research and development there is clearly more justification for confidence in social techniques than at the level of common education. The notable change in thinking about the aims of school and college is the widely spreading acceptance of the idea that to instruct the public in these techniques and to prepare masses of people to accept them is properly a major function of institutions formerly devoted to the education of persons.

This new idea undergirds the reasoning of the Report of the President's Commission on Higher Education (1947). In the view of the commission the "social role" of schools and universities should consist in the improvement and dissemination of "social techniques." The commission proposed that liberal education be displaced or redefined as something which it calls general education, the important change being that education be invested "with content that is directly relevant to the demands of contemporary society." The commission is concerned not only with social attitudes but with social action. It prefers the contemporary world as a subject of study and favors immediate relevance to this, not pausing to ask whether the contemporary world is in fact asking the relevant questions. It proposes that study should "emphasize generalizations," rather than facts and the rigorous thinking by which durable generalizations are made. All this is sound practical policy if the end in view is to establish in the students a definite disposition of mind toward a particular subject, an attitude which has been planned in advance by the teacher. If, on the other hand, the object is to bring students to the mature ability to know and judge vital matters at first hand, the proposal is dangerous nonsense.

The foregoing account of the discussion of the aims of education in America since the first war suggests that, unlike the general drift of opinion concerning world politics and letters, thought about the purpose of education has undergone no important reversal. Except for the shift in 1937 from "Education for the Future," with special attention to the state-supported humanitarian future, to "Education for Citizenship," meaning civic responsibility, there was no remarkable change in it until after the war. Indeed, the appearance of the Report of the President's Commission in 1947 reveals that the ethical prejudices of Rousseau and the instrumentalist philosophy of John Dewey continue to enjoy almost universal popularity in the postwar period.

The influential educational thinking since the 1920's shares with the "liberalism" of the Thirties the following assumptions: men being primarily rational, and the ills of the world arising primarily from bad arrangements, the chief concern of school and college should be the promotion of certain social techniques; mature and critical attention to the individual can safely be neglected or even ignored. Superficially one might argue that, far from ignoring the emotions, recent education pays large attention to them, citing especially the increased study of the arts and of "art appreciation" in the schools following the progressive education movement. Closer scrutiny, however, will show that much of this activity is based on the belief that the arts are an affair of natural impulse and social cohesion little concerned with discipline. Liberalism in education since World War I has taken the form of putting down barriers. It has meant more and more freedom for the student to follow youthful whims. H. L. Mencken remarked of liberals who held such views that they were not really emancipated but only unbuttoned. In this period the elective system in college went to the extreme of eliminating more and more requirements set up by the mature and of inviting the young to do all the choosing of their courses. Liberalism in education meant not only freedom of the student to study anything, but freedom of the professor to teach anything. One subject was considered as good as another. *Education for* All *American Youth* (1944) stated: "There is no aristocracy of 'subjects' in the . . . curriculum. Mathematics and mechanics, art and agriculture, history and homemaking are all peers."[1] It was the period of the "democracy of the subjects." As in the political and literary thinking of the Twenties and Thirties, so in education mature judgments were avoided.

In the face of all this, one important committee report on the aims of education challenged the ideas responsible between the wars for "wrapping the young in romantic cotton wool." It stated in measured and vigorous terms that some subjects are more important to study than others and that the mature must decide which these are; that the study of mankind begins and remains for some time in the life of the student primarily a study of the individual; and that the arts and letters are concerned with adult judgments. Far from treating liberalism as a matter of eliminating more and more barriers, the report states that freedom is submission—"submission to the best and fullest truth that can be known, recognizing that truth cannot be fully known." Education in liberalism can never result from following youthful whims, for it "has a pattern of its own." There are some things of which the liberal is not free to be ignorant. The report was called forth by the worry lest the elaborate and technical problems of war should lead us to ignore the true nature of the study of science and human experience. It is the now famous Harvard Report published in 1945.

President Conant, though heavily engaged with the mobilization of Harvard University for war research and training, and at Washington with such urgent matters as synthetic rubber, a host of scientific projects related to new weapons, and ultimately the atomic bomb, discussed the problem in basic terms: How may the university itself understand better the aims of college teaching? How may it improve such teaching? What is the relation of these ends and this practice to the American democracy? On his recommendation the Harvard Corporation set aside funds sufficient to pay the cost of extensive interviews and study by a very able committee of twelve Harvard professors. Mr. Conant named the group the Committee on the Objectives of a General Education in a Free Society; the committee examined and judged objectives and used the same phrase in the title of its report: *General Education in a Free Society*.

The parts of this volume of utmost importance to the schools and universities of America are not those commending specific reforms in the Harvard curriculum, but two ethical ideas: first, the reasons which prompt the committee to recommend to the faculty that it again assume its ancient obligation and decide what is most valuable for the young to study, and, second, the standards by which it proposes that the faculty come to its decision. The committee makes the former recommendation because it holds that there are some things of which the liberal is not free to be ignorant. The standard by which it urges the faculty to decide what these things are is the standard which is to be found in human nature itself. For themselves the twelve scholars and scientists hold that the long record of human experience, ancient and contemporary, reveals on analysis a definite and abiding standard of conduct, a norm which is discoverable and against which all human thought and action may be judged. The committee quotes Mencius, Plato, and a contemporary, Stephen C. Pepper, in exposition of this idea and then comments:

> Man, these agree, has his norm, and the account of education we are giving here agrees too, without, however, professing to give an adequate statement of the norm. The apprehension of the norm—by approximation to it—is education itself, which is thus its own aim.[2]

If this is true, the learned, that is, the teachers, must decide what to study in order to approximate the apprehension of the norm. "Man . . . has his norm," and we agree that he has. This proposition is at odds with the whole moral philosophy of the Dewey school and thus with the controlling ideas which for a long generation have governed the decisions, the appointments, the practices, and the announcement of aims of the American school system and a large fraction of the colleges and universities, particularly those training teachers.

The Harvard Report was written by a committee of twelve, and it is not surprising that at times it departs from the rigorous standard which its analysis of theory sets. Thus, while the usual reference to human values uses the terms *norm* and *standard*, the sentimental language of the times creeps in on occasion, and the humanities are said to be concerned with visions and ideals. But the report nowhere, I believe, calls them "dreams." In one or two passages the committee is apparently more sure of the objectivity and hard reality of science and social studies than of these qualities in the humanities. But on the whole the report is realistic, talking sense about the nature of mankind, of learning itself, and about the job of teaching and keeping school.

In analyzing the objectives of common education the committee considers the criticism heard for two decades: that there is no guiding principle to unify a student's studies, and that in consequence the university in modern times has become a multiversity. It rejects the four major proposals for reform: to abandon the elective system in favor of the traditional curriculum; to organize studies according to medieval rationalism; to make the solution of contemporary problems the unifying aim; and to find in scientific method the presiding principle. The last receives special notice in the report, probably because, of all the philosophies of learning, it is at present the most prevalent. The committee calls it the "pragmatic solution," which "sees in science and scientific outlook this saving unity."[3] This is the general view favored by the followers of Professor Dewey. Of them, the report says, "Yet, if not the philosophers of pragmatism, at least their disciples seem in practice, if one may put it so, not pragmatic enough. That is, there is always a tendency in this type of thought to omit as irrelevant the whole realm of belief and commitment by which, to all appearances, much of humanity seems in fact swayed."[4] Thus the committee finds in the academic world the same shortcomings which have been observed by critics of liberal thought in general.

The unwary took the report as all very fine for Harvard. But what applies to the oldest institution in the land where students are picked by severe competition is hardly applicable, they said, to the gigantic university and school system of the United States. To think so is to ignore one of the most revolutionary proposals in the book. It is this: that contrary to popular theory, a schoolboy should not be excluded from the best kind of education because he is less gifted than his neighbor. He should not, that is, be consigned to vocational training and wholly deprived of an education because he is not brilliant. Of the less gifted, the report properly says: "They are as worthy and as valuable democratic citizens as anyone else. The problem is to educate them by exactly the same ideals of schooling as everyone else, yet by means which shall be as meaningful to them as are more abstract means to the more abstract-minded."[5] If the less gifted must spend some of their school time at vocational training, they nonetheless have the same right as other citizens of the republic to know and to understand the essentials of our life to the limit of their powers of understanding. The main problem of the report thus becomes: "How can general education be so adapted to different ages and, above all, differing abilities and outlooks, that it can appeal deeply to each, yet remain in goal and essential teaching the same for all?"[6]

That education should "remain in goal and essential teaching the same for all" is a major premise of the present book. Many argue that such commonality of aim is impossible because only the excellent few can think with superior subtlety and refinement. If the chief aims of life and of thought were technical, their argument would stand. The assumption of this book is that the aims are common, central, and human, that while elaborate exposition of them may depend upon subtlety and refinement, they have proved to an important degree recognizable by every man and available to each to the extent of his own powers to read, to think, and to apprehend.

It cannot be said that the twelve scholars and scientists who wrote the Harvard Report taught themselves the fundamental proposition about the norm of human conduct because of what they observed in the most recent of the world's wars. The critical acumen and extensive knowledge of man and nature which went into the report had required a lifetime of reading and inward debate. It is significant, however, that in 1943 and 1944 their opinion was asked, and that in 1945 and 1946 their conclusions were read and debated by school and university communities with approbation.

To find a general change in the reference points of complicated popular thought occurring about the time of the war leads to the natural conclusion that the war produced the change. One may object that while in some of the opinions cited as representing change, the authors of the opinions had in fact confessed their former errors and renounced them, in others the authors had been saying the same thing for years. True. But the attention paid these utterances during the war and since, and the growth in the circle of their favorable acceptance is significant. So impressive is this phenomenon, it can be said to represent an important shift of opinion.

In thought about international affairs the shift amounted to an abandonment of the disintegrated liberalism which left the lover of freedom uncertain who in the world conflict over liberty were his real allies. It led to toughened and more realistic thinking about the individual, to abandonment of the sentimental conception of his natural goodness and his utter rationality, and to a correction of the illusion that scientific observation and logic alone will suffice in the treatment of human affairs. In letters, philosophy, and general ideas the war taught many the meaning of adult responsibility and its relation to the sensitive record of men's impulses, deeds, and thoughts. In analyzing the aims of education one able committee, whose report enjoyed wide circulation, based its conception of the education of a responsible American liberal upon the idea of the individual as one capable of approximating, despite the violent war in his own breast, the norm of manhood.

4

The Critical Basis of the Liberal Idea of the Individual

If in addition to the dogmatic assertion of American liberties the young are to be given the means to understand these critically and to perceive their possibilities in the unforeseen conditions of the future, what, and to what end shall we teach them? They will need skill in thinking and feeling; they will also need to be able to sense and to judge what is important to think about and to what purpose. The foregoing chapters indicate that responsible American liberalism is based upon positive affirmations concerning individual man, his value and inward responsibility.

What is the critical basis for the belief that the individual has value? In candor we must admit that there is impressive evidence that he has little or none. Magnificent cities and states have flourished on principles at odds with this one. It has been reckoned that a very small fraction of the world's population since the time of Christ has lived under systems which assume the sanctity of the individual; some put the proportion at less than one-half of one per cent. In relation to those alive now, the fraction is still small. Within the Christian era the Occident has offered volumes of testimony that the individual is negligible.

Years ago a man, arguing with a friend that there is a personal devil, got nowhere by means of dialectic; so he took him to the

House of Commons: there was proof! The late Sir Walter Alexander Raleigh, in hiding at a garden party where he was being lionized, wrote his famous jingle: "I wish I liked the human race." Swift hated himself and us, preferring the beautiful, clean, reasonable Houyhnhnms to our revolting kind. Timon, the disillusioned communist, says, "I am Misanthropos, and hate mankind." According to Lucian it was Timon's object "to be his own neighbor . . . and if any man implores him to put out his burning house, to extinguish it with oil and pitch." We have but to look within ourselves when the damage we have done to a neighbor or the wound we have delivered to a friend is irreparable, or to consider what we have had to observe at firsthand of rascality, cowardice, or meanness, to conclude that men are snakes.

The longer the whole inquiry and the greater the evidence considered, however, the more puzzling our nature appears. Robert Burns, who knew a good deal of merriment and not a little of dejection, threw up his hands:

> Good Lord, what is man! for as simple as he looks,
> Do but try to develop his hooks and his crooks,
> With his depths and his shallows, his good and his evil,
> All in all, he's a problem must puzzle the devil.

The human record contains a thin vein of testimony that we are all pure and beautiful, being born good and quite able to remain so if society does not interfere. But on the whole this constitutes a kind of adolescent witness, abandoned in maturity. Even the chief English exponent of this view, William Wordsworth, who spoke in young manhood of the infant "trailing clouds of glory," in his later years wrote the Ecclesiastical Sonnets. But we still live in the period of the noble savage; progressive education still holds that:

> One impulse from a vernal wood
> May teach you more of man,
> Of moral evil and of good,
> Than all the sages can.

Many in our lifetime, particularly among the Christian socialists, have concluded that this romantic idea of the individual constitutes the critical basis of the belief that he is precious and endowed with certain unalienable rights. Searching investigation, however, reveals evidence that a person is a more darkly mysterious being than even the lovely child, "father of the man," imagined by the romantic thinkers of the eighteenth and nineteenth centuries. Pope called man "the glory, Jest, and riddle of the world."[1] Sir John Davies in the previous century remarked our vast and growing knowledge, but that of all things man is the least known.

> We that acquaint ourselves with ev'ry zone
> And pass both tropics, and behold each pole,
> When we come home are to ourselves unknown,
> And unacquainted still with our own soul.

But despite self-ignorance man knows something about his own stance in the world:

> I know my life's a pain and but a span;
> I know my sense is mock'd in ev'ry thing:
> And to conclude, I know myself a man,
> Which is a proud, and yet a wretched thing.[2]

Strenuous thinkers have invariably borne testimony to this double character of ourselves, not an angel, but a little lower than the angels, proud and yet wretched.

To establish critically an idea of our nature is no easy task. The testimony is conflicting, and the evidence comes from unexpected places. The result is not subject to mathematical or even purely logical proof, although it has its laws and is demonstrable. As the Harvard committee said, the best that can be hoped for is an approximation, not a simple statement of the character of man itself. To set about the inquiry we must decide what to admit as evidence and determine the best way in which to analyze the evidence we accept.

Clearly the facts first at hand for this purpose are history, including contemporary history. On the principle, "by their fruits ye shall know them," one may set out to inquire what men really have done. There are hazards here, remembering how successfully the record can be written to serve ends other than the truth. Major Swindon in *The Devil's Disciple* puts the question to General Burgoyne: "What will history say?" The General replies: "History, sir, will tell lies, as usual." Furthermore, it is alleged by many contemporary thinkers that history reveals nothing whatever about the nature of man, but is merely the record of cycles and of hordes on the march. But whatever else it may do, history at its best does in fact throw light on the nature of man and upon the question whether or not the individual is considerable.

The study of history to this end cannot proceed far, however, without requiring some special skill in interpretation. What do these pronouncements, deeds, and effects signify in connection with men's nature? Of what light or darkness in the will and mind of their protagonists are they the outward and visible sign? The writing of history requires more of this special ability than is imagined by many historians. To some, the writing of history is simply reporting like reporting for the paper. You see what has happened and write it down. But when matters of great pitch and moment are at stake and the deed is large in its consequence, what the historian seeks to recount with accuracy is not only the outward but the inward deed. What he seeks are the terms of the contest in the hearts of the protagonists. Why did they decide thus, and what did the decision cost them and others, even us? The skill involved here is the skill of poetry, of reading it and writing it, a skill which can be learned by any who possess good powers of perception and average sensitiveness. But such study entails especially a training of the feelings, for all the deeds sufficiently important to demand accounting by the historian involve passion. Necessary also is the ability to perceive what really happened, a mixture of canniness and long experience with human motives (part of the experience can be provided vicariously and the canniness sharpened by endless comparisons). Finally, the skill with poetry essential to our treatment of history as evidence about the nature of man entails experience with the problem of the One and the Many: that is, with discovering by plain observation, logic, or a kind of sleuth's sense, which, in the welter of events, is the important one; what, in the confusion of facts, is worth pondering. Experience with poetry provides experience in sensing the universal in the particular and also in discovering a particular which truly expresses a universal. Furthermore, poetry is of a piece with history, providing some of the events themselves (such as Hamlet's unwillingness or inability to obey his father) which constitute prime evidence in the humane investigation. When later in this book the study of poetry and its relation to history are considered, poetry will prove, like history, to play a major part in the effort to approximate the idea of the nature of man.

These two, history and poetry, cannot be seen critically without analysis of the nature of fiction. Oscar Wilde said that truth can be told only by an accomplished liar. This epigram parodies the solemn observation of the ancients that the highest and most precious truths, notably those related to our nature and destiny, can be conveyed only by means of stories. When history and poetry are thoroughly and richly studied, they involve such reflections as this one, as well as the numerous analyses of virtue and vice which fall within the domain of moral philosophy. They require, too, a grasp of metaphysics, if for no other reason than to try to make sense out of the incredible destruction men have wrought upon each other in defense of or attack upon dogmas.

But there are other reasons. One is suggested in the distress among the framers of bills of rights how to authorize these. Whence came these rights? The American Declaration of Independence has us endowed by the Creator, the Constitution of the United Nations rehearses that we are endowed by Nature, and the International Declaration of Human Rights avers merely that we are endowed, without meddling with the nettlesome question, by what or whom? Who or what endowed us is indeed pertinent to the study of man. However, in this chapter and the subsequent ones we are concerned with the critical as distinguished from the dogmatic assertion of the value of the individual and his responsibility. Thus the metaphysical problem enters here only to the extent that it is germane to a critical appraisal of human experience. Treatment of the dogmatic affirmation of faith is confined to Chapter 13, "To Believe and Doubt Well."

There are still further reasons why all philosophy is required knowledge in pursuit of this inquiry, for the connectives of opinion themselves make a sizable literature, and to relate the opposing theories of our nature requires familiarity with the brightest and most impressive statements of the controversy attained by men. Like history and poetry, philosophy is a corpus of knowledge as well as a skill.

In the critical investigation of whether the individual is precious or not, it is important to work upon the pertinent facts about him, to refine our perception of these by extensive analysis, comparison, and conjecture upon their consequences, and to know something of at least the foremost ethical systems. When later in this book the study of human experience, history, poetry, and philosophy are examined, analysis of them will reveal not only that there is voluminous evidence in men's deeds against the Christian and American proposition about the individual, but that there are impressive schools of opinion against it, too. The purpose of the study is to see how critically the proposition may be supported.

The individual has value and within himself is subject to law—whether or not the second half of this principle is true may also be treated in history, poetry, and philosophy. But there are many who hold that the nature of man, and especially both parts of this proposition, are more effectively studied by psychology in all its branches, including social psychology, than by the critical study of the most candid things that have been thought and said and the most direct reports of what in privacy and in public has been done in the world.

Few would deny the clinical usefulness of both analytical and physiological psychology, or the bearing of its discoveries upon our understanding of the interplay of body and mind. But to regard the measurement of the reactions of the nervous system and the assignment of meanings to the symbols of dreams as the chief basis of knowing ourselves is truly to abdicate our manhood. The illusion is so absurd as to be negligible but for its popularity. Its evil is seen when the able young, sensitive to the fads of the times, are conditioned to regard these studies as the primary key to the critical problems of mankind. When deflected from its proper medical purposes to the gigantic task of describing human nature, clinical psychology becomes a clumsy system of old and frozen metaphors ill-suited to so subtle and lively a task. Its faults lie in its poverty, its ignorance of much human experience, and its removal from experience itself into measurement and jargon. As the Mexican scholar, Edmundo O'Gorman, has said: "Such knowledge is only a representation, a mere image of human existence, which instead of achieving a direct and original contact with that existence, simply offers a theoretical description." Whether or not we agree with him, slavery to a terminology is dangerous; the conformity it imposes leads to slavery itself.

Recently a zoölogist and two research associates made a sociopsychological study entitled *Sexual Behavior in the Human Male* and recorded answers to interviewers and other measurements and statistics about the sexual habits of thousands of boys and men in America. The book undoubtedly has medical and social usefulness, especially in courts and agencies concerned with extremes of indulgence. The phraseology of the volume, however, and its advertising and reception, implied that here was a work on morals. That is, its authors, promoters, and some of its critics implied or stated that here was evidence on the nature of man.

To a very slight degree this is true, for every record of what really happens in our lives contributes to the notion we form of what in fact we are. But the degree is slight, though many regard the findings of this book as of major moral importance. Its publishers advertised that sex education was being revised in the light of this study. The book, of course, is not about morals at all, but about mores, the habits of the people interviewed and those they are thought to represent. But the authors themselves confuse the two, using the word *norm* over and over as if they were referring to what the *norm* has meant historically—a standard of human behavior. The word itself connoted in ancient times the carpenter's square by which he determined the perpendicular, and for centuries *norm* has meant the determinant of the perpendicular of manhood, a meaning emphasized in the adjective, *normative*. But the Kinsey report uses the word to mean nothing more than the mathematical average. Normal behavior in this book is the average behavior determined by the authors' statistics—this means the average of the cases they questioned. When one reflects that manhood is deep in history as well as extensive over space, that there have been whole cities and whole generations in which, like Sodom and Gomorrah, there were no good men, but that the idea of manhood persisted, he discovers that the norm of human behavior is something far more complicated and various than a mathematical average. Indeed the logic of the Kinsey report would hold that forty million Frenchmen can't be wrong; but how wrong they, or one hundred forty million Americans, can be! The "mere image of human existence" created by the Kinsey report has been mistaken for the object for which it pretends to stand, and that image is statistics, which are mistakenly thought in our lifetime to prove something about quality or value, provided you have enough of them.

In the *Saturday Review of Literature*, after publication of a letter by Martin S. Cutler under the title, "Homosexual Minority" (June 4, 1949), other letters on the subject appeared. In the issue for July 16, Donald Fay Robinson of Cooperstown, New York, wrote:

Sir: Special pleading for homosexuals as such creates a minority that has no existence in fact. As the Kinsey report indicates, many men (and women) practice homosexuality with varying degrees of exclusiveness; but a majority of them also have heterosexual relations, and there is no hard and fast line between the "homosexual" and the others. What is needed (and what fits the facts) is not a society for the prevention of cruelty to homosexuals, but a reorganization of our concept of human sex ethics to include also all such important variants of human sex behavior as homosexuality. . . . When we can look upon all the variations of human structure, thought, and behavior as we look upon the color of people's eyes, then—and only then—will we have the possibility of true tolerance and a unified world.[3]

When the norm becomes the mathematical average, deviations from it quite logically become "variations of human structure, thought, and behavior" and no more significant to what is truly human conduct than the color of people's eyes.

The terms of understanding the nature of man and of the individual are the same whether the immediate question is the mighty ethical one posed by the contest of the century or a decision to be made in private life. In advising pre-law students what to study, a report adopted by the American Bar Association said, "Psychology has its uses but psychology never taught a man how to pick a jury—or a wife."[4] For this purpose, the report said, the proper training is to be found in "the boys' club, the athletic field, the discussions around the dining-room table at home, the 'bull sessions' in the college fraternity house, the varied activities of the college campus, the daily newspaper, the people of high and low degree one has met at school or on vacation—yes, and the books one has read and the plays one has seen."[5] One's choice of a jury or a wife—one's abiding opinion about the individual: the subject of reflection and the manner of making up one's mind in each decision have much in common with the process of the others. Stocking and training both one's thoughts and feelings is also similar in all three efforts.

What of man's inward responsibility? Is the individual subject to a law within? The question, like the one about his sanctity, is the primary concern of history, poetry, and philosophy, assisted, it is true, by the physical and natural sciences, but by no means displaced by them.

There are some who imagine that for Americans the basic proposition of our dispute with the Kremlin will take care of itself, persisting naturally on our soil, like baseball. Of course we believe that the individual is valuable and subject to law within! That is assumed. We assume it, they say, in everything we do, including our management of schools and universities. When it comes to determining what and how to teach we need simply to remind ourselves that our object is to maintain the traditional American goals, to keep before ourselves the American dream, and to proceed to occupy the energies of the teachers and the taught with improved social techniques. That program will work in war when the goal is so simple it may be named on a map—Berlin or Tokyo. In peace it might work for a decade, until the brightest of the young began to wonder why on earth all this pother about the American traditional goals, anyway, in view of the charming brightness of something supposed to be "new." One has but to look at the opinions of the most brilliant and most vocal during the Twenties and early Thirties to see what becomes of the American goals when held not critically and imaginatively, but merely as slogans. This was the period when it was fashionable for young writers who were sending home poems, stories, and essays from the Left Bank to quote *Also Sprach Zarathustra* and to say that the best government is a benevolent despotism. This was the period when George Jean Nathan called politics a low concern.

One would hope that America could always afford the rambunctious antics of the young in the Latin Quarter, but we should expect America always to enjoy critical powers mature enough to view them with realism and humor. The proper treatment of the traditional American goals is not to take them for granted—which amounts to consigning them to dogma, slogans, and radio sing-song ("I Am an American")—but critically to reperceive them, which amounts to the long study, at school and college, of the nature of man.

Before reflecting upon the learning and thinking requisite to this treatment of the philosophical basis of freedom, we do well to consider what is at stake. It is surely within the scope of possibility that in conducting the cold war we may become so engrossed in its technique—the transport, the mobilization, the control and manufacture of bombs, and alliances and treaties, the mechanics of the United Nations, the agreements among groups at home, the avoidance of a depression, the securing of industrial peace—that we have no heart for the arduous intellectual labor of redefining and rediscovering in terms of today the subtle philosophical proposition which occasions our disagreement with all totalitarians. The issue of the century concerns the nature of individual man and how order may be maintained without violence to him.

What is at stake is easily seen. For if hundreds of thousands who influence thought, taste, and opinion fail to sense why "we hold these truths to be self-evident," in something more critical and knowing than chanted reiteration of the truths, America will soon agree with the Nazi belief that our quarrel with communism is merely one of territory and power, and we may expect at home some form of dictatorship, whether imported or native.

5

History

THE LEARNING and thinking requisite to a critical understanding of the bases of American liberty begin with some grasp of the individual and his nature. This learning relies upon the constancy of the norm of human conduct, and it has rightly been said that the whole effort of mind called liberal education may be described as the approach to that norm. The object of study is multifarious, rich, varied, disparate, many-faceted. But the end in view is that surprisingly single, integrated, purposeful, and steady creature, Man. To pursue the study requires some decision about what subjects are of first importance, some specification of the ends to be sought within each subject, and some particulars of the manner in which the studies should be pursued. This decision and these specifications are the subject of the next ten chapters.

The immediate responsibility of American education to the United States and to human freedom is to equip the young with the ability and the disposition to think about the twofold proposition that the individual is valuable and within himself subject to law. The critical establishment of this dual statement, over which the whole world is now officially divided, entails at its center the study of history, poetry, and philosophy.

A writer in *Harper's* magazine for June 1943 called the humanities "repositories of lore," a "warm and pleasant" sounding category "to which odds and ends, fads, and the boondoggling demanded by local conditions and pressure groups can be allocated." "History," he said, "represents a peculiar monstrosity in the academic museum. Its principal subject matter is already largely included in, and is in any event logically a part of, cultural anthropology, which is indistinguishable from sociology."[1] The editor, in commenting on the essay said, "These are bad days for the liberal arts." His author proposed one of the views of history which make it utterly useless to the modern mind seeking an answer to the ethical question which now divides the world.

In our lifetime the word *culture* retains perhaps a pleasant antique association with Beacon Street a century ago, but its present import derives from the limited and scientific use to which it has been put by anthropology. It refers to the arts, warfare, religion, and gardening of primitive peoples. Cultural anthropology has also been applied to sophisticated peoples; and thinking with its help to describe with equal effectiveness the whole of ancient or modern Rome, the uninformed are tempted to make wild and sweeping statements about Roman or any other culture. The parody of the idea of history revealed by the *Harper's* essayist eliminates it from usefulness in the modern quest because to think of the events of a people or a city in terms of culture is to deny the importance in these of the decisions and deeds of persons who bore names and hated, loved, and were generous or ruthless like ourselves. We are seeking the nature of man in private as well as man in public, and our dispute with the Russians has to do with the individual—not with cultures, but with the individual.

Another view of history which would debar it from usefulness in this dispute is that it is a mere reference library. Dr. Algo Henderson, sometime president of Antioch College, outlining college education and the century of the common man, said that "the contemporary world must be the focus of post-war college education. . . . If the curriculum were based upon the essential problems of contemporary society, to which illustrative material from the past could be freely applied, the problem might be solved."[2] A historian who had taken part in the new course of studies for trainees in the Army Area and Language Program said that perhaps its success proves that henceforth history should be treated topically, taking its departure from contemporary national and world problems. To confine history to illustrative material in the study of "the essential problems of contemporary society" means in Dr. Henderson's book, and in the reasoning of many, to confine history to modern social problems, again assuming that in history the decisions and deeds of individual men and women are not of special importance.

A third group of thinkers in effect discount any relevance of history to the question: what is the nature of the individual? These are the determinist historians, who hold that dark mysterious forces or trends or tendencies or movements entirely account for events and that the individual is unavailing. They hold that leaders are of so little consequence that if one of them is assassinated and another promptly takes his place in the general anthill, the circumstances of fate will be little altered. They include not only the Marxist historians, but other brands of determinists or inevitablists, extending in their social and political prejudices all the way from Spengler, who became the darling of the Nazis, to the novelist and amateur historian, Tolstoy, a romantic Christian. Arnold Toynbee, the current favorite of Protestant Christians, is not free of cycles and other movements which, even in his pages, enjoy a metaphysical existence. These historians treat their most admired inevitabilities as if they were destiny itself, and though they have posed for decades as "realists" and down-to-earth, hard-headed critics of the "idealists," their work represents, to use Paul Elmer More's phrase, the demon of the absolute.

No one has found an answer to the question: Is history the account primarily of individuals, their failures and their heroism; or is it primarily the record of trends, movements, forces, cycles, never of personal import, but an account of people in the mass, of hordes, tribes, and the struggle of classes? In reading history the student cannot avoid the debate. He will be well advised, in the first place, to learn as much of the recorded event as he can. It is a good plan to remember that history is the account of happenings, and that these are the eventual concentrate of the events reported piecemeal and partially completed in the daily paper. Though these events may be loaded with meaning for the future, when they are only half enacted one cannot be sure of their exact significance; we cannot interpret them, nor divine from their impact what their result will be. Naturally, history in the making is too particular for any theory. For example, remember Winston Churchill's speech after Dunkirk and how single and alone his voice was:

> Even though large tracts of Europe and many old and famous States have fallen or may fall into the grip of the Gestapo and all the odious apparatus of Nazi rule, we shall not flag nor fail. We shall go on to the end, we shall fight in France, we shall fight in the seas and oceans, we shall fight with growing confidence and growing strength in the air, we shall defend our island, whatever the cost may be, we shall fight on the beaches, we shall fight on the landing grounds, we shall fight in the fields and in the streets, we shall fight in the hills; we shall never surrender; . . . [3]

Most men who knew the facts in 1940 were afraid. Almost alone Mr. Churchill was not afraid. It is hard to imagine, knowing what we do of the other Allied leaders, that if one of the bombs had fallen on him someone could have filled his place.

The late Sir Charles Oman, one of the best historians of our lifetime, has this to say about the individual in history:

> Two generations have now passed since the blessed word "Evolution" was invented, and was applied as a universal panacea to all the problems of the universe—historical no less than physical. By this I mean that a whole school of historians have set forth the thesis that history is a continuous logical process, a series of inevitable results following on a well-marshalled table of causes. Of course the logician may tell us that every consequence is the summing up of its antecedents. But that is hollow formal logic. And to my mind it is impossible to turn all history into a continuous and mechanical panorama of logical causes followed by inevitable re-

sults. My humble opinion is that things might generally have happened otherwise than they actually did. The history of mankind is often accidental, even occasionally cataclysmic. It is not a logical stream of cause and effect, but a series of happenings, affected in the most inscrutable fashion by incalculable chances, which were not in the least bound to occur, ranging from natural phenomena such as plagues or earthquakes, to the appearance of outstanding human personalities who "put on the clock" or occasionally "put the clock back." The Whig historians who pontificated on the theme that "history is the history of peoples, as opposed to the personal adventures of kings and statesmen" were far more wrong in their general conception of the world than Thomas Carlyle preaching of the all-importance of the individual in his book on "Heroes."[4]

Of the popes and kings of the sixteenth century Oman makes this observation:

All that we can say is that if some of them had been other than they were, the course of history might have been different. If, for example, Francis I had been another Louis XI—ascetic, economical, unchivalrous, given to intrigue more than to war—the struggle between Valois and Hapsburg would not have taken the shape of successive invasions of Italy always ending in disaster. Or if Charles IX had been a vigorous, self-reliant, strong-handed king, like his grandfather Francis I, there might have been no Huguenot wars.[5]

Without doubt the prosperity and security of the Western world in the second half of the nineteenth century had much to do with the illusion promoted by the "Whig historians," that peoples are a kind of entity independent in their movements of the strong guiding mind and hand of leaders. One of the amusing ironies of history is the fact that in America the century of the common man was hailed by the followers of a president who by his own personal leadership had acquired more power in peace and in war than any of his predecessors. Not many years before, Warren Harding had been the favorite of the "rugged individualists."

An American historian, John Lothrop Motley, held a view of

the individual similar to Oman's. He said of his *Life and Death of John of Barneveldt:* "This work aims at being a political study. I would attempt to exemplify the influence of individual humors and passions—some of them among the highest and others certainly the basest that agitate humanity—upon the march of great events, upon general historical results at certain epochs, and upon the destiny of eminent personages."[6]

History so read clearly piles up evidence about our own nature. At its extreme this view of history concludes that it is entirely biography, and to reason so is to obliterate such gigantic historical considerations as the influence of cotton and the railroads upon the Civil War, of the Industrial Revolution upon all modern countries, of the frontier upon American thought, of nitrates upon World War I, and of synthetic petroleum and American industry upon World War II. One cannot accuse Motley, however, of ignoring such social forces, though he wrote a century ago. The economic problems of Europe and the setting provided by its human geography of the sixteenth century figure in his account and bear upon his judgments. But the wellspring of his understanding of the time is the private and state papers of the period. The reports of Barneveldt's spy, and Philip's, the candid and strictly secret messages to the Council sent by the Venetian Ambassadors, the letters revealing the duplicity of the Duke of Anjou, the record William the Silent left of his inmost thoughts as well as his public utterances—the inside story for Motley was not only the story inside the guarded cabinets of monarchs and revolutionaries, but inside men's hearts and minds and wills, where events lay in embryo.

One cannot read such a revealing public document as Lincoln's Second Inaugural in the knowledge of contemporary opinion and events, and with a sense of what his words cost the president, without enlarging his own idea of what it is to be a man. It is so with the preface to Sir Walter Raleigh's *History of the World*, Vanzetti's letter, the Mayflower Compact, Sir Thomas More's speech before his execution, and his biography by Roper; it is so with *Mein Kampf*. One cannot read these documents on the human race and conclude either that man's private intention and decision has nothing to do with history or that he has acquired no addition to his store of valid evidence about what manner of creature we are.

Lewis Mumford, in the essay from which I have already quoted, offers an example of the sentimental muddle into which the judgment is thrown when history is taken to be exclusively a study of social forces. He is discussing the confusion of the self-styled liberals about the issue of the recent war. The time is 1940.

> The liberals could not understand that the gift of Czecho-Slovakia to Nazi Germany could not appease Hitler: that one might as well offer the carcass of a dead deer in a butcher store to a hunter who seeks the animal as prey—the meat being valued chiefly as a symbol of his prowess. And that is why the talk of mere economic adjustments that would enable the fascist states to live at peace with the rest of the world is muddled nonsense; it assumes, contrary to fact, that fascism springs out of rational motives and pursues concrete utilitarian ends. The bad arrangements of the peace of Versailles did not by themselves create fascism nor will the best results of a magnanimous peace conference be able at once to wipe out its destructive impulses and undermine its irrational philosophy. Unfortunately it is not in Ricardo or Marx or Lenin, but in Dante and Shakespeare and Dostoevski, that an understanding of the true sources of fascism is to be found. Economic explanations reflected a reality in the nineteenth century; they disguise a reality—the claim to barbaric conquest—today.[7]

What is the self-instruction necessary to understand the obstacles to peace in the 1940's, the 1950's, and the 1960's? Clearly it involves economic geography in all its measurable complexity. But to try to account for Mussolini, Hitler, and their would-be successors without some experience of pride would be to explain the explosion without the fuse, the eruption without the subterranean heat. To understand the bearing of economic geography on real or potential conflicts one must master a great many given and analyzed facts. The early and intermediate stages of the study are based almost altogether on set books or at least upon the treatment of set problems. It is the same with pride. Why is pride the deadliest of the sins? What is its relation to the lust for imperial conquest? Why is pride capable of bringing on tragedy, and why did the ancient *hybris* consist simply and exclusively in failure to know and keep one's place as a man—one's place in relation to one's self, to other men, and to the gods? These now neglected questions are undoubtedly more basic to the political problem of our generation than the race question in South Africa and the laying of the dust in the dust bowl.

Clearly, search in history for evidence of our nature relies on mature selection of evidence and criticism. Again Motley speaks of the terms of this judgment in the first volume of his *History of the United Netherlands*.

A vast responsibility rested upon the head of a monarch placed, as Philip II found himself, at this great dividing point in modern history. To judge him, or any man in such a position, simply from his own point of view, is weak and illogical. History judges the man according to its point of view. It condemns or applauds the point of view itself. The point of view of a malefactor is not to excuse robbery and murder. Nor is the spirit of the age to be pleaded in defense of the evil doer at a time when mortals were divided into almost equal troops. The age of Philip II was also the age of William of Orange and his four brethren, of Sainte-Aldegonde, of Olden-Barneveldt, of Duplessis-Mournay, La Moue, Coligny, of Luther, Melanchthon, and Calvin, of Walsingham, Sydney, Raleigh, Queen Elizabeth, of Michel Montaigne and William Shakespeare. It was not an age of blindness, but of glorious light. If the man whom the Maker of the universe had permitted to be born to such boundless functions chose to put out his own eyes that he might grope in darkness, by his deeds must he be judged. The king perhaps firmly believed that the heretics of the Netherlands, of France, or of England could escape eternal perdition only by being extirpated from the earth by fire and sword, and therefore, perhaps, felt it his duty to devote his life to their extermination. But he believed still more firmly that his own political authority throughout his dominions, and his road to almost universal empire, lay over the bodies of those heretics. Three centuries have nearly passed since this memorable epoch, and the world knows the fate of the states which accepted the dogma which it was Philip's life-work to enforce, and of those who protested against the system. The Spanish and Italian peninsulas have had a different history from that which records the career of France, Prussia, the Dutch commonwealth, the British Empire, the transatlantic Republic.[8]

"History judges the man according to *its* point of view. It condemns or applauds the point of view itself." History is clearly a mass of selected facts; this sentence stresses its additional character as a way to think. What is history's own point of view? Motley implies toward the end of the paragraph that among other things it is pragmatic, for it judges the wickedness of the Spanish monarch and his policies in the light of what they made of Spain in the subsequent three centuries. He observes that history deals in comparisons when he remarks the brilliance of the age which surrounded Philip in his darkness. But the center of his judgment (and his judgment will exemplify his notion of history's point of view) is moral. Its standard is nothing less than the norm of human conduct itself. Viewed against this it becomes clear—clear as the silhouette of a ship against the sky—what determined Philip's policy. It was the *libido dominandi*.

If one important purpose of the reading and writing of history is to achieve an estimate of our nature, this enterprise evidently requires two mature and highly sophisticated skills. One is skill in perception of human motives. The other is skill in judging these in the light of manhood itself. In large measure these are skills of village, bourse, and camp. They are the virtues of the sceptical listener to gossip who is able to sense the mote of truth in the beam of rumor, of the justice of the peace who is able to arbitrate in homely and blunt honesty between confused and confusing disputants. Translated into studies and elaborated, as they must be if one is to become competent either to read or to write the history of civilized and consequently elaborately organized people, these two skills are the skills of poetry. Reading literature and trying to write it is a proved and necessary way to develop the skills peculiar to the effective reading and writing of history.

The two abilities concerned may be called perception and judgment—the peculiar character of perception in history being that it must be focused upon the utterances and deeds of men; of judgment, that it be at home in the numerous known relations of the individual to universal manhood. The chapter which follows will deal with both of them.

6

Poetry

IN THIS BOOK the word *poetry* is used in its broadest sense. It connotes all literature which is neither history nor philosophy. It is, etymologically, the thing made, and its characteristic is fiction. Some importance attaches to whether or not it is rhymed and metric, but not fundamental importance. The word *literature* could usually be substituted for *poetry* as it is used here, but for reasons that will appear, the more strict and more ancient word is employed.

Like history, literature is held by some to be useful to the modern mind primarily for the light which it throws upon the known social problems of the present. So, in many quarters, goes the opinion of these times. Like those who treat history as a reference shelf from which ancient illustrations or examples may be drawn, those who thus limit the use of letters hold that all the humanities are a body of dead knowledge conveyed to us by the editors and annotators, a corpus of cultural record saying something about past cultures which it is hoped will be found germane to contemporary culture.

In a few words, what are the humanities?

In the reports of the humanities conference held to celebrate the Princeton Bicentennial, the two best statements were made by a Frenchman and a Mexican. M. Maritain said that among the chiefly significant elements in the humanistic tradition are the invincibility of the inner world and the superiority of delightfulness over usefulness, or the immanence of contemplation over transitory action. Señor O'Gorman said that he understood pursuit of the humanities to entail a passionate interest in immersing one's self in the knowledge of man. With due respect for our intellectual and other accomplishments, Professor O'Gorman found little of this in the United States; in its stead he observed that "all the discussion sooner or later revealed an ultimate concern with problems of a practical nature."

His analysis of our best thought and scholarship merits reflection. He had hoped that scholars in the humanities would be willing to consider the debated question of the historicity of man but found them involved in "academic and methodological problems in the teaching of history, implicitly considered as a discipline in the formation of the civic spirit." He observed that much of our concern for man is confined to experimental psychology. Replies to his letter published in the *American Scholar* aver that O'Gorman is unfair in his report of the conference at Princeton, and this may be true. Whether or not he has been unfair to the conference, he has certainly been fair to much in the profession of the humanities in these days. I regret that he described our shortcomings as a lack of metaphysics, since his criticism would with more point refer simply to the absence of profound critical thinking in the American pursuit of the humanities, and this lack would, in the last analysis, fall under the heading of ethics. Professor O'Gorman named the philosopher Heidegger as one whose thought should exemplify humanistic scholarship. The literary and critical scholar, Werner Jaeger, would be a better example, particularly in his book on the Greek nurture of youth called *Paideia*. Professor Jaeger is now, to our great advantage, a member of an American university, but we cannot boast that the American study of the humanities is characterized by the critical ethical thinking of that splendid work.

A long essay or volume would be required to prove by examination of history, letters, and ethics that the idea that the humanities are merely the culture of the past is wrong and that the view implied by the two scholars quoted is correct. This contrast and its implications should be evident to all. Either inner action, as of the will, is more important than temporary outer action or it is not; if it is more important, it is clearly the concern of the humanities. Either the understanding of the "measure of the fullness of the stature" of man is a constant and lively and ever-renewed obligation of reasonable men or it is not. If it is our obligation, the humanist is something far different from a mere transmitter of the past, and the subject of his studies is something far subtler and more profound than societies and institutions.

The humanities are better represented by Leonardo sketching the faces of the condemned in the executioner's car than by Ficino writing a treatise on Platonic theology. They are the critical discovery of our own nature by use of the most reliable evidence and the most accurate ways available to treat it. The evidence is both direct, in a man's own life, and recorded, the record being important not at all because of its age (its age is incidental, and knowledge of its age is of value only to illuminate its meaning) but because it is first class—that is, nearest to the truth, clearest, richest. They constitute both a body of knowledge and a training in perception and judgment of the kind necessary to the interpretation of history and all human experience.

Some say that the object of liberal studies is historical, philosophical, and global perspective. This object has a genuine, if limited, usefulness; and in some parts of systematic knowledge to master the idea of a culture also is of assistance, particularly in reasoning about primitive societies. But resultant generalizations are not basic to the problem in hand, which concerns the nature of the individual. They are not basic; indeed, they may be downright misleading. What the century needs is a valid account of particulars, of particular man, and a valid understanding of how to judge him against the composite generality, manhood. A moratorium should be declared upon the word *culture;* consign it to the deep freeze, along with *heritage, tra-*

dition, and *the past*, so long as these are regarded as virtuous not so much for the active ideas and vigorous life they contain and its quality, but primarily because they refer to what happened long ago. When important only because of its age, the past is indeed "a bucket of ashes."

The center of the humanities is poetry. How does poetry help us deal with the critical issue of the century? In two ways: as training in perception and judgment; and as the embodiment of much human experience. Reading and writing poetry imparts a skill that is essential to thinking in human terms about men. That is its first usefulness. The second lies in what poetry says and is its intrinsic value, poetry itself, which is evidence and judgment combined. The subject of this chapter is the training and skill which poetry supplies.

In our century we are peculiarly subject to misleading stereotypes of word, symbol, and judgment. All about us we see the plausible but false account of ourselves pass for the accurate and the true. Men and women in the slick magazines are usually a standardized sentimental version of ourselves. The boy going fishing always has a bandaged toe, a broken straw hat, and a can of worms; the man in the Abercrombie & Fitch angler's outfit has no fish and an embarrassed look on his face. When the second-rate playwrights put a small boy in a dialogue, he does the stage-standard tricks of squirming and kicking his feet; it is disclosed that he failed to wash behind his ears. Old ladies sit in a chair, not really imitating old ladies, but a cliché idea of an old lady in the popular mind which has been provided, for instance, by Whistler's mother or the harridan made popular by *The Whiteoaks of Jalna*. Early in the war someone back from danger in a foreign theater got out of the transport and kissed the American earth. The passionate idea may have been his own. Then someone was photographed doing this, and soon there were dozens being photographed, overjoyed, beyond doubt, to be safely home, but expressing as much the image they had seen as the object in their own understanding. Life copies art as much as art copies life. The little girl has a doll carriage and roller skates, and she squeezes the doll at the neck under her elbow as regularly as the communist cartoon of the capitalist shows him with gross fingers and a torpedo cigar. The extent to which we prefer the stereotype to the real representation of ourselves and the world is colossal. Most of the joke-book stories told after dinner are beside the truth; indeed, some famous raconteurs are so adept at reducing what happened to the surefire formula for a laugh that you soon learn that what is being told is going to be slightly falsified. I know of a grade school in the country where children in the drawing class are not encouraged to look at the rabbits, which are numerous where they live, but are taught to trace a Walt Disney monstrosity with bad teeth, and to use kewpie stencils for people.

"The proper study of mankind is man." So elaborate have become the images by which we in the twentieth century now talk about man and study him, one might say that we have improved on Pope: "The proper study of mankind is mannikins." In our century, mannikins are in great favor, as you will see not only in the store window and in the image of man which emerges from most of the works on sociology, psychology, and education, but also in the image visible in the movies, advertisements, slick magazines, and many of the best sellers. Censors of the mail of American soldiers and sailors during the war observed that most of them wrote the same letter home. Here the mannikin symbol had sunk so deep that it had frozen into almost meaningless form the private and most precious thoughts, not of the old and tired, but of the young. This intimate fact about how in our hearts we fail to see objects for what they truly are and with our own eyes is alarming indeed, more alarming than the pathetic acceptance by those wishing to cheer someone dear to them, of the ready-phrased congratulations sold by the telegraph company.

If you have ever tried to paint or draw a portrait, you have discovered that your chief enemy is the mannikin whose symmetrical and wooden face you are tempted to place on the canvas instead of the character-revealing countenance of the sitter before you. So beset are we in this age of inexpensive pictures, print, and the transmission of words, with the image which obscures and substitutes itself for the object, we may say that the first purpose of literary studies is to get into our minds in place of the conformity seen by the undiscerning, man, as directly, and vividly, and truly as we can understand him.

The imperious demand of the times that one master the clichés accentuates this duty of education. For in the city you can hardly go about without learning the essential formulae. To move quickly enough to earn a living, you must have these clichés at your tongue's tip—nay, you must think with them. If you doubt this, ask directions of a policeman in good and idiomatic English, but by means of words and sentence structures not common in the talk of civilians to policemen. You need not use one word with which the officer is unfamiliar, yet he won't understand you. Or try in your own words to place a long-distance telephone call. You will waste time and nerves until the policeman and the telephone operator have translated your unconventional sentences into the speedy formulae which they have been trained to hear and act upon, or the waitress has successfully referred your desire for coffee to the list of "beverages." Apparently, mastery of the clichés of the organization of trade and social intercourse is intended in the theory that education is adjustment. See how speedily the adjusted adolescent succeeds at a party, once he has mastered the stereotypes of the younger set—a parody of youth, really, not youth itself.

To fail to see objects and live in a world of images—this is a description of middle age at its worst. It is also a description of much serious writing and thinking which passes for scientific in our century. Images organized into systems are responsible for what Francis Bacon called the Idols of the Theater. The fixed categories about ourselves constructed into so-called sciences are responsible for removing many from a direct and authentic touch with the world and the men in it. The reasoning which relies exclusively upon dialectic has a fallacious sound, and the fallacy lies here—the images are what is reasoned upon, not the reality beneath them.

The avoidance of misleading idols in our thinking is a task of education. Perception of various kinds can be taught. As an amateur painter, I can testify to what teaching will do to the eye. I had thought that the observation of elaborately combined and elusive color indoors and outdoors was a sensory power with which others were born but not I. Fortunately for my pleasure in the world, I have enjoyed the instruction of two or three distinguished painters, in classes in which many of the other students were committed to painting for life. My teachers did nothing but ask questions: what did we see; did we really see in nature what was there, rather than what years of looking at other men's pictures had led us to expect to see? Gradually this Socratic process enlarged the complexity of our vision. I now can see in nature numerous colors whose names I had heard or read about, but whose existence I had accepted merely on authority. By comparison and analysis of what is seen, the eye can be refined. Observe the object in motion, in its own shadow cast by blazing sunlight, in rain, under the elbow or the legs, and from the edge of the eye, and try always to state the color on the canvas. The process is intellectual as well as sensory; the effect upon one's powers of perception is astonishing. In a similar fashion the perception of incidents and objects in the world—the mind's perception of them—may be recreated, sharpened, and refined. The process is the process of poetry.

Poetry is a way to think, and it is available to every man. Its chief practical usefulness to us lies in improving our ability to see the world as in itself it really is. Poetry's chief concern is faithfulness to the fact. Its usefulness is enhanced because of the kind of fact which engages it most, for this is the hidden fact, and usually the human fact, often charged with emotion and difficult to understand or even to see—it is what, in human and down-to-earth terms, may be called the spiritual fact. The first question about a thing or an incident to be answered by a poem is: what is it, really?

These remarks sound odd to those accustomed to think of poetry as a series of sighs about the evening star or a canoe in the moonlight or who confuse poetry with something written on a birthday package. One distinguished teacher of poetry, on hearing one of the Ah-poems read in class, slapped the desk and said: "You go down to the brook and *look* at a skunk cabbage, and don't come back until you have seen one." Poetry's faithfulness to the fact will surprise anyone who holds the illusion that it deals primarily with never-never land—in short, anyone who has not read much poetry.

To be specific, consider the example of literature called a poem. Ignorance of what poetry is cannot be dispelled by describing poems. Poems should be spoken, written, and ruminated upon. To teach many people poetry would be to provide what Professor O'Gorman calls a direct, original, and authentic knowledge of man instead of a representative, descriptive, and imaginary one. To teach many people poetry, however, requires first of all schooling in imagination in order to improve the skill in sensing what is valid and tends toward truth and what is sentimental or fantastic. It requires also the highest type of accuracy—spiritual accuracy. It requires time and a special kind of learning, for what is being learned is a way to think which is different from the way to think in other studies.

What happens is that in poetry one refines and elaborates a natural and naïve way to think; in other sorts of learning this naturalness and naïveté, for good reasons, are discredited. Gertrude Stein may have said some silly things, but now and then she said a trenchant one, as when she remarked that in early childhood the image and the object are coincident, but imperceptibly as we grow older the object steals away from behind the image more and more, leaving us in an adult world composed almost entirely of images.

To train the imagination so that by it one may learn to continue to see objects instead of images and to prize objects above images—that is the task of the teacher of the humanities. The higher learning by and large is the Lady of Shalott. Literature alone makes it possible to look out of the window as well as into the mirror—not to judge by appearances. There is but one thing more red-blooded than poetry and this is life itself. Cultural history is the reflection of poetry, little more than images. If experience is to be described by its circumstances—economic, political, historical, and geographical—then experience itself will never be understood. Description of circumstances without foundation in the human law is the enemy of any truly humane understanding unless it is kept, as John Livingston Lowes said of the footnotes to *The Road to Xanadu*, "severely kennelled in the rear." Cultural history is stage directions and belongs behind the scenes. Even backstage it must be kept in its place. When John Barrymore, for example, undertook *Hamlet*, he eschewed all prefaces, critical commentary, and footnotes, isolating himself in the woods for two years with nothing but the bare lines of the poem. He was determined that every inflection should be controlled by the meaning of the whole play, and the result was a production of *Hamlet* which by its unity and new discovery of meaning or humor in the lines was the marvel even of the "authorities." In order to teach poetry with honor, the way to think peculiar to poetry must be held in honor, side by side with the historical and dialectical processes, which, when they become overweening, discredit literature.

A good practical way to train the imagination to see objects instead of images is to translate some prose or verse out of Greek or Latin into English, or the reverse; for to make a fair representation of the ideas in another language requires both imagination, and in the process, a disciplining. For the imagination is applied, if the foreign literature is a good one, to the subtlest and most elusive and most important ideas of mankind. To write a sonnet in English; to write a story and make it a story and make it come off; to produce a play or act a complex part: these are exercises both in the development of imagination and in the discipline of it. Most of all to read poetry or the best prose and understand it—perhaps to prove your understanding by the perfect and only inflection in reading the passage aloud: that is an accomplishment.

How does this training begin? It starts small and remains at its highest reaches dependent upon understanding the elements: metaphor, overtone, innuendo, lyric, and story. These are not mere techniques of analysis. When I say understanding metaphor I do not mean the tagging of tropes, learning the difference between the definitions of metaphor and simile, and the Virgilian simile. I mean the way the poet thinks and the way, if he is to understand, the reader must think. That is, to think with metaphor, lyric, and story.

Metaphor is as essential to the understanding of poetry as interpolation to trigonometry. Without a lively and active knowledge of metaphor in use, you could no more read *Moby Dick* or "The Eve of St. Agnes" than you could expect, without algebra, to deal with the quantum theory. Let us name over, textbook fashion, some of the departments of using metaphor: it carries you toward precision in both the visible and the invisible world; each metaphor has its own limitations; if carried one step beyond its own proper use, a metaphor turns away from accuracy and quickly offends you by its untruth (consider the dead idea of "perspective" in the committee opinion about culture); to use Robert Frost's phrase, there is "metaphor of the whole" and "metaphor of the part." When Thomas Hardy was dying he had read to him again and again Walter De la Mare's poem, "The Listeners," which contains the lines:

> "Tell them I came, and no one answered,
> That I kept my word," he said.

Undoubtedly the reason Hardy asked for the poem is its metaphor of the whole, which allows one to take supreme comfort in the fact of the existence of virtue which is oblivious not only of rewards, but even of responses or recognition.

Metaphor of the part without metaphor of the whole produces sayings, epigrams, and witty conversation. Metaphor of the whole without metaphor of the part produces dead raw arguments, the mere prose thinking of logical metaphysicians. Metaphor of the part when reiterated becomes fixed in symbols (cherubim and the dove); some of it has further hardened into language (*spiritus*, spirit). In a poem, metaphor of the part must be wild, free and surprising, and to order the amazing revelations into a poem all metaphor of the part must serve the metaphor of the whole. Some consider metaphors mere "beauties," the cloves to the ham. They are, of course, the substance of poetry, as of thought.

Metaphor may be physical on both sides, as when you say the cook's face was as red as the lid of the stove. Or it may go from material to immaterial, as when you say, "He is the kind of person who wounds with his shield." The unmentioned sword is there, the sword with which most men deliver wounds. But to speak of this is to become, as Mr. Frost says, "too thorough." Those five words of the metaphor itself contain a full novel. Walter Pater made a metaphor so elaborate that one would think it could not stay in our consciousness to assist thought—"to burn always with that hard gem-like flame"; but in spite of its complexity this idea remains among the working tools of our minds.

There is also a lyrical way of thinking—for the poet and for the reader. Those who associate with the word *lyric* the textbook idea that a lyric is the private and sometimes unintelligible cry of the human heart should remember that song in poetry is far more ancient than the nineteenth- and twentieth-century romantic lyrists. A lyric is a song; the best songs, like those of Ben Jonson and Shakespeare, have become the common possession of the most objective of all critics, everyman. The lyrical way of thinking is the way of thinking in song. It is the way the poet celebrates his theme—"Arms and the man I sing." This lyrical way of thinking is to be found in all the arts—dance, painting, music—for the chief business of each of the arts is to describe and celebrate the world.

Most things seen or thought about have a very slight third dimension if any depth at all. In the arts the third dimension is so real that the object stands surrounded by air and light, separated from the world behind and beneath, all by itself and undeniably a thing in itself. It is placed in the world, but for the moment isolated and vivid to the eye, as vivid as the figure in a Renaissance portrait, bright, dark, warm, and present, cutting with its contour the pale blue shapes of the landscape background. It has light and weight and depth, like a loaf by Vermeer. We say it sings; something glorifies it. If it is a snake, it is more snake—"tumbling in twenty coils" or "parting the grass as with a comb"; if a drunkard, more surely drunk—"This is my right hand, and this is my left"; a rascal, Iago; the lovesick, "If music be the food of love, play on"; a lover,

> She bids you on the wanton rushes lay you down
> And she will sing the song that pleases you.

Eric Bentley recently remarked that a potato by Cézanne would be superior to a crucifixion by Holman Hunt. The reason is that Cézanne was the better celebrant. By glorifying the object in the light of reason and imagination he made it more truly itself. The counterpart of this quality in poetry is lyric. Why, for example, is the ugly story of Medea a poem when Euripides tells it, and little more than a shrill scream when Robinson Jeffers tries his hand? Because the Euripides play is lyrical, even in tragedy, while the Jeffers is not. Chaucer has a reputation for telling stories; part of it rests on the fact that he is a lyrist.

To celebrate an idea is not to gild it; on the contrary, it is to see it as in itself it really is. The cock stands up in the barnyard, surrounded by the sun, and when he crows

In all the land of crowyng nas his peer:
His voys was murier than the murie orgon.

In short, he is more truly cock, the representative cock, supported by a poet's delight in the physical world. Shakespeare, a master of the metaphor of the part as well as of metaphor of the whole, seems to make unendurable pain more bearable by means of singing lines:

We two alone will sing like birds i' the cage.

But becoming endurable, the tragedy deepens; the pain has not blacked you out in a faint; you are still conscious, and there before you, intensified, is the terrible destruction of the unfilial and unimaginative mind. The awful fact is the longer and more accurately regarded.

When something is celebrated in song it is held under the eye for a span and we see that it is worth notice. As celebration proceeds, for example, in the songs of Ophelia, not only the eye but our whole inward apprehension observes, and what we see is many times greater than what can be conveyed by prose. In artificial light a painting by Renoir has a few strong colors and that is all; by daylight, a hundred unsuspected ones. It is so when by means of celebration we see a thing or a person or an idea.

Like familiarity with lyric, familiarity with story is acquired by use, not by precept. These lessons take long to learn. History proves that all kinds of people learn them: fishermen, bank presidents, the C-grade student, the disciplinary case, the Phi Beta Kappa, the general. To know a story and why it is a story and why it cannot be translated into exposition and remain the same, and that the rarest and mightiest possessions of the human spirit can be discovered only by means of story and by no other process of thinking—to know all this and to have it as your own is to have much. The beginnings of this knowledge are available, like general education, to every man, and to each according to his capacity to take and use.

For most American youth, Greek and Latin are gone and have been lamented. In the search for something to take their place, we should remember the real usefulness of those honorable studies. They trained the imagination. This was possible even in the old, harsh grammatical and translating disciplines for four reasons: because the literature to be read was peculiarly refined and strong; because the languages were two of the best; because the pause necessary to deal with phrases in a strange tongue gave time for the meaning of the phrases to work upon the student; and because the difficult task of conveying as nearly as possible in our own language the subtle intent of the ancient sentences required extensive trial of little-used resources of our own tongue. If and when something is found effectively to take the place of the old schoolboy Greek and Latin, it will be something which also requires long meditation upon words, and their meanings and elaborate associations, and upon the affairs of the human heart which produce wars, marriages, and harvest festivals. No thoughtful boy is the same after beginning to master in the few years of the end of adolescence the meaning of *hybris*, *nemesis*, and *areté*. It may be that by reading and writing literature and dwelling upon the voluminous significance of the words with which we carry on privately the soul's own conversation with herself, that is, American English words, young people will come equally far by beginning to master the meaning of such loaded words as lust-in-action, charity, felicity.

These matters may sound small, not to say trivial, in the presence of discussion of the Bomb and the United Nations by the President's Commission, and their opinion that the guiding principle of general education for all youth should be the discovery and dissemination of new social techniques. But very fresh in my mind is the example of a boy back from the Burma Road who tussled and struggled with the ballads, finding no connection between those old wars and war as he had seen it. The class read "The Ode to Melancholy," and on this he spent fearful travail. Asked what the poem said, he replied after much thought: "Don't be downhearted!" Sent back to try again, he reported that the poem means, "*Always* be downhearted!" So he labored on poetry for a fruitless year and a half, and tried to read *Paradise Lost* without ever having read the Old Testament. One day he came to say he had heard on the radio "The Twelve Days of Christmas." "Gosh! I had no idea there was anything like *that!*" It was the entering wedge. Understanding one poem, penetrating beyond the fantasy and symbols in it to the truth they stood for, made possible the comprehension of other poems. This one ballad converted the operative idea in his mind of part of what it is to love a girl—translated it from the shallow and impoverished conventions of Hollywood to something more intelligent and particular. Other ballads and poems further refined his reading and perceptive powers, until afterwards, when he read Southey's *Life of Nelson*, his understanding even of that biography so far surpassed his best performance six months before, one wondered if he was the same boy.

This student has endurance, humor, and wholesomeness, and probably one day his teachers and parents will be the more proud of him because his eyes have been opened, and he is no longer a victim of blind and even cheap conformity. He is but one, and the schools and colleges are populous. If we could multiply his small discovery and the genuine instruction in understanding and the emotions which followed, we would enrich the quality and increase the maturity of judgment in American life.

The part which poetry can have in the discovery of our nature and whether or not the individual is precious and subject to law is so central, the discerning reader will wonder, "Why begin a discussion of poetry by treating it as a means to an end?" So far this chapter has laid down but one proposition: that literature assists every man to discern the fact and absorb the feeling beneath the current and popular half-representation of these, and that this assistance is essential to an accurate reading of history or any reliable estimate of contemporary affairs. The chapter will deal with one other use of poetry as a means of reasoning. Previous discussion stated that to read or write history requires two abilities. The first of these is perception of human intent, feeling, and overtone of meaning, a skill peculiar to the reading and writing of poetry. The second ability is that necessary in reaching the critical estimates demanded by history. Its necessity is evident when one speaks of the point of view of history and discovers that this entails not only a summary of historical events, but primarily a picture of man. The skill needed is skill in comparing the particular human deed or opinion with something universal in men.

One might expect this task to be assigned to philosophy, whose explicit business is to define and state relationships, but the chief viable example of the skill in question will be found to be a special characteristic of poetry. History's business is poetry's business, too: the accurate assessment of where a particular man stands in relation to manhood. Poetry is instructive to history because, like history, it is so lively, because like history, its subject is the event, and because history, like poetry, is shot through with tragedy and comedy.

The beginner in the short-story course puts into the mouth of his hero coming out of a swoon the words, "Where am I?" But the instructor red-pencils this. Almost anything else is allowed: "Who hit me?" or "Edythe!" or "Water!" Modern man is said to have been clopped on the head, and the authors of the dialogue seek words to put into his mouth as he comes back to daylight. For all our cleverness, we who represent the higher learning have managed to think up nothing more original for his next speech than "Where am I?"

I refer to the new general education courses and their lust for location. They assume that what men need most is to learn where they are, and they try to give bearings on the past. As one reads more closely the reports of committees and prefaces to new courses one learns that the real subject of study is not man but societies—how this society emerged from some other and how it compares with a third or even a future one. I have quoted some of the ablest university leaders to this effect. The report of the President's Commission on Higher Education says the same thing.

I am willing to grant that it is usually a good plan to know your way about, but let us not forget the many brilliant and able minds of our acquaintance who get lost in the streets, and for whom ignorance of the compass is nothing worse than an amusing joke. Let us remember also how downright destructive map-mindedness can be. I once watched a group of tourists "do" the Louvre, camera on chest, guidebook open in hand. They trooped into a room containing a famous small head by Lotto, finding their way by their feet as they read the compass card in Baedeker. By some miraculous museum habit their feet stopped before the picture; they finished reading, looked up, and exclaimed, almost in unison, "Lotto!" and left the room.

Location courses are designed to meet the objection that the university has become multiple and to give not only unity but "integration." The argument runs that while a century and a half ago theology, often dispensed in lectures by the president of the college, gave centrality to studies, such supernatural assistance is no longer available (perhaps because the presidents are no longer supermen) and history, including the history of ideas, must make whatever sense can be made of the fascinating welter of modern knowledge.

Western Civilization; the Humanities: as we read the description of these courses we observe a kind of *mappa mundi*, and it is by no accident that in this *nouveau moyen âge* we have turned to making maps. In austere rationalism, barely warmed by imagination, and lacking the courage and abandon which goes with humor, we have earnestly studied, as did our cousins, the scholastic thinkers, the connectives of knowledge. Academic people like to regard the educational plans of St. John's College and the University of Chicago as medieval oddities in the twentieth century. Some of the efforts to implement the academic proposals of these institutions are certainly unusual, but the intellectual reaction which they represent is fairly general in our lifetime. It is a force in most committee thinking about the higher learning, the reaction from disorder to system.

The fact that "Where am I?" is trite means that there really is some reason for the question. One of our concerns is, in truth, location, and the trouble with locating ourselves by means of *mappa mundi* or chronology or philosophical system is that no one of these compass cards nor all taken together have the important directions. And by studying and accepting merely the facts of history or the movements of society or the systems of philosophy, we may in effect abuse our sense of where we are within ourselves and in relation to what in truth confronts us. The explicit location in these various studies—history, philosophy, politics—is surely useful. But it becomes significant to the individual only if simultaneously he has mastered some more basic way to think, the foundation rock for his house of education.

Know thyself. The ancient phrase has probably been made to mean literally everything which anybody ever thought important. A university professor once publicly said he thought it meant: Know your cells and organs; for he emblazoned the slogan at the Chicago Century of Progress Exposition over formaldehyde exhibits of the human embryo and foetus in successive stages. For the ancients, γνῶθι σαυτόν referred, among other things, to location. "Know thyself" meant "know where you stand." So Critias in the *Charmides*, speaking of the inscription at the temple of Delphi, said: "That word, if I am not mistaken, is put there as a word of salutation which the god addresses to those who enter the temple; as much as to say that the ordinary salutation of Hail! is not right, and that the exhortation Be temperate! would be a far better way of saluting one another. The notion of him who dedicated the inscription was, as I believe, that the god speaks to those who enter his temple, not as men speak; but when a worshipper enters, the first word which he hears is Be temperate! This, however, like a prophet he expresses in a sort of riddle, for 'Know thyself!' and 'Be temperate!' are the same. . . ."

The mayor of Chicago said during the 1893 World's Fair: Chicago can achieve whatever it purposes, and it has fixed its purpose upon a star. Since apparently the mayor took himself seriously, location would have been important for him; he might have avoided talking like a fool by knowing where as men we all stand. Location in these terms involves dimensions difficult to grasp, the important dimensions dealt with by poetry. It is the knowledge acquired at fearful cost by the protagonists in tragedy. "This knowledge," says Professor Bowra in speaking of Sophoclean tragedy, "is about themselves, but primarily about themselves in relation to the gods." "For Sophocles," he goes on, "this is the essential and fundamental knowledge. A man does not know himself or his place until he knows how he stands with the gods."

How one stands with the gods sounds archaic to any but those acquainted with Greek tragedy. The gods are not worshipped nowadays. No. But one cannot see the translation of the *Antigone* prepared during the occupation of Paris in order to present to the brave men and women of the Resistance a reason for their faith in France without sensing that how Antigone stood with the gods was precisely how a man or woman in any time preserves or wins his own self-respect. Maxwell Anderson asked the ancient question in examining his own plays and the musical comedies, tragicomedies, and tragedies on Broadway. He put it this way: "Why does the audience come to the theatre to look on while an imaginary hero is put to an imaginary trial and comes out of it with credit to the race and himself?"[9] He found the answer in the demand of the audience that the play prove "that men pass through suffering purified, that, animal though we are, despicable though we are in many ways, there is in us all some divine, incalculable fire that urges us to be better than we are."[10] This expectation by the audience, regardless of their professed religion or lack of it, can be taken to constitute in twentieth-century men as much as any others a concern with how they stand with the gods.

Poetry's supreme demonstration of the relation of this particular man to universal man is tragedy. There the light is in keenest focus. Poetry shows the relation also in comedy, for the fun in comedy, known by every audience without a split second of taking thought, arises from the flick of insight we have of ourselves and our kind in foibles, failures, and predicaments, against a well-known and understood picture of manhood. The comedy usually refers to manners, and here the standard is a stiff and fragile pattern, usually of conventions of the time. The comedy sometimes is gigantically human, as in Falstaff, and then the picture against which at every comic moment the comparisons are made is human dignity in the large, *virtus*.

By means of its familiarity with these comparisons, and the skill in judgment which experience with poetry imparts, it equips us to reason about history and to see the well-perceived person, place, or event, not from the point of view of our own times or of our party or of the age under consideration, but from history's own point of view, which is human.

7

How the Free Man Decides

When each man asks himself privately what he thinks about the individual and his responsibility, what will he say? If he is a reasonable and alert person he will have accumulated a numerous series of instances which bear upon his opinion, a succession so long that he has forgotten most of them, retaining only a sensation about them or about what he thought they meant at a time of reflection. He has behind him when you put to him the all-important ethical question of democracy a set of opinions like this: the people in that affair proved themselves despicable; or, the principals in that dispute were of two kinds: some of them acted out of greed alone, but A, B, and C appeared to have a sense of honor or in some way to be affected by the probable consequence of their deeds upon others, or upon their own self-respect.

The instances will come from everywhere, many from family and private or business affairs, many from the newspapers, history, and literature. Those from literature will be especially peopled with events seen upon the stage or screen; directly or indirectly the tales from the Old Testament, Aesop, Grimm, the Arabian Nights, and the ballads will figure, whether the reasonable and alert person has heard any of these in early versions or at many removes in the retelling which continues in all languages. This is true because the stories of Job, Jacob and Esau, Samson, Sinbad, Hansel and Gretel, and the Fox are at once so violent and so clear.

For the purpose of analysis we may divide into two categories what the reasonable man has in his mind to draw upon in treating the ethical question of democracy. The subject of his reflection is made up of people and plots. The only rule of evidence by which he admits or eliminates a person from his consideration is whether he believes that what he knows about him is true. This rule admits on equal terms the fictitious people of literature and the real ones of daily life and history. To all three kinds of character he applies the same question: Do I have authentic information about him? Is this what he really is or was like? If so, the whole private acceptance or rejection of him as evidence concerning the human race is this: Do I believe he exists? For example, what I happen to know intimately of Hamlet is both more extensive and more persuasive than what I happen to know of Lorenzo the Magnificent; so for the private purposes of making up my own mind about men, I find the Dane more real than the Florentine. This is, of course, not merely a question of the extent of my knowledge or its vividness, but primarily a question of whether I regard as probable what few internal facts I possess about both men. Do the reports I have about a particular man convince me that it is likely that such a person may truly have done what I am told he did? By contrast the campaign biography of a politician is readily rejected as evidence and would probably be so rejected by any careful reader even though ignorant of the purpose of the book, simply because to a thoughtful person it would usually not ring true.

Nothing is gained by trying to draw sharp distinctions between the people of fiction, of history, and of contemporary life. To call the last real and the other two successively less and less so is to pin reality upon nothing but immediacy. The "realistic" effort of contemporary educators to explain, expurgate, or change the fairy tales, miracles, and mysterious ancient stories by "science" has the effect of explaining them away. The impoverishment forced upon childhood by such nonsense is incalculable. By this one aberration of modern education alone countless children have not only been crippled in imagination, they have been deprived of some of the most tried and accurate evidence possessed by the race concerning its own nature. To read the prophylactic versions of the Bible, Grimm, and the Greek and medieval legends now sold by "enlightened" educationists is to witness a wilful destruction comparable to the bombing of cities. The prissy discussion of these as myths and folklore is the ultimate desiccation of the academic mind. Tales of gods, giants, fairies, elves, and devils are documents about ourselves. We need them to think with; they are admitted evidence in the private court of one's own judgment. Why? The frog and the beast must persuade someone who loves them to strike off their heads. Only if they succeed will they be restored to their rightful forms. In other words, your best friend *will* tell you, and is willing to wound you in order to correct or save you. This is as much a daylight fact as any other. In the Middle Ages there may have been danger that men confuse stories with the measurable fact by which they gained their daily bread. But despite the prevalence of voodoo and gypsy-craft in modern cities, the chief danger now is all the other way, that the ethical truth of stories will be missed. The danger is that their ethical truth *has been* missed by the literal-spirited philosophers who control in a vast monopoly the motivating ideas by which the young in these matters are robbed of their birthright.

No child intelligently taught has suffered long or seriously in discovering, between the ages of about seven and ten, the distinction between the figures of fairyland and those of his daily routine of home and school. On the contrary, the discovery is a natural one and raises surprisingly few questions for the child. Far from suffering, the child permitted to know in all their fierceness and evil the people and contests of fairies, gods, and giants has made an essential start upon his own long road of discovery and judgment of what manner of creature he and his kind actually are.

The question of mature judgment about the individual involves childhood stories only incidentally. At its center lie the great stories, both historical and fictitious, which men rehearse to each other on the stage, in history books, on canvas, and in all the arts. In the mind of the well-read man there lies a populous city, where dwell the mature men and women to him important because intimately, accurately, and vividly known. The list is long, and the variety great. The mean and the magnanimous are there: Salmon Chase and Abraham Lincoln, Iago and Cordelia; there also are the humbly innocent and the humbly prideful: Bottom the weaver, Heep, and the unnamed soldiers who brought David the water from Bethlehem.

We are here concerned with the practical question, how may the normally alert and reasonable person construct for himself an idea of what as men we are like? He begins with his own experience. After that, the class of evidence which is at once most nearly accurate and most clearly pointed—the best, most useful, and most reliable records—are all poetry; though those of history run very close seconds. The best records may lack rhyme, meter, or external form; people are more comfortable when you call them literature; but in the broad sense of "the thing made" they are poetry. The raw experience of our lives related to them is best understood in the terms of poetry—that is, by superimposing upon experience an order and a form, not necessarily an old form, perhaps an altogether new one, but a form, as when Browning used the records of an old court trial for *The Ring and the Book*.

The primacy of this treatment of human experience was flatly stated by Aristotle. When one mentions Aristotle in these days, he is accused of being esoteric; but let us remember that the *Poetics* was an analysis of public opinion, of the reaction of common people in a crowd at the theater, then and now the most popular kind of thinking. Those who have read the essay with care are still inclined to deem it superior in precision to a Hooper rating. "Poetry," said Aristotle, "is something more scientific and serious than history," φιλοσοφώτερον—more scientific or more philosophical or, as sometimes translated, more nearly true. This sentence, illuminated by the Aristotelian idea of the universal and of fiction, gives the key to the nature of the humanities—not, obviously, because Aristotle delivered it, but because the predominating evidence over two millennia, in scores of nations, by millions of theatergoers and hecatombs of critics and philosophers points to its viability. It implies that the subject of the humanities is man in action—inward as well as outward action—and it states that the peculiarly human way of representing, examining, and reflecting upon this action is poetry—or what, using the more general term, we call literature.

The people of fiction, said Aristotle, are imitations of the people of history and contemporary life, but he hastened to define imitation as something much different from a copy. They are emulations of the idea of the person which the person himself was trying, unconsciously no doubt, to be. These persons of fiction, like the happenings of the story, must be probable. That is, the reader must be led to say: they *would* behave like this on receiving the letter or learning the truth about their king. People in real life are eccentric; sometimes they are too eccentric, that is, too special, for art. It is the same with wild nature. If you put the colors of the Grand Canyon on a canvas, it will doubtless look like a color postcard, which no one entirely believes. G. K. Chesterton found the same to be true of Dickens's Little Nell and decided that she is so improbable she must be a copy of some unique person Dickens had observed. If this is true, Dickens fell short of art itself in presenting her and became what the sculptors call "model-bound." "Nature," said Chesterton, "is as free as air, art is forced to look probable."

One fruit of discerning reflection upon people revealed to their possessor in poetry, experience, and history, is a growing sense of what it is to be a person, and of the distinction between a person with a name and an individual with a number. Mark Van Doren describes the difference as follows:

> The person in an individual is the man in him, the thing that politics respects when it is wise and good. It is what the doctrine of equality respects. It is the medium through which individuals understand one another; it is the source of language and the explanation of love. And it solves many mysteries of the thing called person-

ality. Individuality is less powerful; it is uniqueness, it is eccentricity, it is something we lack tongue to praise. He who is most a person is, strangely, the least personal of men; he is least hidebound by a notion he has of his own integrity. He is surprised when he hears of that, having all the while been occupied by the world's variety. There are many things he prefers to himself and tries to be. What he tries most steadily to be is a man. And when we praise him we praise his humanity. We compliment individuals; we praise persons for the virtues in them which they share with other men. An old way of saying that is that good men—that is, men—tend to be alike. Virtue is single and general; courage is not what one is but what one has.[1]

A man who can sense this distinction between the individual and the person and know it in history and in contemporary thought has progressed far in liberal education.

Mr. Van Doren's analysis, a distinction unpopular in our lifetime, has often been attacked, when expressed by others, as a mere vestige of the "genteel tradition." None will accuse Igor Stravinsky of being "genteel," yet in this particular he agrees with those who find that a person is something elevated because he is common and that what gives the individual his value is the possibility he shares with all people of becoming more and more, as he grows, a person. Ours, said Stravinsky, is the "new age that seeks to reduce everything to uniformity in the realm of matter while it tends to shatter all universality in the realm of spirit in deference to an anarchic individualism." Universality in the realm of spirit, he said, is represented by "the dignity of the human person (which must not be confused with the individual)."[2] Thus the worth of the individual, his dignity, and the reason why liberalism always respects his integrity and worth and treats his house as his castle, lie in his universality, the same human universality which sets the standard for character, be it fictitious or historical, and the standard of right.

The literary, critical, and artistic prejudices of the times, of course, have been at odds with this classical distinction between the individual and the person. *Personality* is thought popularly to be described by a man's unusualness, not his usualness. The man with a personality has queer hair, or an odd nose or laugh, or distaste for dogs or oysters, or extreme enthusiasm for tap dancing. He is, in short, a man of humours, one whose uniqueness lies not so much in the quality of what he does as in the odd direction which his peculiarities take. Genius is thought popularly nowadays to consist in such intense cultivation of foibles. Progressive education made much of eccentricity. Its concern with "interests" led at times to a solemn preoccupation with whims. Its votaries boasted of a college girl who in her freshman year arrived with a pet turkey of whom she was passionately fond. Progressive education, so its apologists maintained, turned that pet turkey into a liberal education! Uniqueness of all kinds has been in favor in this century, and not many years ago a wag, observing the lust of the arty to be unusual, said that the cup of our uniquity is full to overflowing. Mr. Van Doren is at odds with the worship of oddity. He is saying that the peculiarly human element is what we have in common with all men; he is reiterating in a different context the Aristotelian principle that to be truly great a character or a story must be universal, that is, representative or probable.

The abiding judgment of the question whether or not the individual is valuable rests upon the observation that each individual has implicit in him the possibility of becoming a person. What we know of people tells us this, not argument nor demonstration in the Euclidean sense. There is no guarantee that extensive knowledge of humanity will lead one to this conclusion, but history shows that most informed and clear-thinking men and women, when left alone by bigotry and inquisition, arrive in their own way at this remarkable conclusion. It is popularly supposed in many quarters that the significant thing about human judgment is its variety and inconstancy. So various have been opinions, some holding Caesar admirable, others, a rascal, that it is fashionable to believe in our lifetime that human judgment is a mere feather in the winds of the time, wavering and unreliable. Many of our contemporaries hold that these ethical judgments are all a matter of taste and that *de gustibus non est disputandum.* A thoroughgoing analysis of critical judgment of historical figures and incidents and of the epics, tragedies, and comedies of world literature, however, reveals something quite different. The surprising fact is not the disagreement of the critics but, considering the disparity of the centuries in which they lived, the governments which ruled them, and the religions or lack of religion they professed—the notable fact about their opinions is the extent of their agreement. The area of common judgment about the great protagonists of history and of literature and about the evident influences at work in the human breast is considerable. This body of agreement, never precisely delimited, and always the subject of review and reappraisal, constitutes the best account we have of the norm of human conduct.

Liberal thought is never permitted to depend upon a party line, not even what appears to be the enlightened party line of the democracies, Western style. It can never remain liberal if its ends are assumed, even though the assumptions be such evidently fine ones as the traditional American goals. Ultimately it is able to rest on nothing more explicit than this constancy of human critical judgment of which I speak. On the side of reason, as distinguished from the side of dogma, the sole foundation of liberalism is this steadiness of human opinion when free, highly serious, and refined by the great public debate of contemporary and all civilized minds. The impatient have often deemed this establishment of our liberties both complicated and vague, and many times in history they have attempted to found government upon specific divine revelation, the edicts of a single seer, or the uncriticized will of one mounted man or group.

The ideas among which to choose the ethical basis for the government of men are not numerous. Among the principles which have been tried, one alone has been found sufficiently alive, sufficiently various, and sufficiently steady to make it possible to guarantee civic freedom for large numbers of people for very long. The constancy of the discovery that every individual has it in him to become a person has made it possible to achieve and maintain democracy. For it is this ethical discovery which establishes, in critical terms, the value of every man.

No one can attain manhood without discipline; is it true of the individual that he is subject within his own mind to law? The first half of the issue of the century—whether the individual is important—is contested by the avowed totalitarians. The second half (as we observed in the third chapter), that he is subject to the law for man, is distrusted as well by extreme adherents of authoritarian religion and of the welfare state. How may the man of free and informed critical judgment privately reason to decide whether he thinks the assumption of American representative government in keeping with human nature?

As in dealing with the first half of the democratic proposition about the individual, we may expect in treating this half neither proof nor disproof. We ask simply, how does the alert and reasonable person reflect upon the question and make up his mind? He will cope with one of the inmost issues of human life, and in his reflections we must expect him to refer to the mode of thought by which such issues can be considered critically. Clearly the judgment he will try to make will occupy territory also occupied by religion, and probably few modern men would be able to divorce altogether their secular thought upon the problem from their religious experience. So far as these aspects of ethical judgment are separable, however, we shall restrict this part of the inquiry to human judgment, eliminating revealed religion and—to a considerable extent, though not entirely—natural religion.

The fact that the law for man works within us should not lead one to think it private, whimsical, or eccentric. On the contrary. The law within is centered and common. Far from being whimsical, it is responsible to the common agreement among men determining what is decent, fair, and just. Nor is it private, though it occupies our private thoughts. While it is true that when we break the law we sense its existence by means of conscience, we also know the law in our minds and express parts of it by words which will win the recognition and assent of others, relying, for this purpose, on the great convention: that is, the coming together of the best opinions of the most discerning men and women. Thus, though individual, in the sense that the law for man holds each man, by himself, accountable, it is social, in the sense that men are social beings; in the sense that our obligation is not only to ourselves, but to other people as well; in the sense that we understand the law for man by the study of men in society as well as men in private; and in the sense that we receive much of our knowledge of the law for man directly from the society in which we live.

The subtlest and most central facts about our lives have never been conveyed from man to man by exposition or argument, but by stories. One has but to reflect upon the ethical propositions of the Old Testament to observe this fact. To be sure, the blunt prohibitions placed upon the Israelites and upon all men in the Decalogue are prose imperatives. But the descriptions of our nature are conveyed in the stories, whether fictitious or historical or a mixture of the two, the stories of Moses and Aaron, Ruth, Lot, Nahum, and the rest. Christ voiced the classic understanding of the nature of a story, and Matthew referred to this in quoting the psalmist.

> All these things spake Jesus in parables unto the multitudes; and without a parable spake he nothing unto them: that it might be fulfilled which was spoken through the prophet, saying,
>
> I will open my mouth in parables.
> I will utter things hidden from
> the foundation of the world.

Aristotle expressed the proposition in his preference of fiction to history because it is nearer the truth.

Reference has been made in these pages to the dependence of that Aristotelian dictum upon Aristotle's idea of the universal, particularly as it relates to character. Is this fictitious person convincing? The answer is always given in terms of whether or not he seems to represent the human race. Would someone be like that; behave or speak like that? Is he probable?

The same question of universality applies to plot. Not the improbable possible, said Aristotle, can be permitted in fiction, but the probable happening, even, in extreme instances, though it might actually be impossible. Upon the question whether the individual is subject to law within, great light is thus thrown by the very restrictions of character and event in a story.

Paradoxically, the first requirement upon a story is that it be true. In a sense a joke also must be true, unless it is a Scandinavian whopper. There is a distinction between a joke, an anecdote, and a story, but in this they are similar: that their success—that is, their being a story, and not just a lot of words—depends on whether they *would* happen. You may feel obliged to give an ear to all sorts of talk, some of it pointless, but what really sets you off is a story which has probability.

A visiting Scottish divine was told one of the then popular jokes about the plumber or the undertaker or the mother-in-law, and was asked by his host why he did not laugh. "I wadna laugh at what didna happen," he said. Unfortunately much that passes for a story plausibly recounts the implausible, thus taking advantage of thoughtless people and making propaganda possible. This is true of many of the so-called stories in the slick magazines and a great many movies and advertisements. It is not primarily that the movies have happy endings that makes them false. It is rather that they usually have the same ending and that the action and even the dialogue of most of them are so cliché and dull and without ingenuity that after you have seen a few you have seen them all. If the movies were all dull we could forget them and stay away. The annoying thing is that once in a blue moon a picture like *The Ghost Goes West* or *The Macomber Affair* comes along, the reality of which we should not care to miss.

Two elements in genuine stories provide evidence concerning men's private accountability to something at work within themselves. These are the chorus and the plot. Chorus spells out the feeling and judgment of the neighbors concerning the action and the characters of the play. On the ancient stage the chorus sang or chanted the ethical opinion which right-thinking people were bound to hold; the neighbors were mankind in general. In the novels of Thackeray or Trollope, the author breaks in with comment, now amused, now censorious, and—whether mild or severe—always ethical.

In the modern play, *Our Town,* the function of chorus is performed by the Stage Director, who not only gives the geographical and landscape setting, but implies the ethical setting as well. In the Anouilh version of the Antigone story, the chorus, spoken by one man, lectures the contemporary audience on the difference between melodrama and tragedy:

> Tragedy is fitting and good. It is quiet; it is sure. In melodrama, with these treacherous ones, these continuously evil, this persecuted innocence, these avengers, this new world, these rays of hope, one may escape death, as in an accident. Perhaps one may save himself; the good young man perhaps can arrive in time with the gendarmes. In tragedy you are still. You are all together. You are all innocent, in fact. It is not that there is one of you who kills and the other who is killed. It is a question of distribution. And then, above all, tragedy is quiet because you know there is no more hope, filthy hope; you know that you are trapped, trapped like a rat, with all the heavens falling, and all you can do is shout—not complain, not moan, but shout at the top of your lungs what you have to say, what you have never before said, what you have not, perhaps ever before known. And for nothing: in order to say it to yourself, to teach it to yourself. In melodrama one argues because he hopes to get out. That is ignoble, mercenary. In tragedy, it is free. It is for kings. And there is nothing left to try.[3]

The chorus does not persuade us of the truth nor even attempt to establish it; that is the function of the story itself. But the chorus underlines the ethical facts, lest the unwary miss them. Some assume that the purpose of this exposition by the chorus is to draw a preachment from the story, like the almost illogical "moral" which Coleridge was persuaded by the times to tack on to that magnificent story of "The Ancient Mariner"—"He prayeth best who loveth best." This is not at all the purpose of the chorus nor (usually) of the novelist when he speaks in his own person. His part is, rather, to clarify the action. The whole intent of everything said on the stage or rehearsed by the teller, when the tale is well told, is simply that: to clarify and forward the action. The fact that in order to do this it is necessary to underline the relation of the deeds and thoughts of the protagonists to the common standard of conduct illustrates the private accountability which works within the mind of every man. It illustrates also, what the discussion of plot will elaborate, that the plot could not exist without this private accountability.

Plot shows forth the inward accountability of persons more convincingly even than the chorus. For if one thinks over the great stories most often acknowledged through the centuries to be real stories, it is evident that every one of them would fall apart and cease to be a story if there should be eliminated from it the assumption that the protagonists are inwardly accountable and in varying degree made aware of the law within by the promptings of conscience. "Thus conscience doth make cowards of us all"; "Macbeth shall sleep no more"; Judge Gaunt in *Winterset;* Willy Loman in *The Death of a Salesman:* what makes the story is the understanding, increasingly clear to the chief characters as the action becomes intense, that there is an inward law which is like a natural law; it exists and is implicit in what men do and think. It is a law also, like a law of the city, for before it all men are tried. This is understood and progressively becomes vivid to the protagonists as the action works upon their own inward understanding of what it is to fail to be manly, what it would be to be heroic.

Something similar happens in comedy. The comedy of manners is a special case. In it the fun usually consists in showing up the absurdity of fashion by comparing fashionable with candid people. How is it possible for a person to see himself as, we say, he really is? He may accomplish this by freeing himself, one by one, of his illusions about himself. In pure comedy and tragicomedy the action and the sharp words of the other characters in the play work this gradual correction in the self-estimate of figures like the Duke in *Twelfth Night* and most of the characters of *Dear Brutus*. The inward accountability here is not an affair of guilt, punishment, and heroism, but of mere common sense.

In both tragedy and comedy, whether enacted or on the page, the story will come off only if the audience shares with the author the standard of accountability by which the plot measures the characters. Thus in fiction of all kinds there is a double demonstration that the inner law for men exists and that men sense it by conscience: the fact that without the existence of the law and our apprehension of it there would be no plot; and the fact that without the common possession of the inward law by all men the audience could never see the foundation, let alone apprehend the purport of the story. The social behaviorists are fond of saying that all this agreement among men about norms of conduct is nothing but artificial social convention having little to do with our nature. In the presence of Aeschylus, Aristophanes, and Sir Thomas Malory, it is difficult to take this opinion seriously, because in the great stories there is verisimilitude–similarity to the truth we know about ourselves.

In considering the place of letters in studies, the Commission on Liberal Education of the Association of American Colleges stated in December 1947: "Literature has always been a powerful force for illuminating our true nature and for influencing men in their separate and their social lives. Its study was never more necessary to education than now." "In showing forth the various kinds of life, evil as well as heroic," said the commission, "literature reveals the moral problems and meanings of experience. It therefore acquaints the student with moral choice and the consequence of action. Proper teaching of literature should create in the student resistance on the one hand, to corrosive cynicism, and on the other, to narrow and unenlightened fanaticism. It should make him aware of the variety as well as the constancy of moral responses to experience. The full understanding of a piece of literature entails the commitment of one's affections and sometimes even one's beliefs, and thus the effect of the intensive study of literature should be growth in the extent and clarity of one's allegiances. So literary study, both secular and religious, provides moral enlightenment by making more elaborate and more firm the understanding of what it is to be human."[4]

The critical establishment of the proposition that every man within himself is subject to law is a great mixture of experience, hunch, strong feeling, reasonableness, and logic. Rarely does anyone of average mental abilities enter into a series of the great stories well told without concluding for himself consciously or unconsciously that both the characters and the action of the stories must be reckoned with in his own life. That is what makes the true fascination of fiction. It is the same when a discerning person sees at first hand and vividly the account of historical events in which life, death, and the light or darkness of whole cities of men are at stake. At their best, for these purposes of ethical inquiry, history and letters here occupy common ground. The superiority of letters lies only in their responsibility to the universal, where history is responsible to the dated event.

A juvenile court in Brooklyn discovered that many delinquents suffer because they feel themselves unique, and they are comforted and stabilized when through the reading of novels required by the judge they are made acquainted with accounts which match their own against other experiences. The tension and nervousness from which we are supposed to suffer, anxieties and fears from which we constantly run to the psychiatrist's couch, are appreciably decreased by contact with the examples in story and song, and the possibility they offer of comparisons with ourselves. For, as Deor said in the midst of grief over being neglected in old age, "Yet these strove on and overcame; I can endure as well." The resultant dignity of both physical and spiritual bearing is perhaps the most precious thing we can ever acquire.

A man about to break up his home for a second love appeared to feel no compunction about the effect on his children, for he said that no other love had ever been like this one. Certainly all loves, lives, persons, are differentiated like snowflakes, or leaves on a tree, and to that extent are unique. But the preponderance of entity within classes is on the side of similarity. We grasp the similarity in human life by means of literature, and, seeing it at last as a great and unfinished frieze, on the entablature of some great Parthenon—"the march of the ages"—can more readily perceive ourselves as an orderly rather than a chaotic part of it.

The opinion of the Commission on Liberal Education bears upon the nature of the decision at which the reasonable and alert person may arrive in trying to decide for himself about the value of the individual and his responsibility. "The full understanding of a piece of literature entails the commitment of one's affections and sometimes even of one's beliefs." When you read poetry well, that is, when you read the great stories, you not only give your mind to it; you give your heart. You enter in. As the French say, you are engaged. Your ultimate commitment to the purport of the story is yourself. The poem, if it is a truly great one, is about you. It is this whole-souled quality of poetry, warm, lively, at once possessing mind and feelings, which makes it the supreme evidence, the final witness before our judgment of human nature. Is there a debate in the twentieth century whether the individual is precious and whether he is, in fact, responsive to the law within? History shows it, and poetry, encompassing history and transcending it, knows it for a truth.

8

Philosophy

IT IS FOR the foregoing reasons that poetry should lie at the center of the general education of everyone. This is true for what poetry itself says about human nature and the ethical contest of the century; it is true also because even the elementary mastery of poetry provides the skill necessary to any accurate reading and reflection upon history. History lies pretty close to the center also; and not far out lie two or three other disciplines. Their relation to the ways of thinking important to the western democracies today will occupy this and the next two chapters.

Sooner or later, consideration of ways of thinking and the cultivation of skill in reflection must treat what is officially known in the college catalogue as Philosophy. Professional dialecticians, if they have pursued these remarks this far, may be annoyed that I have delayed until Chapter VIII the direct and explicit treatment of systems of reasoning and value. Professor Ralph Barton Perry provides the explanation:

> The place of philosophy in a liberal arts college will depend upon the extent to which other subjects realize or renounce their humanistic possibilities. If the natural sciences confine themselves to technique and technology, then it will fall to philosophy to delineate the spectacle of nature in a course on "cosmology"; and to present the scientific spirit of man in a course on "the philosophy of science." If the social sciences yield their autonomy and become

a province of natural science, then the meaning of society and the purposes of human institutions will be left to a course on ethics, theory of value or social philosophy. If history ceases to reconstruct and interpret the life of man, then that task will fall to a philosophy of history. If literature and the fine arts are superseded by their accessories and adjuncts, the history of philosophy, or esthetics, or a philosophy of criticism will become the sole exponent of the intuitions and values of which literature and the fine arts are the vehicle.[5]

The discussion of literature and history in these pages has assumed that literature is the vehicle of intuitions and values and that history's chief task is to assist in the reconstruction and interpretation of the life of man. Translated into education these propositions will mean that letters and history may be taught in such a way that they will not renounce but will realize their humanistic possibilities. The contention of this book is that all the central disciplines of modern thought are susceptible of liberal treatment or of illiberal, the liberal being the effort, within the several disciplines, to understand the nature which surrounds us, and which we find within us, the human nature, and the physical nature, nothing more. This cannot be done by the substitution of scientific techniques and technology for science itself, nor by the social sciences if they forget or repudiate their original intent to find the meaning of society and the purposes of human institutions.

If all the rest of the curriculum fails to be liberal, says Professor Perry, the Department of Philosophy must do its best to show students what the liberal study of all the other subjects should involve. This, in effect, is what now occurs in many colleges, notably many which are lodged within gigantic universities, though they still pretend in their titles and public avowals to be devoted exclusively to the liberal arts and sciences. This, in effect, is the reasoning which underlies the movement to establish the new survey courses in western civilization. Since any genuine, lively, and single-minded preoccupation with ethical and humane meaning is now lacking in so many departments of learning, the college has created a new one to comment on the proper subject of all the others. By this means, although the student may not have gained much experience in direct critical reflection upon the issues of human experience in courses dealing with the detail of physical and human nature, at least he may get an idea of how useful his college education might have been if in spirit and in truth it had all been liberal.

Part of the trouble arises from the fearsome acceleration of modern discovery and theory itself. Knowledge has grown so fast that every mind concerned must sense the growing pains. And if philosophers preoccupied with principle, that is, the One, upbraid scientists and scholars concerned with particulars, that is, the Many, the particularists are ready with their retort. The trouble with the philosophers, they say, is that they are too rational. Nature, physical or human, as they can easily demonstrate, was not designed by a logician. The trouble with philosophers, they say, is the trouble diagnosed by Sir Francis Bacon. They are deluded by the Idols of the Theater, systems of notions which we present to our minds instead of the specific world which we may observe. In judgment upon this debate the informed bystander must certainly admit that not nearly all professional philosophers are famous in this decade for their approach to the norm of mankind; not nearly all show a grasp of what the professional philosopher, Professor Perry, has said about the "humanistic possibilities" of all the disciplines, including natural and physical science. At a recent conference on the use of philosophy in contemporary thought, for example, twenty-five instructors of philosophy from nearly as many institutions held that the sole obligation of philosophers is to examine the postulates of the social problems currently stated and identified. They were uninterested in the obligation which presided over the inquiries of Socrates to find out the "right" questions and ask them. On the other hand, among professional philosophers in America today there is a considerable group who have been proposing for two decades the idea of liberalism reflected in Professor Perry's statement. They and their like-minded colleagues in the other disciplines should be supported in their effort to bring back the higher learning to its human and critical center, before it is utterly dissipated in trivialities.

To do this would be to recognize that though the ultimate purpose of studies is informed and active manhood, the immediate purpose is understanding, nothing more. This is true of all kinds of essential knowledge—that is, of all kinds of knowledge which is central in our experience: knowledge of men in private and in groups, knowledge of the earth, knowledge of what intimations we have of divinity. Its purpose is that we may understand nature, notably our own nature and that of the cosmos where we dwell. Such knowledge is liberal knowledge. We distinguish it from utilitarian knowledge or unexamined knowledge by saying that it is philosophical.

If we understand things not only in relation to their obvious kin but also in the large, we say that our knowledge is philosophical. The true scholar obeys two kinds of accuracy—the accuracy of the letter or the measure, and the accuracy of the implication. It is the latter which concerns philosophy when we demand that knowledge be philosophical. The higher accuracy demands a correct account of a thing in terms of good and evil or in terms of cause and effect or in terms of being, or in all three.

The mechanical subdivision of learning into courses, and the assignment of courses to departments, have had an especially unfortunate effect upon the teaching of philosophy. The fault arose not from the philosophers, who have protested against it, but from the mere arrangements of instruction. The conventional way to impart knowledge and to require the student to train himself in reflection often commits the fault of keeping these two halves of the single process of learning separate. Information is dispensed—let us say, Spanish history—on Tuesdays, Thursdays, and Saturdays, and values (a course in philosophy) are taught on Mondays, Wednesdays, and Fridays. Value is intrinsic as well as relative; we know it when we know something valuable for its own sake. But to study value by itself, or even partially divorced from valuable things, is to reduce it to a mere medium of exchange like the currency. Such study stresses the fact that we often know the value of something by comparison with something else; and philosophy studied as a "course" by itself tends to become less interested in intrinsic value and more and more to treat relationship and to deal with little more than the connectives of thought—the *ands*, *buts*, *ofs*, *fors*, and the intransitive verbs. The nouns, or things we think about, and the transitive verbs, or the action they perform, are left to the "information courses." Because of this separation the student rarely if ever tries to write a full working sentence for himself—that is, an affirmation of the value and meaning which he himself has observed in some part of the experience of the race which he has studied. The separation has been known to tempt the professors of philosophy themselves to avoid such affirmation.

The conventional system cannot be entirely wrong, for some impressive things have come out of it. But for undergraduates it seems to me that there may none the less be a better method of teaching philosophy. Perhaps this would involve no department of philosophy at all, because all teachers of the liberal arts and sciences would be philosophic.

How would it be for the departments of philosophy to close up shop? The same suggestion, for the same reason, has been made to churches. The reason is that, like religion, philosophy probably has to be rediscovered; people must first find out that they need philosophy. Now, it would prove embarrassing if, unlike the emperor who didn't know he was naked, people never woke up to their need. So instead of the whole radical proposal, I make half of it. Suppose the professional philosophers give up their departments and courses and teach for a season in other departments.

The move would have the following four advantages: *a*) the philosophy professors who had never mastered any other fundamental discipline to the point of teaching it could absent themselves for a period from the general and enjoy what for many would prove a kind of holiday in the world of particulars; *b*) their teaching of the new subject would probably be more liberal than their former teaching of philosophy, certainly more liberal than the conventional teaching of the new subject, because they would naturally consider the particulars of it not only in particular, as the college catalogue demands, but in terms of good, cause, and existence: in short, this treatment of the new subject would turn it into philosophical learning; *c*) once master of a subject to the point of teaching it, they could talk to the proud specialists of the subject; *d*) those who had mastered another fundamental discipline would be relieved of the temptation to talk to no one but other professors of philosophy.

Advantages *a* and *b* accrue to the former professor of philosophy and to the improvement of his lectures and his books; advantages *c* and *d* accrue to the better understanding of philosophy in the learned world and in the whole community. With justification, the rest of the faculty think some philosophers inexact and esoteric, reasoning without sanction from any of the ranges of experience and evidence which legislate for the other academic disciplines. Philosophy professors are thought to talk a private argot for the amusement of their colleagues. They have, indeed, been known to boast of technical secrets hardly explicable to laymen. Of course, every art and science and craft has its own freemasonry, but the arcana of the order invariably represent elements incidental to it, not its purport. For a philosophy professor to learn and teach another science and to teach it philosophically is to demonstrate the simple truth that philosophy permeates and upholds all the ranges of experience and evidence, and in particular to show professors of the sciences in question in what way philosophy is responsible to the evidence of their own science and how their particular subject is responsible to philosophy.

The experiment I propose might have further good results. The professors of the invaded departments might discover what it is to teach their subjects liberally—that is, with a strict and disciplined analysis of the subject in terms of common value as well as of its own technical values. Many a professional philosopher has done what I suggest, to the profit and pleasure of his students as well as himself. During the war when one single and simple end—victory—engaged us all, and our whole intellectual effort was directed toward it, not a few philosophers taught mathematics, language, cryptanalysis, and social science. Some are masters of history, architecture, and music. To keep alive and useful in their minds the apprehension of these disciplines by undergraduates, professors of philosophy should be given the opportunity every few years to teach a course or two in departments other than their own.

If philosophy departments should close up everywhere for a period of time and the whole curriculum should become more liberal than it is, one might inquire whether they would ever reopen. In practice, of course, the systematic and self-centered study of philosophy should and would remain the primary and exclusive concern of some philosophers. But how much richer and better understood this study would be if it were replaced in its old Greek position! In losing its life, it would find it.

Besides this, two important parts of the philosophy curriculum would prevent the closing of the departments. The first is the classics of the subject. The student has a right to these, and to more of them than he usually gets. Few untutored students can with profit read them alone. If no other department is competent to guide the student in his reading of large parts of Plato and Aristotle and a dozen other reflective thinkers, the philosophy department must guide him. The full study of politics involves a strict and truly philosophical knowledge of ethics, including political philosophy—not a merely sociological study of it. Many of the classics in ethics and political thought can be studied outside of the Department of Philosophy. But such study becomes valid only when the professor understands the philosophical context in which the ethical and political thinking has been done. Ethics itself belongs in many places in the curriculum—among them, in literature. Sad to say, few teachers of literature have read or systematically analyzed the great ethical essays of the world, and many are incompetent to deal with the principal theme of tragedy and epic poetry. (Perhaps a visiting philosopher in the literature department, *if he had learned to read poetry*, could open the eyes of his colleagues.) I have the impression that it is largely by default that ethics, neglected in history and literature, has been isolated in the Department of Philosophy, and that cosmology and metaphysics have suffered a similar fate.

The second part of the philosophy curriculum which would remain, even if all the other teaching should become more liberal by becoming more philosophical, is its training in the craft of reason. Mount Holyoke College from 1897 to 1946 maintained, side by side, a Department of English Literature and a Department of English. In recent years the academic world has supplied a gossipy explanation of this unusual arrangement: there was said to be a clash of personalities. But this was not the central and effective reason why these two groups of teachers, scholars, and writers continued for nearly half a century to teach brilliantly and to turn out such an unusual number of able graduates that inquiries about their method of teaching were continuously made on the part of graduate schools here and abroad. The operative reason was that the Department of English, concerned as it was with critical and original reasoning and with writing, maintained under the particularly strong leadership of the successive chairmen a functional treatment of literature, history, and the rest of the human record, while simultaneously the Department of English Literature, composed of an unusually able group of scholars, conducted courses and studies organized in the conventional manner by special attention to the material, whether in periods or in sequences of historical or generic development. The Department of English was governed by a theory of learning to be found today in some of the best departments of philosophy: that skill in reasoning and imagination may be taught and improved, and that this may become the major pursuit of an advanced student provided he is held down to facts, including those presented in all the rest of the curriculum—history, literature, science. Students who pursued an English major in those years at Mount Holyoke, and those in some departments of philosophy at present, learn a more active use of knowledge than many of their classmates. A substantial fraction of their upperclass work is devoted to writing and reasoning. The object of their major instruction is to help improve the quality of this, to refine it, and to elaborate its variety and applicability to facts of all kinds and to affirmations and denials of all sorts. Something similar happens to the honor student in a laboratory science who is permitted to devote a great deal of time and energy to solving scientific problems, under relatively little supervision once he is started on his way, but with strict accounting at the end of his major work.

The teaching of philosophy, English, and science in this fashion might be called functional to distinguish it from the conventional mastery of blocks of material often associated with learning. Such teaching is risky, and when the treatment of fact becomes sketchy or cavalier, it is downright destructive. Where, as in the two parallel departments at Mount Holyoke, there is rigorous attention to fact, both within the department devoted to writing and reasoning, and in the other departments in which sudents also take courses, the fruitfulness of this kind of teaching has been abundantly demonstrated.

To a degree, all liberal teaching should be functional. All students, whether majoring in chemistry, history, French, literature, or government, should write a great deal—considerably more than, with their present organization, most faculties can require. One simple reason for the remarkable success of some of the European universities lies in the immense amount of writing which the student must do and which the instructors take the time to examine with care both for thinking and for construction and expression. Those universities enjoy the advantage of a strict pre-university training in the schools, an advantage which most of our own universities do not share. Without a sound preparation in writing, language, and mathematics, the American student usually must waste his time on a certain amount of school work even in the university; the university teacher also must devote valuable time to remedial training. He must correct in detail the faulty reasoning which is inevitable on the misspelled, ill-paragraphed pages written by the brilliant boy or girl who was not well taught at school. He must correct the flaws in mathematical calculation as well as mathematical reasoning which might have been avoided by better pre-college work. Not many colleges and universities can afford a staff large enough and skillful enough to perform these school functions, while driving forward the critical mastery of the higher learning. Not many university teachers, despite their remarkable ability in their specialties, are equipped to teach elementary skills in reasoning and expression. So the task of functional teaching in American universities is often neglected. Departments of English which are alert and vigorous must often take, on behalf of the whole faculty, the entire responsibility for functional instruction. Sometimes the obligation is assumed by the Department of Philosophy. Sometimes, in fact, a genius of a teacher, imaginative and conscientious, in any department whatsoever, manages, along with presenting the material of his courses, to do a thorough job on the writing, reasoning, and calculating of his students. He sets so many laboratory problems and so many collateral papers and works so painstakingly on the results of the assignments that it is by him that the students are truly taught how to use knowledge: that is, how to put it to work in their own minds, how to reason imaginatively upon it, and express it.

Philosophy provides both skill in thinking and an account of the most famous and successful expeditions of the human reason. As studied in the universities it offers good training in disputation, its common process being dialectic. Whoever tests the thinking of these times to determine its quality as a technical performance is inclined to call it good. The logic of the editorials, the reasoning in the serious magazines, the syllogisms of responsible public utterance are adept, clear, varied, and skillful. While the same cannot be said for the yellow journals and the rabble-rousing orations, it is certainly true that the discourse read and heard by the thoughtful public is remarkably free from fallacy. Probably in our country the audience for good hard reasoning conducted with technical integrity and within the limits of valid discourse is now much the largest in history. One reason for this is undoubtedly the fact that the engineering problems which we have solved so brilliantly can be treated only by use of extensive common sense, and this commodity, being much in demand, has been extensively produced. Another reason is that the type of issue to which the thoughtful American most commonly gives his whole attention—that is, a social issue—is almost entirely, so far as public debate deals with it, understood in terms of logic.

Notice the disputes on the editorial pages and the letters to the editor. They are all concerned with alleged errors: errors of reporting, which turn out to be errors of perception, errors of ethical standard, errors of interpretation, especially errors of assignment of motive, and errors of logic. Of all of these the last is the one most thoroughly denounced, and it is about the only allegation to be disputed at great length. We are a nation of arguers, and we argue well.

Skill in argument and even in dialectic is gained in many places outside the study of what is officially known as philosophy. Familiarity with the philosophical systems can be gained only there. Many astute and reasonable men, self-taught, or instructed almost entirely by experience with the application of science or shrewd bargaining, see little importance in these old and current efforts at systematic abstract thought. Without question, their own discourse is irresistibly logical and frequently brilliant; but it is often so confined in postulates and conclusions that it never proceeds beyond an elaborate analysis of means. These are the men responsible for the incredible American know-how. It is difficult for them to see in the systems of Kant, Hegel, Aristotle, Aquinas, Dewey, Kierkegaard, and the others, anything but an elaborate and perhaps fascinating game of chess—fascinating, that is, to the quaint men who enjoy such oddities.

The spiritual enlargement provided by philosophy is similar to that produced by history and poetry. History and letters people the streets and the market-places of the mind with such a plenitude of men and women so accurately presented that we say, on becoming familiar in daily life with a new acquaintance, "I have met him before." Philosophy supplies the mind with many of the known alliances of ideas. To a degree, the man knowledgeful in philosophy may, on grasping a new idea, say, "I have been here before." While the internal logic of contemporary editorials is impressive, their ignorance of the necessary alliances of ideas is impressive, too. One reads many paragraphs of truly brilliant reasoning, but particularly where morals, religion, and political theory are concerned, he is led to exclaim: "This writer, never having been here before, is unaware, philosophically speaking, where he is now."

I doubt if any alert and reasonable student acquires a "philosophy of life" directly from the study of a few great systems. He is lucky if at thirty he has a "philosophy of life" which he can recognize. But it is true that in early manhood and womanhood a person begins to confirm or revise his tastes and opinions so that they are related to each other. That is, his ethical judgments begin to have a reasonable relationship to his religious ones, and these both, in turn, to his political and even artistic opinions. Robert Frost in conversation once described this process by saying that a kitten or calf is so disorganized that you may poke it or lift its foot and what you do to one part of it calls forth no response in the rest. But as the animal grows older, he becomes more and more one piece. This is true as a person grows older, until in maturity you irritate him with respect to any one thing and his whole self is involved. Speak of politics or painting and you touch all his major beliefs.

The maturing youth becomes more and more of a piece in feeling and thought, and the singleness of this feeling and thought becomes his "philosophy." What is taught in the philosophy department is the disembodiment of the order discovered in experience. The original and direct discoveries of this order are poetry and the other arts. Necessarily, the child becomes acquainted with the order by means of the arts before he undertakes systematic abstractions, and the first of these which he masters are some of the clearest and most beautiful—rhyme and arithmetic. As school is now kept in America it is likely that he will enjoy the benefit of little of that original and direct discovery of the order in human experience and considerably less arithmetic than he could grasp and use. Instead, his attention will be occupied at an early age with a great deal of predigested reasoning about men in groups, and he will be taught, as the President's Commission on Higher Education advises, by generalities. Thus his opportunity to develop critical skill and knowledge of his own will be impeded. It is true that skill with generalities will be useful to him. However, such skill is beyond him until he has had fairly extensive experience with men, ideas, and feelings, all mixed together as he sees them in history and contemporary life. They must be presented to his mind alive and whole, but in such a way that they reveal an order, as he began to find the order in childhood poetry, before the aridness of the aim of much of his schooling made his imagination and his perception die of thirst.

The unexamined life is no life at all, said Plato. Well taught, philosophy cultivates the skill of examining. It leads the student to theorize, recognizing that theory, etymologically and in fact, is a viewing, as of people, happenings, and things upon a stage. To theorize is to see them thus removed and ordered. Like letters and history, philosophy is a skill as well as a corpus of experience, and it becomes useful when the student learns how to hold skill and substance together and make them work for him. Letters, history, and philosophy: they are present in all fruitful reflection upon fact, from the infant beginning, when Red Riding Hood was distinguished from the wolf, and these three disciplines lie at or close to the center of the common education of every man.

9

Social Science

HISTORY, poetry, and philosophy, which view man from within and according to the law for man, give a partial account of our nature unless supplemented and criticized by the study of externals—the nature of human groups and of the physical world. This and the following chapter will comment on the relation of social science and the science of matter to the central purpose of liberal education.

Social science cannot say positively whether the individual is in fact precious and subject within himself to law. It can and does consider two important negative tests of the statement. Social science when true to itself inquires into the laws, that is to say the customs, the habits, the operative principles of men in groups. These are natural, just as much so as those which describe men's thoughts, feelings, and deeds in privacy. If there is less agreement among the knowing about these social laws, we must reflect that of the bodies of systematic knowledge, the social sciences are the youngest. That is, they were the last to be separated from the other analyses of nature and treated in isolation.

One negative test which social science puts to the ethical proposition on which democracy rests is whether it runs counter to the natural phenomena of group behavior which have been observed and verified. Two considerable schools of social scientists hold this to be true: the Marxists and those recently in favor with the Nazis. The second negative test has little to do with the truth of what in our Declaration of Independence we hold to be self-evident, but it bears upon the use of those ethical affirmations as the foundation of government. Social science asks the question: Can a system of government be developed on these postulates and be made to work?

The answer to the ethical question concerning the truth of the Declaration's statement about the individual comes so readily to the American mind that it may be tedious to devote eight chapters to a critical discussion of it. The same applies to the question of its workability. We all know that the Declaration of Independence was the start of something which has worked phenomenally well. In the present discussion we are concerned with the education which will make it sufficiently understood to be applied in a new half-century and to be explained, exemplified, and defended against the skill and gigantic energy officially supporting its denunciation. To analyze the learning involved we must observe the painstaking and voluminous study necessary if its workability in government is to be confirmed in this pragmatic test.

How may government be devised to guarantee to all citizens the respect before law which ethics demands for all men? We are still refining the political and economic theories necessary to accomplish this; great institutes of our best minds are devoted to nothing else but the development and dissemination of new social techniques designed to put into practice more effectively the new and the old theories. In our dispute with the Kremlin it is the principles which are of utmost importance to the student, for it is they which will be useful to his reasoning for his lifetime as a voter and a participant in the national town meeting. He will learn the theories partly by seeing them exemplified in techniques; as a citizen already called upon to express opinions, he will, of course, need to know many of the techniques for their own sake.

It should be clear from the foregoing that social science is a highly advanced study. American school children benefit by some of the introduction of social questions into school discussion, but the illusion has become current in schools and colleges that these complicated superstructures of reasoning, which stand upon direct experience, letters, history, and critical thought, may themselves provide the starting point of the intellectual life. The unhappy result of this impatience of the educators is that many an eager-eyed young political and economic and social theorist at the end of his studies simply does not know what has happened to mankind in the recent or remote past and, more important, what has really happened in the age-old war in the cave, the cavern of man's own private mind and will. As an example, consider Max Lerner's advice to those dedicated to "democratic socialization," which was quoted on Page 17.

When undertaken by students of a little maturity who have at least begun to master the particulars of human nature, the social studies become fruitful indeed. Their necessary elaborateness in the twentieth-century contest of theories of government and economics needs but to be mentioned to be admitted. Successfully to win the war of ideas in which the nations of the earth are now engaged, we need great numbers of men and women informed and able to think originally both about the principles and about the techniques of all the social sciences, but whose theories have particular meaning and ethical foundation because developed in the knowledge of the internal as well as the external facts of human experience.

The pre-eminent example of a social technique is a court. Concerned for the thorough training of lawyers, the American Bar Association in 1942 asked Arthur T. Vanderbilt, then Dean of the Law School of New York University and now Chief Justice of the Supreme Court of New Jersey, to prepare a report on pre-legal education. The question posed by the Association made specific the general question later to be posed by the President's Commission on Higher Education: What are the educational requirements for the improvement of this social technique? The President's Commission, publishing its report in 1946 and 1947, treated not one technique but techniques in general. The more explicit inquiry of the lawyers, scholars, and judges was a down-to-earth and working one. It examined law offices, government agencies, and juries. It analyzed the needs of plaintiffs and defendants and the accused; it consulted the most famous judges in this country and Canada. The question at hand was: What does it take to become a good lawyer? The fact that the lawyer may become a judge, a legislator, and a government official with extensive powers figured in the analysis. The findings are entitled, "A Report on Pre-Legal Education," and it was adopted in 1944 by the House of Delegates of the Bar Association and in 1945 by the Association of American Colleges.

Liberal education, though constantly described, criticized, attacked, and defended, seems to defy definition. In this particular it is like the idea of a man. The most useful proposals concerning its nature are those employed in reasoning upon a particular use or application or problem of liberal education. The law committee considering the strictly vocational problems of the lawyer so thoroughly analyzed the ethical and natural elements of the task of obtaining justice that their account of pre-legal education is of great practical usefulness in representing what in practice genuinely liberal education is. The committee holds with Plato that

> Education is . . . the art of converting the Reason. . . . It is worth repeating that law is an aspect of life and accordingly as broad as life itself. The pace in law school is so fast, the amount of ground to be covered so extensive that it is inescapable that the student who knows how to reason and how to express himself, who knows something of human nature, who understands in broad outline at least his environment—physical, social and moral—and who knows how to assemble information rapidly and accurately has a great advantage over the man who is deficient in one or another of these particulars. For the well-prepared man, each case he reads is a continuation of his liberal education, for law properly studied by

a properly prepared student is just as much liberal education as any subject in the college curriculum. Thus studied and taught, law is worthy of a place in a university, but not otherwise.[1]

It is hardly necessary to remark that the author of the report and the 118 leaders of the American Bar consulted agree that legal education should follow the full and completed course for the bachelor's degree. The view that law is liberal expresses the assumption of the whole report that its concern and the concern of all its worthy officers is the virtue of justice.

Much is said in the report about the nature of the social sciences, training in them, and their techniques. But mastery of their techniques is consigned to the graduate professional school. Their pertinence to contemporary problems is stressed in the famous remark of the late Justice Oliver Wendell Holmes: "For the rational study of the law the black-letter man may be the man of the present, but the man of the future is the man of statistics and the master of economics."[2] Mr. Holmes said that about fifty years ago. At the time few lawyers studied either statistics or economics and with his accustomed foresight Holmes saw the coming need.

The fundamental disputes of humanity, such as those about our nature and those concerning the purpose and manner of teaching the young, oscillate like a long pendulum. Hardly an important opinion is expressed which is not in its time proposed as a corrective of other opinions thought to be dangerously extreme. As Martin Luther said, mankind is a drunken peasant on a donkey. You heave him up on one side and he slumps over on the other. As years go on, the corrective utterance comes to be regarded as the norm; it stands alone, unqualified as a central doctrine, until it, in turn, needs critical correction. In modern educational discussion, a classic example of this oscillation of opinion is presented by the contest between Matthew Arnold and Thomas Henry Huxley, the one defending a circumscribed and almost entirely historical humanism, and the other proposing the virtues and usefulness to the mind of natural and physical science. What Huxley urged as a corrective—as an addition to the old education, as a peer among the ways of treating experience—has now become the predominating and, in many quarters, the exclusive way to think.

Properly to assess the Arnold-Huxley dispute and its meaning for the middle of this century, it is necessary to reflect on Huxley's own education. He had read letters and history, and like Arnold, he was surrounded in boyhood by people who assumed that this was the only way for the mind to mature. I should like to know what Thomas Henry Huxley is thinking now, if he watches us from limbo, and what he thinks of the exclusion, in the name of reforms which he instituted, of the humane knowledge which in his own youth and maturity he was able to regard as the natural right and common property of every grown-up mind.

A similar analysis of Justice Holmes's dictum that "the man of the future" is not the "black-letter man" but "the man of statistics," is necessary to an understanding of his intent. Holmes himself enjoyed a lively and imaginative youth, surrounded with the human riches of history and letters. When in maturity he reflected on the growth of society and of the law, he saw what he would have to add to his own education; he saw what he no doubt would have welcomed as an addition to the studies of his own boyhood. I question if he was at all prepared to sacrifice, as have many of those guided by his corrective sentence, the black-letter learning which provided the basis of his understanding of justice.

Fifty years after his remark, the entire serious and effective education of many a prospective lawyer is economics and statistics; for not a few the whole of elementary and secondary school has been controlled by the intention to use the schools almost wholly for the improvement and dissemination of social techniques. As social techniques are commonly studied, and, indeed, as much genuine social science is treated, the prevailing process of thought is argument. The object of the teaching is to persuade the student by logic that one social technique is absurd and another necessary. Holmes's own opinion of the argumentative tenor of the education and practice of a lawyer he expressed as follows:

> The life of the law has not been logic; it has been experience. The felt necessities of the time, the prevalent moral and political theories, intuitions of public policy, avowed or unconscious, even the prejudices which judges share with their fellow-men, had a good deal more to do than the syllogism in determining the rules by which men should be governed. The law embodies the story of a nation's development through many centuries, and it cannot be dealt with as if it contained only the axioms and corollaries of a book of mathematics. In order to know what it is, we must know what it has been and what it tends to be. We must alternately consult history and existing theories of legislation.[3]

In preparation of the report on pre-legal education, questions were sent to leaders of the American and Canadian bars and replies were sent by 118 Americans, including the then Chief Justice of the Supreme Court, and 21 Canadians. In general the Canadian replies agreed with the American. In general the practicing lawyers, judges, deans, and law scholars agreed that study of social science is important to the pre-legal student, though not of first importance. But the status of the social sciences in the higher learning and the effect of the manner in which they are taught received sharp criticism. The report states:

> Many leaders very definitely believe that too much attention is being diverted to this field. Chancellor John Stewart Bryan of the College of William and Mary, an outstanding newspaper publisher, speaks of "the cycle of adoration of the social sciences." Mr. John W. Davis, a distinguished practitioner and former Ambassador to the Court of St. James, expresses the view that "a great deal of what is thought to be science in economics, sociology and psychology does not fall under that head. If a student or graduate lawyer has an interest in these things, he can acquire his knowledge by general reading." It is the belief of many that the ability to understand and weigh the forces which mould human life and institutions can be

better acquired through literature and history than by the pursuit of the social sciences.[4]

However, most of the distinguished men consulted and the report itself express the opinion that the social sciences should be studied, both because "a clear understanding of governmental, economic, and social problems and of the results of man's experiences with all of the various panaceas for governmental, economic and social tribulations is a necessary part of the lawyer's equipment"[5]—both for this reason, and because the particulars of constitutional and economic history and the current events related to these must be known in particular.

It is here that the chief criticism of the lawyers is leveled at the teachers of the social sciences. College graduates, they say, do not know the facts. "All too often the student comes to law school with his mind full of theories or a verbal echo of them, but either ignorant of our social environment or extremely hazy about it." Dean Pound put the matter as follows:

> The student of these subjects [sociology and economics] may be taught so dogmatically that in a few years what he has learned will have been superseded and yet have been so thoroughly fixed in his mind that he is much worse off than if he had had no instruction in the subjects at all. Even more, as these subjects are commonly taught, in my experience they seem to produce students who believe that there is value in a plausible argument that two and two make five, and consider that wise-crackery is a substitute for consecutive thinking and reasoned argument.[6]

The preponderance of opinion both among those consulted and in the body of the report is that the study of most importance to the future lawyer is language and literature. One would expect that this might be true at the level of learning how to write and reason clearly, two skills for which the study of English and the classics is directly responsible, and Dean Pound voices this opinion, properly coupling with skill in language, skill in mathematics, the training of the reasoning powers to which language and literature are most closely allied. Dean Pound says:

> In my experience in forty-two years of teaching law, on the whole, students who have gone far and done well in mathematics have stood out exceptionally. Students who have pursued an old-fashioned curriculum in Greek, Latin, and mathematics have usually learned to observe accurately, think consecutively, and use language critically. These things are very much more important than an apparatus of information in the social sciences, since the information is apt to be obsolete before the student gets into practice.[7]

But the judges, lawyers, and law scholars go much farther than this. They state with great emphasis that language and literature are the studies of most importance to the future lawyer because of what they say. Regrettably, there is much professional teaching of letters in the universities which disagrees with this. Letters are enjoyed by many for their technique. To these academic critics literature is like the talk of the talkative wife. Her husband was up for desertion. "Why did you leave her?" asked the judge.

"She talks and talks. She talks all day and all night."

"What does she talk about?"

"She don't say."

Literature is important for what it says. It is a human possession to be used, by soldiers, lawyers, doctors, every man. Its use is largely a use to the mind, for by it we present to ourselves, judge, and enjoy the world—enlarge our *common* sense. The use of literature to the lawyer described by the committee is the correct use: that it shows forth our nature; and for this reason, its study in college is of first importance to the future advocate.

> The lawyer's interest, however, in English goes far beyond his mastery of it as a tool. I have never known a judge or a practitioner or a law professor who deserved to be called great, who was not well versed in the best of English and American literature,

especially the Bible and Shakespeare. Great literature widens and deepens our knowledge of human nature. It stimulates the imagination and the emotions and so enlarges and enriches life. In an age preoccupied with society and social problems it safeguards the individual; for literature, like all the arts, is concerned with the emotions and the emotions are always personal. This, great literature does for all men, but it especially serves the lawyer. The lawyer's life is spent in solving problems. He is in some danger of becoming a thinking machine. Darwin in his Autobiography relates that many years of scientific research and reflection dwarfed his early love of poetry. The lawyer, living and working with people, cannot afford to become intellectually lopsided. Moreover, the lawyer is likely to see the pathological side of life. He needs literature to heal him, to restore his balance, to give him perspective, which is one of the characteristics that distinguish the great lawyer from an ordinary attorney. And by example it constantly aids and enriches his power of expression. No wonder, then, that the language and literature of England and America stand first on the list of recommended studies.[8]

The study of literature naturally entails some study of language. The report entitled "Liberal Education Re-Examined" to which I have referred has this to say about the character of thinking which results from the neglect of these studies:

> We are, as a nation, so largely inarticulate, and our thinking is so sentimental and banal, partly because our schools and colleges are failing to give our young people the linguistic training to which they are entitled.[9]

Few will disagree that the all-encompassing purpose of the American social techniques, with the exception of national defense, is to protect the rights of the individual and promote his well-being. Yet paradoxically, the earnest intrusion of the study and dissemination of social techniques into education has had the effect of crowding out from consideration, and even from general knowledge, the individual himself. Judge Vanderbilt rightly observes that in this age, "preoccupied with society and social problems," the individual needs to be safeguarded. The Commission on Liberal Education holds the same opinion:

> Ours, we are reminded, is a mass age; people are living and thinking in standardized fashion. Military censors observed during the war that all American soldiers wrote the same letters. In peace, not less than in war, the mass attitudes of a highly complicated society persist. The idea of the declining importance of the individual, already widespread in political and economic thought, is gaining acceptance in educational theory. The effect of many well-meant reforms in education during the first half of the century has been to magnify the importance of social welfare and efficiency and to minimize that of the individual. Attention to the group welfare has brought ways of thinking and teaching that deprive young people of the conceptions that mature the individual.[10]

Milton described a "complete and generous education" as "one that fits a man to perform, skillfully, justly and magnanimously, all the acts, both public and private, of peace and war." Social techniques are now studied at school and college to the neglect of humane knowledge and discipline of the imagination. The purpose of the substitution is to lead young people to enter politics and in other ways assume civic responsibility. The educationists say they will have "motivation." The opinion of the legal minds contributing to Judge Vanderbilt's report contradicts this view. The lawyers hold that the result of teaching social science is poor motivation.

> The most serious complaint against the way the social sciences and government in particular are taught is that the men from the colleges do not come to law school with any abiding convictions as to their personal responsibilities as citizens. What William James has termed "that lonely kind of courage, civil courage" seems to be peculiarly lonely in our college graduates.[11]

Changes have recently occurred in the teaching of government; and thanks to the visits by students to the bureaus of government, internships for graduates, and other devices, an increasing number of undergraduates are looking forward to government as a lifetime job. Unfortunately, however, the stress appears to be upon specialist training for the civil service—a valuable and important service, to be sure, but not the crux of the governmental problem. The question of motivation of college students most vital to American political institutions is to get them to run for elective office, beginning with the simplest ones and with humble participation in the raw work of parties turning out the vote. Judge Vanderbilt reviews this problem. Defending the poor political record of twelve of the most distinguished preparatory schools (out of 67,000 graduates, but 27 United States senators and one associate justice of the United States Supreme Court), the president of a New England college a few years ago said, in the words of the report, "that politics in the United States is such a dirty game that no gentleman can afford to become mired in it."[12] Liberal education has a clearer idea of politics than that.

American democracy will be saved not by intelligence alone, but by intelligence endowed with power. So we may not expect salvation from the civil service, and if the colleges are to contribute anything of deep and lasting significance to government, they must provide something more than technicians, specialists, and civil servants, valuable as they are. Politics itself, elected and appointed office, is hazardous indeed. Political jobs are insecure, and, probably, for this reason, a little wicked. The new decalogue asserts: Thou shalt not be unsafe. Safety first. Life insurance, health insurance, accident insurance, unemployment insurance, seniority, pensions, tenure—in the political creed of the young these have become graces and virtues. But public office is risky. "When the party goes out," says Robert Moses, "it goes a long way out. The opposition is usually without influence or public respect."

In many cases public officials have walked the pavements and worn out typewriters looking for any job which will keep their families going. "Are we justified," Mr. Moses continues, "in attempting to train people for public service under these conditions?" In politics a man runs risks. Indeed, not only of body, but of soul. F. S. Oliver, the biographer of Robert Walpole, said: "If there is not another [profession] in which a man can hope to do so much good to his fellow-creatures, neither is there any in which, by a cowardly act or by a mere loss of nerve, he may do such widespread harm. Nor is there another in which he may so easily lose his own soul."[13]

But courage is not dead, and the colleges, teacher and learner alike, have recently given thought to dangerous duties. What can be done in wartime could, of course, be done by men of will power in peace. If the colleges determine to do their political duty, two contrary courses of action present themselves, based on two different theories of democracy.

Professor Murray Seasongood concluded his lectures on "Local Government in the United States" with a preachment: "It is the duty of those who have had the best educational advantages to become . . . leaders for civic, as well as national, righteousness. The struggle for civic ideals put into practical operation is worthy of the greatest devotion and self-sacrifice."[14] Lincoln Steffens and Norman Thomas, said Mr. Seasongood, say "that there is no chance for efficient local government because privilege is too widespread and cannot be deracinated."[15] Mr. Seasongood expects that the use of religion and courses in local government will change this. Instead of conventional morality, he proposes: "Thou shalt not steal," and "Thou shalt love thy neighbor as thyself." According to Mr. Seasongood's view, good government and the university world's part in it is a matter of ideals, devotion, and self-sacrifice. Ideals, let us observe, are wobbly steppingstones for critical judgment, but are in their place effective stimulants to action. Our concern here is with action, or rather, motivation.

Professor Pendleton Herring holds a contrary view of the college's part in good government. He is against admonitions. Men take part in politics, he says, because of their interests. "Only as government is charged with greater responsibilities affecting their well-being do citizens follow governmental activities with more attention."[16] But Mr. Herring does not altogether oppose Mr. Seasongood, for he states: "The problem of popular participation in government can be met only when men find personally significant values in public affairs."[17] Self-sacrifice, ideals, and devotion may, it is clear, lead a man to "personally significant values." But realism bids Mr. Herring warn college professors that educated men will begin to play a significant part in politics as their own interests become affected.

Certainly mere preachment will not "convert the reason" of the young sufficiently to lead them to a crusade in politics. But among contemporary youth, superficially blasé, *noblesse oblige* is not dead. What converts the reason is ordered fact, in this instance the fact about our nature as men and as political animals. If a college believes in self-sacrifice for ethical ends, it will surround the student with all kinds of influence, curricular and extracurricular; will provide him with ethical and religious standards; will attend not only to his studies of government but of all other human experience in order to lead him to devotion and self-sacrifice for his beliefs. To follow the other view—that an educated man will take part as his interests become involved—means, I take it, to instruct a student about his own interests and those of his group or class. A college should, by this principle, give the student as wide a technical knowledge as possible of contemporary parties, lobbies, pressure groups, minorities, majorities, patronage, and the like. But by implication he would usually remain aloof from politics until self-defense or defense of his own involved him willy-nilly.

If a college decides that government can become better by the devoted self-sacrifice of serious men, it will do many radical things. The professors of political science may take the lead. If so, they will demand that their colleagues in classics, philosophy, and literature do their job. They will have little patience with philology for its own sake and with historicity as an end of literary study. They will demand a general enrichment of all humanistic study. Instead of enlarging political science and economics courses, they will demand that more students spend more hours in the studies concerned with private as distinguished from public ethics. As they do this, they will no doubt look with disfavor upon the "elective system."

Young men trying to be useful in politics must meet certain requirements. It goes without saying that they must like people, individual people; and they must be of a warm and outgoing nature. Their learning must be warm and particular, too, peopled with individuals to the point where they have a firm idea of the character of Everyman.

A few years ago at Kenyon we restricted the course elections of premedical students, not to give them more science but to give them less. With the entire approval of the leading medical schools, we now require that they take more work in the humanities than heretofore. We want doctors to know more about human life even if on entering the medical school they know less about biology. It would be altogether as reasonable to require "pre-politicians" to know about human life, critically and in depth.

The instruction accorded by the social sciences is clearly relevant to the issue of the century made vivid by Communist aggression, a relevance nonetheless important for being negative: that by the social sciences one may test whether the liberal idea of the individual and his responsibility is at odds with observed principles of group behavior; and whether it is practicable to maintain government and other institutions in defense of his sanctity and in reliance upon his inward responsibility. These studies of mankind in groups are clearly advanced studies, deriving meaning and pertinence when pursued by those at least reasonably familiar with human nature and history; but the practical task of strengthening democracy by leading the able into social activities such as politics and economic reform appears as much assisted by allegiances of an individual and private nature, as by analyses of social institutions.

These considerations represent the most important usefulness of the mature study of social science. Without the central human knowledge about ourselves which in studies can be imparted in no other way than by poetry, history, and philosophy, social science is a menace, for it quickly descends into mere techniques of manipulation. Without humane understanding at its center, social science displays men governed not by the law for man but the law for thing. By making the law for thing operative in human affairs dictatorship establishes itself.

In our country there is now an ominous ignorance of the dual nature of constitutional democracy. Many an educated person will tell you that the genius of law and order in America is the will of the majority. Virtue, they say, abides in the majority. Whenever in history this terrible half-truth has been let loose, order and freedom have been destroyed. What has preserved them has been the rule of the majority tempered by justice. The will of the majority is a social study; justice, individual as well as social. Why should so many educated men and women, some of them in high place, now fail to grasp the meaning of that truism of American government? Because not only they, but the teachers of most of them have confined their studies and their reflections almost entirely to mankind in quantity. The logical conclusion of any account of mankind which assumes that the whole human problem is a group or collective problem is dictatorship.

That old human truth, forgotten in our generation, demands an immediate review of education. If understood now, that old truth would lead to the abandonment of the chief "reform" of studies since the first world war, for this "reform" consisted in teaching "social science" earlier and earlier in school. The story is too familiar to need rehearsal. Mature and advanced considerations of society, refined and made useful in social philosophy, economics, sociology, and theory of government, have been watered down and translated into terms thought available to very young students. What has been offered is a description of society to pupils too young to reflect upon it with any authority of their own. The studies have given an illusion of understanding—the illusion that the student understands not only social institutions, but man himself. But to the student who knows nothing but social science, man is known only by his function or participation in the group. If man himself is most notable because he is a member of a social institution, no matter how exalted the institution, he is already a slave.

10

Science

A FEW scientists recently have been saying or implying that the poverty of the humane studies is matched by a similar weakness in the understanding and support of science. This view has a fantastic sound in the midst of federal and industrial appropriations for scientific research, the popular admiration of scientists, and the rapid increase in general scientific knowledge and interest. Against these undeniable gains of science in the past twenty years stand two ominous facts, perhaps clouds on the horizon no bigger than a man's hand. One is the deplorable neglect of arithmetic and the lower mathematics in the common schools; the other is the recent phenomenon that rarely is science praised in public for its own sake. Its claim to support and admiration is almost universally put in the utilitarian terms of Francis Bacon—the conquest over nature for the improvement of man's estate, meaning his physical welfare.

Our part in the amazing bomb was largely to organize and apply the ideas discovered for us in Europe. This was a social and engineering achievement more than a scientific one. Why is it that Sweden has many more original scientific thinkers than Ohio, though Ohio is richer in money and more populous? A third worry for the bright growth of science should be the extent to which we have been assuming, since the engineering achievements of the war, that science is something which, like industry and an army, can be mobilized. Being, like human nature, an elusive, mysterious, and deceptive thing, physical nature gives up its secrets only to men of disciplined imagination. This fact, along with the necessity both to sharpen the imagination and to woo it by giving it play, would seem to represent the needs most important to make known to the informed public. It is true that informed talk about science has been much deflected by the clear necessity to establish a national science foundation; and to gain political ends is so difficult, people say that any argument should be employed which will get a vote. The danger in this opinion lies in the fact that the general expectation among thoughtful people of what science will do is in fact operative upon the fair or the mean estate of science itself. If people respect science largely because it supports technology, science will reduce itself more and more to mere technology.

Dr. Karl T. Compton, while president of the Massachusetts Institute of Technology, said:

> I am increasingly concerned over the fact that a major portion of the fundamental scientific discoveries and theories have been coming from Europe, in spite of the far greater number of students and generally superior laboratory facilities in this country. The field of nuclear science and atomic power is a good illustration, where, out of say a dozen of the fundamental ideas, some nine or ten have come from Europe, including the original discoveries of radioactivity, of artificial transformation of chemical elements, and of nuclear fission. Even in the field of invention a surprising number of inventions which the American public customarily ascribes to American genius have actually originated in other countries. The U. S. need not be ashamed of its share, but this share has certainly not been proportionately outstanding. The one thing which we in America accomplish to a superlative degree is to develop the new ideas, from whatever source, into useful applications engineered in superior manner for production and use. Why has the U. S. not been relatively more prominent in the production of fundamentally new ideas?[1]

There is no question about the value of natural and physical science. There are, it is true, many public attacks on what is labeled science. On examination these accusations misname the malefactor, who turns out to be not science at all but something less than science and perhaps transformed out of science.

There are four important attacks on what popular usage sometimes misterms science. First, there are those who think natural science malevolent because it makes modern wars more horrible and more universal than ancient ones. The argument could as easily be applied to the other half of knowledge, our knowledge of man. The perversion of science is a tank; the perversion of the humanities is propaganda. Thinking of France in 1940, who will say which proved more destructive, perverted science or perverted knowledge of man?

Second, science is accused of irreligion. On close scrutiny it is evident that the accurate description of the physical world and its laws at no point conflicts with worship or belief. Galen, the ancient physician, said that some think it religious to sacrifice hecatombs of oxen to the Creator, but he deemed it true piety to set down accurately the apparent crossing of the optic nerve. Clement of Alexandria, a Christian, said that the Epicurean view of matter (philosophically not unlike our own) made it more possible for man to believe in God than the Stoic view, which held that God is present in matter. When in the nineteenth century the right to teach and study the natural world was challenged by the theologians on the authority of the Book of Genesis, what was at fault was not science but the humanities. Not the chemistry or the biology but the biblical scholarship was poor.

Third, science is accused of teaching, to quote a current magazine writer, "that man and all his works are a part of the natural world, and can be adequately studied, without residue, within the framework of natural science." Real scientists do not talk that way, but pseudo scientists do.

Fourth and finally, technology has been mistaken for science, and it has been accused of focusing the whole energy of men's minds upon creature comforts. Chancellor Brüning said that if he were to name one cause of the rise of totalitarianism in Europe in the 1930's it would be the almost exclusive confidence on the part of European universities since the previous war that technology would solve the problems of mankind. Technology is not science but the application of it. Science itself, pure science, the accurate description of physical nature and its laws, does not pretend to solve all the problems of mankind. It is not so arrogant.

Obviously peace, like war, needs technology. Peace also needs science. It needs pure science because no modern man could use his powers freely and honestly while neglecting the wide unknown of the natural world, a periphery of our ken which we have pushed outward for thousands of years, knowing well that each increase in the area of our knowledge increases the extent of mystery which we face at the limits. Peace needs pure science also because to inquire in honesty and with all our powers of imagination and logic confirms us in a habit of dispassionate judgment and subjects us to the legislation of our best approximations to scientific truth. How valuable is this state of mind to man we may see by acquaintance with any man, famous or obscure, who has truly dedicated all his powers to improving man's account of the physical world.

The cultivation of the scientific state of mind is of the highest importance in liberal education. Happy is the college whose scientific energies are concentrated upon mathematics and the basic sciences, basic to thinking because of extensive use to the mind wherever it confronts the mysteries of the physical world. Fortunate, also, is any college in which the science instructors are able to show in their own sciences the difference between the liberal and the illiberal study of the subject. The former in general will prove to be inquiry into the subject for the light it casts on the nature of the physical world, and the latter will prove to be study exclusively for the sake of something else, such as medicine, engineering, or pharmacy. Much is made of the value of original research as a means of keeping the instructor on his toes and of enlarging knowledge. As much, perhaps more, should be made of the advantage of the instructor's research to the learner, for the presence of a consistent effort to observe something new or construct a new theory cannot help vivifying in the mind of the alert student the fact that the whole intent of his own study of chemistry or physics or biology is to understand the nature represented by these phenomena under view.

Science, when everybody who spoke the word spoke Latin, meant knowledge—*scientia*. *Scientia* comprises two kinds of knowledge: knowledge of man and knowledge of the physical world; and although for a considerable area these two kinds of *scientia* overlap, the data and methods of one being relevant to the problems of the other, they have distinct and clearly separated centers. I am aware here that I am stating a philosophical proposition, the evidences for which are far too numerous to admit even of mention in a short chapter. The assumption which underlies all my remarks about the two natures surrounding and inhabiting us, is stated in Emerson's rhyme about the law for a man and the law for a thing, quoted on Page 8.

Natural science is the law for a thing; when it runs wild the fault lies in our inadequate comprehension of the law for man. While none seriously questions the value of the law for a thing, our peculiarly human relation to it is not, in these days, commonly observed.

The management of scientific study within the laboratory appears to be in very good hands indeed and to be guided by a reasonably clear idea of its own aims. Within the school and college system the education of a scientist appears to be in fairer estate than the education of a man. That is to say, we seem to understand throughout what it takes to equip ourselves to reflect upon the law for a thing. Whatever shortcomings there are in the extent of our devotion to the pure effort to understand the law for the sake of understanding, they do not seem to impede seriously our application of science to the national welfare. If they retard the rate of scientific discovery, that fact hardly shows up within American science itself, but only on comparison between our own discovery of natural laws and the discoveries of Europeans. In our lust for material progress we devote insufficient attention to nature itself; the most serious effect of this deflection of science is to be seen in the common thinking of these times.

It is true that in America there are a few informed amateur naturalists, but one would expect that this populous and wealthy nation, with leisure time guaranteed to millions, would occupy itself with more science for love than it does: that is, more of the science of the amateur, recognizing that we assume that this is the age of science and that this is a scientific nation. True, there are plenty of amateur engineers making television sets, motors, and model airplanes. But where are the amateur botanists, geologists, weathermen, and naturalists? There are some, but a genuine curiosity about the law for a thing would, it seems, call forth many times our present number. What in fact is the intellectual result of the universal attention to science in the public schools? The advertisers of electrical, mechanical, and chemical products hold that such instruction fulfills its social purpose because by disseminating information it increases the demand for complicated gadgets. Undoubtedly it does, in addition, stimulate curiosity about how things work—not only how television works, but how the moon works. Yet the extent of this active and directed curiosity about nature itself does not appear to be commensurate with the energy expended on science in the schools.

The problem which science teachers now face is as many-sided as that of the humanists. On the one hand, they are concerned that young people extend in quantity and quality their direct childhood touch with the natural world; on the other, they must train people to live with motors, jet propulsion, and the photoelectric cell. As usual in American education, we take the short cut and deal with these elaborate applications of elaborately abstract reasoning before the young student can possibly grasp the steps of observation and hypothesis. The applications of science which surround us in household, shop, and the air arise largely from microscopical observation and mathematical reasoning; so the student proceeding in his youth to master the rudiments of these applications is immediately removed from raw nature for a fairly long apprenticeship in the laboratory and with the logarithm tables. Meanwhile, his childhood and youthful sensation of natural phenomena and his growing curiosity of intellect, which is capable of reasoning upon his sensations, lie neglected, unless he has the good fortune to fall in with a real amateur naturalist in the Boy Scouts or a geology club.

The usefulness of science to common thinking might more readily be conveyed to young persons if along with the necessarily long apprenticeship in abstractions and prepared observations upon miscroscope slides, they had the opportunity to study some of the macroscopical sciences as well, such as the sciences of the earth: weather, climate, and geology; field zoölogy and botany. However the trick is to be turned, it is reasonable to ask teachers of science, who of all the groups in the academy have exhibited in recent years the greatest resourcefulness and ingenuity, to find a way to provide thinking in general with a more immediate sense of nature–nature under the hand and foot, nature observed by ear and eye and tongue.

The reason for this request to the professors and teachers of science lies in the fact that innocent curiosity concerning the law for a thing is a part of us, and no full sense of manhood can be achieved without it. I say innocent, because the curiosity of which I speak is devoid of any *arrière pensée;* it has no mercenary or other ulterior motive whatever, not being inspired by the demand for either bread or bombs.

The introduction to science for young college students and advanced school pupils is now undergoing a change which is popularly thought progressive. It is the substitution, under the banner of "general education," of the study of broad general conceptions for the observation of specific things and events in nature. When Thomas Henry Huxley lectured to working men in this fashion the educational effect was splendid. "General education" has brought it about that youths who have been taught nothing but "general concepts" will be asked to teach the meaning of a piece of chalk.

It is a part of the hyperrationalism of our decades that advanced educators urge the substitution of "philosophy of science" for direct and specific scientific study. This lust for abstraction abets the current murder of imagination in the schools. If one had to choose between science for the sake of abstract thinking and science for the sake of specific description of the world, the answer would reveal the importance which the chooser places upon imagination. The rich and lively and applicable imagination needed in these days is ill served by too much systematic and rational thinking. We live in the age of the *esprit géométrique*, but the trials which beset us may be understood not by syllogisms and logic but by that other reasonableness called by Pascal the *esprit de finesse*.

The teaching of science in school and college bears directly at this point upon the quality of thinking in general. William James in his early twenties on an expedition up the Amazon with Agassiz recognized the bearing of science upon the quality of all his own thought. "I have profited a great deal," he wrote, "by hearing Agassiz talk, not so much by what he says, for never did a man utter a greater amount of humbug, but by learning the way of feeling of such a vast practical engine as he is. No one sees farther into a generalization than his own knowledge of details extends, and you have a greater feeling of weight and solidity about the movement of Agassiz's mind, owing to the continual presence of this great background of special facts, than about the mind of any other man I know."

There is, in truth, no absolutely good choice between knowledge of details and generalizations. Details without generalization are childish; generalization without details is so dangerous it is devilish. The problem for the teacher is one of sequence. Which come first? If the cultivation of the disciplined imagination is the teacher's object, there will be no question that a considerable amount of direct observation of specific phenomena will have to come first.

The discerning visitor to American schools is struck with the colossal unconcern for imagination. Latterly it is not so much dry knowledge of static facts which has occupied the place belonging to the training of imagination—not so much knowledge as the conditioning of vague emotional generalities called "attitudes." The President's Commission on Higher Education proposes to emphasize generalizations in what prove to be brief and easy courses of study. Legitimate generalization can come only the hard way, after and in the midst of direct and fairly extensive familiarity with fact. I have said that one of the uses of science by the human spirit is the rich description of the physical world. Another is the cultivation of imagination. This is true because of the constant obligation put upon the student on field trip and in the laboratory to take his own direct step from sensation to meaning.

To describe the innocent question in men's minds which has called forth the most central discoveries about earth and the cosmos, it is difficult to avoid religious terms. But these, especially, we must eschew lest we appear to associate ourselves with the twentieth-century assumption that the man of astronomy and atoms is by definition an authority on God. The historical fact is that there is something in us that wants to know, and that it has appeared to the most thoughtful men a violation of their self-respect to abstain from inquiry with all their powers. By the seventeenth century, when science had entered its modern phase, it was generally admitted that curiosity was natural, but there was a debate among sensitive men about whether undertaking the long and systematic study of similarities which gradually resulted in the classification of species was a worthy pursuit of the instructed intellect. They found in themselves an impulse modestly and with intelligence to cherish the natural world. Sir Thomas Browne, the physician and scientist, stated the impulse to science itself as follows:

The Wisdom of God receives small honour from those vulgar Heads that rudely stare about, and with a gross rusticity admire His works: those highly magnifie Him, whose judicious inquiry into His Acts, and deliberate research into His Creatures, return the duty of a devout and learned admiration.[2]

When the occasion for scientific observation and reasoning is stated in this fashion, it is confused by our contemporaries with the religious polemic called the Argument from Design. Sir Thomas sounds to modern ears to be proposing that we study nature to "prove the existence of God." This is not his meaning; he speaks of admiring and magnifying the Creator, not of proving anything. One cannot read the words of the old scientists who set us on our way to discovery after discovery and be convinced that it was their own private and secret purpose to roast chestnuts for the theologians. Something of their own, peculiar to science, led them on. In its way it was probably religious; at least it was thoroughly human, and what it was and is figures in the stature of man.

Either the purpose of science is this human and virtuous thing within us, related to the fullness of our life and the intention of manhood, or Robert Frost's jibe at his scientific friends is true. To tease them he sometimes says, "All science is domestic science." Domestic science surely is what it is in the slogans of Francis Bacon—the improvement of man's estate. In more serious vein Mr. Frost has said that science is one of the humanities, a minor humanity. Faustian it may be, but not minor. When properly related to the law for man it is, of course, a positive good, and humane in the sense that it exhibits our restless curiosity concerning the sensible world and especially its edges.

II

Imagination

LIBERAL EDUCATION means not only learning certain things, but learning them for certain ends and in a certain way. The way of learning is imaginative; the ends have to do with commitment and belief. The present and three subsequent chapters will treat the place and nurture of imagination and faith in liberal studies.

When modern education ceased to be literary, we gradually lost our understanding of the real nature and uses of imagination. We forgot that the disciplined imagination is ethical; we made it into a game of chasing butterflies. We forgot that the imagination leads on to reality and truth; we thought it an escape from truth. The change is revealed in a passage from the S. N. Behrman comedy, *The Pirate*, produced a few years ago by the Lunts. Manuela says that her "imagination is just an escape, the less it has to do with reality the better."

> SERAFIN: Well, you are the most extraordinary mixture of fantasy and realism it has ever been my good fortune to encounter.
> MANUELA: Am I? Well, there is the practical world and the world of imagination. I know which is which. I don't mix them.
> SERAFIN: There I don't agree with you. Not two separate worlds. One an extension of the other. If your imagination cannot give direction to reality—increase its potential—direct its course—then it is a mere lie, a mere delusion.[3]

One has but to reflect on any of the greatest products of the imagination to observe that it is the loadstone swinging always towards reality. *Macbeth* is the story of a man and a woman finding out the truth about themselves; so colossal is the story, it is about mankind—mankind in need of salvation under wrath. The Greeks, in analyzing how the work of imagination may be achieved, noticed that the poet begins with historical fact and legend—things given—and that to these he does something, he retells, and in the retelling "makes" a little. Observing all this they remarked that he imitates. He does not copy, but imitates the universal idea or image of manhood, of magnanimity or cowardice. The end of all his reflection and his "making" is to state what really happened or may happen. In the work of imagination, as in the work of mowing a field, "the fact is the sweetest dream that labor knows."

There are three popular errors about imagination, and the paragraphs above refer to the first: that imagination releases us from reality. The second is that it has nothing to do with science; and the third is that it grows like an orchid but may not be trained.

The second illusion arises from the error that when the scientist discovers something he is forced to the conclusion. The popular idea seems to be that the scientist gathers a myriad of observations, measurements, and other facts, and that his new conclusion is inevitable. But scientific discovery is not inevitable. True, the original scientist is sometimes forced to a conclusion, but as often as not he leaps to it. He and his colleagues later devote whole batteries of measurements, tests, and logic to checking the new hypothesis. They do this in natural science much as the critics examine by logic and reasonableness any new statement in the arts and morals. But high scientific thinking is peculiarly imaginative, as anyone will agree who reflects on what happened when Galvani observed the twitching of the muscles of the frogs hanging by copper hooks from an iron railing, or when Sir Alexander Fleming saw the effect of mold on the culture plates of bacteria.

What happened was first of all a good guess. To be sure, it was based upon a vast store of measured and systematized knowledge, and the guess itself was disciplined. The scientific thinker had learned not to waste his reflection upon utter impossibilities. He had learned, also, to image forth to his mind an account of unexplained phenomena which others might call absurd; when something he saw surprised him, he made a right guess. What he had in his mind was recognized and generally known fact. With this he "made" something, and what he made of old materials was new.

The third error is that the imagination may not be trained. Henry Mencken, the popular spokesman in the 1920's of the romantic idea of genius, compared the author's part in the production of a book to the hen's part in the laying of an egg. Indeed, the imagination was thought to be nothing but the wild and elemental force of the *Sturm und Drang*, whence, in America, the favored conception of it had been derived. So irresponsible was it thought to be, so unrelated to critical judgment and value, that its utter insulation from the commonsense world was everywhere proclaimed. As a result, one heard teachers on all sides clucking over the precious early outpourings of the very young. They looked with sentimental reverence upon the merest glimmer of originality among their charges, and these little gushes were thought, echoing the nineteenth-century romanticism, to represent the lava of the inward volcano. They were collected into volumes of prose and verse in most of whose titles appeared the word "creative."

Historically, imagining means making images. As men have presented to their minds and to each other what seems to be true, the process called imagination has played a key part. No image that has been used about it quite conveys it to our minds in its fullness. It is the spark which occasions the combustion, the yeast in the dough, the motion of the engine, the breath breathed into the dust to make it a man.

The purpose of a man is an action, inward action or outward. The action peculiar to a thoughtful man is inward before outward, but if clear and truly human, it always issues somehow in a deed which others may judge. Even when a man acts so fast you say, "he shoots before he thinks," if he is thoughtful his outward action has been informed by reflection and inward decisions, accomplished, perhaps, months before he acted like a flash. Inward action is the result of reflection and always entails some kind of decision, judgment, choice, or commitment. Often it is represented by selecting things in the mind to put together in order to make something new, or at least something new to the one who is reflecting and deciding. To be valid, inward action must always be translatable into outward, though often the steps from reflection and judgment to doing something are many and complex. The characteristic action called forth by reflection is writing and speaking, the result of putting together experiences, impressions, and ideas in one's own way. At its merest beginnings this process may be nothing more than "saying it in your own words."

Imagination might be called the bridge from thought to action, or it might be called the gear between the motor and the wheels. Without it each may go its own pace independent of the other. Without it action is thoughtless, thought is sterile. But it is not precisely a bridge or any separate thing between thought and action, for imagination is either a quality of thought, or itself a way to think. To think in such fashion that what you think affects what you believe and hold dear and what account you will give of your own private experience, it is necessary to think imaginatively. So rather than serving as a bridge from one side to another, imagination belongs on both sides of the chasm, to thought and to action. It is the quality of thought necessary to relate it to action. If a man thinks unimaginatively, his action will remain thoughtless—controlled, it may be, by custom, but unaffected by what occurs in his mind. If his deeds are informed with ideas and a reasonable account of man and of the physical world, one may be sure that his thought is no mere dead description of things, no lifeless encyclopedic account of facts, but a living and working and producing process—a lively part of the life he lives.

Making, represented in the Greek word for poet, is by no

means confined to belles-lettres or the fine arts, but signifies a broad, extensive way of using all knowledge. *To make* is to put things together, to see similarities: that is, to make metaphors. In the universities we give ourselves very little practice in "making." We hardly write at all and we do not commonly reason from the ground up for ourselves by means of any symbols, a necessity of thought. Most of the students do not write; most of the teachers do not write. To most young people we do not teach the disciplines of writing–grammar and rhetoric; many an instructor is not experienced in these nor even familiar with them. We prefer our knowledge dead and catalogued, not alive in our minds.

Imagination has largely been excluded from the working center of universities. Two main bodies of opinion are responsible for its virtual elimination, one held by an able group within the universities, and the other entertained by those either at its fringes or altogether outside the walls. One body of opinion holds that the working mind gets along pretty well without much use of the imagination; the other, that imagination is something arty and irresponsible.

The former view is reflected in one of the best of all the recent committee reports on the state of liberal learning in America: "Liberal Education Re-Examined: Its Role in a Democracy" (1943). This volume was sponsored by the American Council of Learned Societies, and its importance lies not only in its brilliant auspices but in its faithfulness to the operative reasoning and the current practice of the best universities and in the fact that its recommendations reflect the commonly held philosophy of *academia.*

Quite properly the report states that assured leadership is absent from the field of liberal education. "Many humanistic faculties have lost their way and forfeited public confidence." "Our academic 'humanists,' " the report continues, "must make a resolute effort to reorient themselves, to clarify their own objectives, and to provide the academic community with a type of guidance which reflects genuine comprehension of basic issues."[4] If the report had done this, it would have fulfilled the promise of its accurate and internal description of American universities. In regretting its shortcomings, one must praise the report for finding that the weakness of the humanities is the major source of our confusion. Much has been said recently about science misapplied and about the pseudoscientific pretenses of many social and humanistic thinkers. The illusion that the humanities are good if they can call themselves scientific is clearly a dangerous illusion, as bad as the attempt of some scientists, usually not the best, to find in their studies of mathematics and matter a solution to human problems. Our real intellectual troubles arise not from science but from the humanities, for they have lost their active inward vigor.

After referring to the famous definition of Milton—"a complete and generous education: one that fits a man to perform, skillfully, justly and magnanimously, all the acts, both public and private of peace and war"—the report paraphrases: "Education has a double function—to make men free and to teach them to bear freedom when they have it." To *make* men free. Here the objective of education, like the objective of democracy, is stated in terms of action. It may be significant that the title of this report, like some others, speaks of liberal education "in" a democracy. Barbara Ward, recently commenting on the idea that democracy is something we have and that education's place within it can be located, puts liberal education into its properly active terms. It is literally the job of liberal education, says Miss Ward, to evoke and train the thinking which will *make* men free and will *make* for the city and the world the conditions of freedom.

But to conclude, as does "Liberal Education Re-Examined," that the best ways to think are historical and philosophical is to propose that the thinker remain a spectator of the human and earthly show. This is an incomplete description of liberal education because it takes no proper account of action. In preparation of the report, systematic faculty discussions were conducted in several academic centers, and in these many proposed with vigor the idea that university teaching is primarily concerned with knowledge, not at all with commitment and action. This may be true if action is mere activity, but if action is interior—making a decision, declaring an allegiance, affirming something—the end of liberal education is commitment and action. An educated man is committed to reason—really committed; that means committed to the truth, so much committed that he will not renounce it, as did many professors of German universities, even in mortal fear. The only conclusion one can reach, in contemplating the silence of so many great scholars in one of the mightiest university systems of the world, when every premise of their calling had been violated by decree, is that however vast their knowledge, they were not products of a truly liberal education.

Discussing the descriptive and unjudging temper of humane and social studies in the era of scientific method, a philosophy teacher coined a word to describe a sin of the academic mind: *non-committalism.* The report here considered illustrates its faithfulness to much university study and teaching in its non-committalism. True, the university stands pre-eminent as the center of objectivity, as the "haven," in Thornton Wilder's words, "of disinterestedness." Bare fact, recorded and uncriticized, must stand alone in the light of dispassionate reasoning. But where the facts are human ones, either private or social, a moment arrives when the scholar, in his manhood, must decide and use.

American scholars—schoolboys, college students, scientists—must be liberally educated, actively in their minds, morally in their wills, so that they will know in their hearts the supreme value of reason and truth, a value superior to their own lives. Courage and action are trained in many ways other than by schoolbooks, but they surely enter into thought, and the development of a student's mind, if it is to be manly and full, must take account of these along the way. It is difficult to imagine a man of moral courage who has not by long practice required himself to use what he knows, and to submit his deeds, over and over again, to some of the thoughts and principles established in his mind by study and reflection.

At one point the report notices the excellence and clarity of medical education in contrast to the vagueness of liberal education. The reason for the contrast must lie in this: that while what characterizes medical education is performance, almost all performance has of recent years been eliminated from liberal education. What is the performance peculiar to the liberally educated man? It is writing and speaking and calculating; that is, the active mastery of the arts appropriate to liberal thought.

The report is sicklied o'er with the pale cast of the encyclopedia. Things cannot be understood, it says, unless one knows their whole historical context—economic, political, sociological. Is this true? Is it true of the parables or the Psalms? No. The fresh and even naïve mind may grasp them. The disciplined soul—that is, the mind with a rich and informed imagination—may understand them. It is possible, indeed, that he may understand them a thousand times better than the encyclopedic scholar, because the knowledge most pertinent to the inquiry about ourselves speaks straight out and directly.

If one may refer to the Platonic tradition, the belief that the good life is speculative and theoretical, the report falls within the Platonic tradition. The theoretical life is the life of seeing things as one sees them on a stage. In opposition to it is the principle of Aristotle—that the purpose of a man is an action. It is no accident that the Aristotelian philosophy also prefers poetry to history as a closer approximation to the truth. We should not conclude from this that universities should attempt to produce poets, but it is not impractical for university learning to regard the "making" type of thought as the excellent way of the mind towards which all teaching and study should strive. Imaginative thinking, in the true sense of that word, should be preferred to the merely temporal and systematic. The disciplined and informed imagination includes and makes use of history and philosophy and is operative upon the present experiences.

Imagination is evicted from the university by the utterly systematic mind. It is detained without the walls by the merely arty. It is here, of course, necessary to distinguish between the controlled imagination, which tends towards reality, and the vain imaginings, which are an abomination. In our generation the authenticity of any kind of imagination is often judged merely by its eruptive force, and the word *imaginative* means nothing other than unreasonable, fantastic. Associated with this view is the cult of creativeness which swept the schools in the 1920's and which still hangs like a moor mist above each of the arts.

An extreme expression of the irresponsibility of imagination occurred in the recent quarrel over the award of the Library of Congress prize to Ezra Pound for his *Pisan Cantos* which was mentioned in Chapter 2. During the debate the editors of *Poetry* magazine dealt not only with the poem but with the poet, who was under indictment for treason, and they expressed the opinion that because Mr. Pound's "rather cross attitude towards America" had proved itself for him the "creative" attitude, it was therefore the "right" one.

Two words now favored in discussion of the aims of American education figure in that amazing opinion of the editors of *Poetry*. They are *creative* and *attitude*. Emerging as they have done out of the Dewey romanticism, it is evident in that context what muzzy words they have come to be. In the 1920's we had not only "creative writing" and "creative education"; we had "creative editing" as well. In the opinion of the editors of *Poetry* about Mr. Pound, we have Rousseau's idea of the individual supported by the neosemantical illusion that words have no meaning which abides. In awe of the undisciplined individual romantic genius, it defends a man's irresponsibility as a man. This is anarchic individualism.

Popular illusion has held that imagination may not be trained, but progressive education has made acceptable the idea that, among children at least, it should be encouraged like a tender plant. The lamentable effect of the popularization of ideas set in motion by the progressive education movement, however, has been to estop from mature and effective use of imagination the very children whose infant originality is so gaily cherished. This has occurred whenever, in the name of the child's immediate interests, he has been deprived of the necessarily tedious mastery of the instruments of imaginative thinking: chiefly letters and numbers; and wherever the praise of his unthoughtful and sometimes effortless childhood creations has given him the illusion that he should not inhibit his native genius by criticism and discipline.

The record of this sentimentality on the part of teachers toward the brightest and most promising of their pupils is extensive and sad to behold. A mother once seriously said in the presence of her daughter seeking admission to college, and in approval of the daughter's poor showing to date: "Judith is waiting for her native genius to show itself." At a progressive college Mrs. Chalmers, talking one afternoon with students after she had read and lectured, beheld through the window a girl dressed in a long white Greek-fashion gown and gold sandals; she paced slowly back and forth among the pillars of the porch. "Who is that?" Mrs. Chalmers asked. "That is Millicent," said one of the professors; "she is solving her problem."

No teacher of any of the sciences or the social or humane studies who has critically dealt with the original efforts of his students questions the susceptibility of the imagination to discipline. The conscientious teacher does not exclaim with praise over every product of the spontaneous overflow of unpowerful feeling on the part of his pupil. Rather, he may at times be so severe that what he does may appear cruel. The late Ralph Boas, a superb teacher and an able one at training the imagination, was known, when the occasion demanded, to take the hard-wrought pages of a student and tear them up in his presence. An even greater teacher, Ada Snell, now and then did the same.

The instructor is not paid to praise the student but to be harsh, to represent the common mind and to show up absurdity. The student's business is to try again, as in the famous story of Agassiz. Day after day, as the carcasses of the fish became more noisome, Agassiz sent students back to complete the assignment, which was simply to find out on their own all that could be found in the specimen. For days after the students thought they had come to the end of every observation, they continued under his unremitting pressure to make discoveries for themselves.

The fact that the imagination may be disciplined is a mystery, but any who doubt its possibility have only to read the letters of John Keats and observe the incredible speed with which that youthful mind by self-instruction and conversation matured itself. One means of discipline lies in the mere symbols by which imagination expresses itself, for these have rules and restrictions of their own. They are the arithmetic and the grammar of the symbols. In painting, sculpture, and music there are languages similar, in their relation to what the imagination may present, to the languages of science and letters. Imagination begins to be disciplined when it tries to be intelligible by means of one of these systems of symbols. That is the first step. All imagined statements of any value deal with truth or opinion. The chief discipline of the imagination is the demand that in some context or other it talk sense: in mathematics, that it be consistent with its own system of logic; in expressions dealing with human value, that what is said be probable—or, if purposely fantastic, droll, or monstrous, still intelligibly related to common sense.

At this stage, the discipline of the imagination demands that it be ethical. Let us remember that ethical means the ethos; what we really are and do, the facts of life. It does not mean manners or gentility or prudery or the rules of the boarding school. When imagination is disciplined by the ethos, it has arrived at an advanced stage, but even the young student in his writing or other composition should sense the responsibility of his inventions to the norm of human nature. If, as will almost inevitably come about, he deals in any way with right and wrong, or fair and foul, the way in which he imagines value, the fashion in which he bodies it forth and brings it into being by argument, character, or incident, must be related to the ethos. Such requirement has no relation to the taboos of the Watch and Ward Society. It is simply to demand that the attempt to imagine life be not false to the life which the imaginer and any other candid and thoughtful person may know. That is all.

The obligation to state what one truly sees rightly begins early in childhood. No service is done a boy or girl in praising the bright and surprising colors or sounds or stories brought forth in intended childishness without any effort on the child's part to state the matter clearly, to put the thing straight, according to his own intention and by means of whatever he knows of words or tones or color. This is a delicate business. Only the most skillful teachers are successful at it. It is my observation, however, that if the aims of teaching the imagination were better understood in the critical discussion of the times, and particularly in the philosophy which governs the training of teachers, the number of those now on the job who would be capable of helping in the discipline and the self-discipline of imagination of their pupils would increase tenfold.

The conventional treatment of imagination by educationists is to suppose that it is concerned only with pleasures, a source of brighter holidays but not essential to the work of the world or of the mind. This opinion is responsible for the talk about beauty and exposure to it, for "music appreciation," for the sugary terms in which otherwise down-to-earth thinkers refer to the arts. What is the pertinence of imagination to the cold war? Nothing less than the responsibility, first of all, to understand the terms of liberty in whatever new circumstances, political, economic, and military, the 1950's will bring; and in the second place, to make it possible for the thoughtful, young and old, to state for themselves and each other why freedom is necessary and how its guarantee will be possible.

That small book of the trained imagination called *The City of Man*, to which I have referred, observes that the totalitarians think democracy weak because, they say, it "rests on opinion, it has no conviction." Intelligent conviction is the business of liberal education. As the authors of *The City of Man* say, "the concept of a vital democracy must be dissociated from the notion of a disintegrated liberalism, which is a precursor of tyranny and a prey to it." To contemplate knowledge merely in the temporal and systematic mode afforded no hindrance to the disintegrated liberalism especially evident all about us in the 1930's; indeed, to do so and no more may promote it. To hold that the imagination is wild and irresponsible and cannot be informed by the ethos contributes to the same end.

Under the illusion that there is no such thing as the disciplined and ethical imagination, people rush into action untempered by meditation and belief. To do this is usually to pretend to translate slogans easily into quick physical action and to deny the intellect altogether. But to discover inner action in the ways of the mind and will is to revitalize not only the humanities, not only liberal education, but liberalism and democracy themselves. This may be done by a strict, fresh, vigorous discipline of the imagination, the faculty which, according to Napoleon, rules the world.

This chapter has already mentioned some of the practical ways of training imagination at school. Mathematics taught by truly discerning teachers who are accorded time enough for the conjectures which even the lower mathematics entail, is also excellent training ground for imagination. In the colleges and schools there are numerous publications for original literary work of students. Why are there not an equal number of similar publications for imaginative work in mathematics and the other sciences? The sheer discipline in these subjects is so evident, it often desiccates the mind; and that is a pity, since the sciences have so recently developed out of the vigorous and trained imaginative reasoning of so many gifted minds.

The chapters in this volume on the educational system will deal with the substitution in our lifetime of means for ends. One of the ironies of the energetic and expensive American system of schools and colleges is that millions of money have been spent by foundations, states, and university trustees to relieve the student and the teacher of the very necessities which bring about the most efficient and practical of all training of imagination. I refer to the expensive establishment of testing bureaus and the abandonment of examinations and written papers in favor of the voting machine. Was Othello black, brown, or beige? Underline one. Let this question, quoted from forms printed and used at a famous university, stand for the whole idea. The test may be machine-graded, and the saving in wages, even deducting the initial cost of the machine and the recurring cost of its operation and upkeep, is said to be immense. But looking at the platoons of testers, the stacks of printed matter, the cabals of testing specialists retained to think up tamperproof and guessproof and unambiguous questions, I wonder if any disinterested cost accountant has ever thoroughly compared the alternative costs and what his conclusions would be purely in dollars. True, by means of machine-graded tests you can sort out students after a fashion, picking these for further study and eliminating those. The argument runs that if the job can be done by machine-graded tests, let us be efficient and buy the machines and train the mechanical brains necessary to prepare the teasers.

The important question concerns the effect of machine-graded yes-and-no questions upon teaching and learning. We can afford to buy the machines and to hire and train the mechanical brains. Can we afford to encourage the mechanical thinking which the tests encourage? That is the vital problem. "What is the use of knowledge, young man?" "To pass the examinations." "How can you do that?" "Mark the right questions right and the wrong questions wrong." For this should be substituted the following: "What is the use of knowledge, young man?" "To make something of my own with it." "How do you do that?" "By my own reasoning." "How may I know that you are doing this so that I may help you to improve both your knowledge and skill?" "By my reasoning and using my imagination in the ways found most fruitful to men, that is, by writing with letters or numbers or both."

Avoidance of papers, papers, papers by the student—original papers, long ones, papers assigned, and papers volunteered—is no economy in education, no matter how much is saved or appears to be saved in the budget and the energy of the professors. Papers written and not read or but casually read by the instructor are a discouragement to the able young person. Papers written but merely graded with a cheery word or letter or number in red crayon help the student little. The economy of teaching, sad to say, requires that the instructor work almost as hard on some papers as the student himself, on a few, harder. The machine has proved itself notably inadequate to this important pedagogical chore.

As the imagination copes with the mysteries of human nature and the nature of men in groups, one excellent means of its discipline is the imaginative work of experienced thinkers. The old-fashioned process of digging this out of the chaste and loaded sentences of Greek or Latin afforded a peculiarly rich discipline of the student's own imagination. This is true partly because of the pause necessary in converting the packed and definite meaning, along with its overtones, out of the sophisticated language of the ancients into our own looser one. The imagination was also trained by the way, in the necessarily ethical discussions which most ancient discourse of the first class called forth. This was true even at the elementary level of translating the direct account of wars written by Caesar. It was true of the more complicated and subtle ideas of the dramatists, Homer, Virgil, and the lyric poets.

To read in our own language the good translations of any strict writing, such as Plato's dialogues, or a modern book like G. H. Hardy's *A Mathematician's Apology*, entails not only skill in dialectic but skill in imagination. The latter is true because all good and informed writing, prose as well as poetry, omits on purpose some steps in the reasoning, recognizing that full apprehension requires the reader to sense what is implied and perhaps to weigh it as thoughtfully as what is stated.

A college textbook in psychology admonishes the student to eliminate all emotion from his thinking, proposing that the grown-up and responsible and college way to think is to accomplish thought without feeling. Max Lerner and others warned self-styled liberals in the Thirties that they were victims of a similar illusion. As if you could truly think in this fashion! As if you would want to! Show me, if you can, one good fundamental passage of human reasoning conducted without emotion!

While in the teaching profession it was said and taught that the imagination may be encouraged but neither instructed nor disciplined, a similar theory of the emotions persisted. They, too, are something which flares up and cannot be schooled. But one has only to remember how he learned to like something, be it coffee or Sibelius, to be reminded that feeling may be disciplined. Education is usually described by the mature. To see it from all sides we should hear an account by babes and sucklings, too. They, if they knew what was coming to them, might well look upon their cherished wildness, and the days of unrestrained Indian existence, remarking how all this savagery is teased, cajoled, sugarplummed, and spanked out of them. A conspiracy, they may call it, a gigantic middle-aged conspiracy designed to lead them to abhor this grime, these dead clams and alley cats, this sweet revenge—a conspiracy calculated by systematic and timed propaganda to graft upon them an actual enjoyment of collars and ties, shoes, and grand opera. So the infant may recount the old human convention: instruction of taste. This is just what it is, a conspiracy to substitute for the delights of barbarians the delights of civilized men. "His taste is in his mouth," say the Germans of the utterly vulgar. Converting the reason entails transplanting the taste from mouth to eye and ear and mind.

The training of the emotions follows the forms made available for their expression: the sentence, in its beautiful and devilish variety, the sonata, the sonnet, the proportions of the human form. So are the pleasures ennobled; so are the emotions converted, along with the reason.

In school the fault with talk about culture, background, tradition, the past as a corpus, knowledge as chronology and system, is that such considerations imply what, lamentably, under guidance of aims derived from such conceptions, education has actually become: elaborate concern for ideas which do not come alive. The search for truth, particularly in the humanities, is too often a search for the corpus delicti. The ancient Indian philosophy spoke of the imagination as the active implement by which we may penetrate Maya, the veil of illusion, to the reality or truth behind it. In the absence of its operative force, we may add all the books and pamphlets conceivable to our libraries, in a never-ending stream, and they will not do us a sentence worth of good. Genuine teaching when wedded to genuine learning is lively because its central purpose is lively—the imaginative use of experience. This means a use disciplined both by fact and by the ethical and scientific context of our life—by the law for man and the law for thing.

Some years ago when faculties were asked to approve the new degree "Bachelor of Philosophy," cynics remarked that it guaranteed nothing but an ignorance of Latin. The implication was that the peculiar virtue of the Bachelor of Arts course was a knowledge of Latin. But when well bestowed, the honorable title Bachelor of Arts or Bachelor of Science refers to nothing which its holder cannot put to work. Without imagination the arts cannot exist; under undisciplined imagination they become not the liberal but the black arts. The arts of the truly instructed refer to something lively and contemporary; they are the arts of meditative thought and discourse not only opening up the hitherto unknown, but always affecting in new ways our action both public and private.

12

Belief

SOCRATES held that the wise man is he who asks the right questions of nature. In the dialogues, however, he so regularly had the better of the argument that his students undoubtedly thought—as does the modern reader—that his wide knowledge of geometry, history, literature, and politics, rather than his inquiry, constituted the major part of his conception of wisdom. He sounds, as you read, like a very clever man concealing the fact that he knows all the answers. But in the *Meno* he confesses not to know. The subject of investigation is immortality, and Socrates has suggested that perhaps what we think we know is merely what we remember, it may be from a previous existence. A slave boy is led to see a geometric proposition which he had not known before simply by seeing the lines drawn on the sand and by answering the questions one by one which Socrates has put to him. Socrates says to Meno:

> And if the truth of all things always existed in the soul, then the soul is immortal. Wherefore be of good cheer, and try to recollect what you do not know, or rather what you do not remember.
>
> MENO: I feel, somehow, that I like what you are saying.
>
> SOCRATES: And I, Meno, like what I am saying. Some things I have said of which I am not altogether confident.

The thoughtful man must often deal with propositions of which he is not altogether confident. That is, he does not have final faith in them, yet these tentative opinions, these hypotheses, these essays into understanding which we know to be mere tries, not absolutes—all these ideas of which we are not altogether confident are involved in a real and reliable faith, the faith of a student.

To come up against the many things not known to man in any absolute fashion is constantly to remind ourselves that all things end in a mystery. The skyscrapers in New York are cemented to the core of rock which makes Manhattan Island. But in Chicago the skyscrapers float in mud. Caissons and pilings go down deep enough to make a great expanse of friction, friction against the soft soil sufficient to keep the buildings relatively upright and relatively in place. Human knowledge is like the Chicago buildings rather than those in New York. We spread out our friction against the world as far as we can. Love, loyalty, sacrifice, hatred, greed, envy, humor, honor, generosity—the elements in life we rely on most are none of them rooted in any absolute which we can prove. We know they are there only by our own personal experience checked against the most extensive testimony we can get. Spreading out our knowledge of humanity thus, we make ourselves as stable as we can, instructing ourselves approximately where we stand.

The knowledge most important to a man, the knowledge of himself, is none of it absolute; of much we are not even confident. The worth of inquiry, however, is a very different matter. Socrates follows up his confession of uncertainty of fixed statements with an avowal of faith in search and in its outcome, a faith so strong that it was to lead him willingly to his death. He continues: "But that we shall be better and braver and less helpless if we think that we ought to inquire, than we should have been if we indulged in the idle fancy that there was no knowing and no use in seeking to know what we do not know; —that is a theme upon which I am ready to fight, in word and deed, to the utmost of my power."

Socrates had faith in reflection as well as inquiry. The faith of the enemies of free inquiry is also a real faith, but a mean one. The report from Berlin about the destruction of the *Bismarck* may have been edited; but, if it was true, the men about to meet their death on the battleship radioed: "We shall fight to the last grenade. Long live *der Führer!*" Perhaps they said "*Deutschland über alles*," or "Long live Germany"; but the report reaching us had it, "Long live *der Führer!*" The faith in which the Nazi soldiers and sailors were trained for years is a simple one, expressed in marching, saluting, shouting *Heil*, and repeating slogans such as "Strength through joy." This small faith built an effective army—effective, at least, for a few years.

Our faith is more complex and difficult. It involves the faith of a reasonable man, which in turn requires a mature, self-reliant, and responsible life for the individual. Those who have chosen it have, like Socrates, done so at the peril not only of their lives, but, while they are growing up intellectually, of their peace of mind. As persons of full stature, they have found in this faith not all of life, but one large share of it. The understanding which it has brought them has been durable, not only for themselves, but for their children and the cities where they have lived.

What is this quest which we have in our minds and hearts and which we further by study? At first glance it strikes us as modern and largely of our own making. Recent history suggests that it springs from the Renaissance and the Reformation, when men began to shift the object of their admiration. So many men of the Dark and the Middle Ages were obscurantists, holding it a virtue to worship the Lord in ignorance, to despise nature, and to ask no questions of authority. But in fact the spirit of inquiry is very old in us. It was, of course, far from dead in the Middle Ages; it was notably lively in ancient times. Christ exercised it upon every principle of a man's own secret life and upon his life with his fellows. In ancient Egypt, in India and China and ancient Greece, the same human gesture was made, a gesture of the eye, seeking, seeking. So early is it, and so constant, thoughtful men regard it as the most human element in their lives, distinguishing us from brutes.

Inquiry is only one element of faith. A man could not be

complete with this alone, but he could not be complete without it. The Book of Revelation makes a promise to the faithful, that they will receive the crown of life if they endure to the end. Tested by our own time the victorious statement of a musician to his friends reveals what is signified by Saint John's metaphor.

Bruno Walter had been pursued from place to place in Germany and Austria by the pogroms of central Europe. His son-in-law, crazed by the horrors, killed his wife, Walter's daughter, and then committed suicide. Walter said in the winter of 1940–41 to his friends, referring to the Beethoven opera *Fidelio*, which he was about to conduct: "This music says 'yes' to all who ask if courage and sacrifice and endurance and fortitude can win against a cruel tyranny. . . . Somehow this music tells us that happiness is deeper than unhappiness. Many of you know the tragedy of my life, yet I can say that. There is joy to be had even through grief. In the depths of my heart I know it, and I know that ignorance of this may lead ultimately to defeat and suicide."

I call these words a crown of life because the ability to say them is the desire of so many and the accomplishment of so few. In saying them Walter undoubtedly expressed the fruit of his confidence in reflection and inquiry, which in his particular experience was bound up with music. It is clear that faith in reflection, the student's faith, brought Walter to another faith, faith in the brightest promises that life and its prophets and heroes have made to us.

In the depths of their hearts most men do not really know that "there is joy to be had, even through grief." It should be the object of their lives to show this to themselves. Socrates was sure, to the extent of giving away his life, that to inquire makes us better and braver and less helpless than not to inquire. Walter confesses that ignorance of the knowledge that "happiness is deeper than unhappiness" may lead us ultimately to defeat and suicide. What both of them knew is not proved, not founded on the bedrock of absolute reasoning. If they were alone in these convictions, we should suspect them; but many men whose honesty we trust and whose minds have been unfolded to us have reported the same faith.

The fruitful doubt of the world, typified by the questioning of Socrates, has been established on anti-doubt: that is, faith. But in the books and committee reports on the aims of American education during the past decade, affirmations of belief have been notably absent. Among the American books of national influence there is one remarkable exception, the Harvard Report referred to in Chapter 3. That book is written by twelve scholars and scientists whose business is to be sceptical, yet they base their whole work upon belief. This fact is notable indeed, for the committee does not, like so many of its contemporaries, state that the curriculum begins and ends in intellect and assume that belief is extracurricular. How many institutional plans do just this! How many plans for postwar education add an item number 6 or 7 at the end, to the effect that the student Christian association or fraternities or athletics or humanitarian activities, all matters involving belief, are good extras to be attached to the intellectual life of students! The Harvard committee puts faith at the start of the intellectual enterprise and at the end of the book emphasizes that faith is the guiding star of the whole curriculum.

It might shock "godless" Harvard to think it was being called religious. I am talking, however, not about religion, but about something close to it and important to it. At the basis of all reasoning on what should be studied and to what end, says the committee, is a concept "partaking of the nature not of fact but of faith." The committee then states its creed. Its main article is not exceptional, for at its base stands "belief in the dignity and mutual obligation of man."

It is important, however, that the committee holds that the whole structure of liberal learning is built upon *credo*. Another distinguished committee, the philosophers who prepared the report on the tasks and opportunities of philosophy in American education,[5] examine this same problem. They ask, on what belief can they agree? They conclude with something comparable to the basic credo of the Harvard committee. They can agree on the value of inquiry—but this, they discover, is as far as they can go. This is as far as Socrates was prepared to go in the *Meno* passage quoted, but not, according to some of the dialogues, his limit. Before it has finished, the Harvard committee—faced, let us remember, with a different problem from that of the report on philosophy—took three important steps beyond the committee of philosophers.

The second affirmation of faith by the Harvard Committee is the belief that men can reach "agreement on the good of man at the level of performance without the necessity of agreement on ultimates." This is a long step beyond the first article, and it involves Christian and other religious belief in a fashion which I shall presently describe. It is the faith of humanism. Here a distinction is necessary. Those who confuse humanism with humanitarianism think the former a denial of religion. But for the Harvard committee, the humanistic faith is not inconsistent with Christian faith, but altogether in keeping with it. Indeed many theologians, Catholic, Jewish, and Protestant, regard humanism as essential to religious faith. They are right, for without humanism religion can find no adequate account of man's nature; humanism itself demonstrates man's subjection to the higher will. It is this article of faith, the faith of the humanist, which frees the committee of the charge of Neo-Scholasticism and orthodox or secular Thomism; it is this article which permits the committee to discover, as in my opinion it does rightly, that ancient life and thought is more modern and relevant to us than that of the Middle Ages. It is this article which leads the committee to complain of current pragmatism, and the educational movements set in motion by Professor Dewey—that they are inadequate because they are not pragmatic enough.

Third, and most important, the committee of twelve scholars and scientists at Harvard holds that the long record of human experience, ancient and contemporary, reveals on analysis a definite and abiding standard of conduct, a norm which is discoverable and against which all human thought and action may be judged.

Fourth, to relate the third belief to the first, the committee holds that the primary "belief in the worth and meaning of the human spirit . . . rests on that hard but very great thing, tolerance not from absence of standards but through possession of them." The popular philosophy of our day holds that freedom is release; in education, that liberalism means throwing down more and more hurdles until the college which follows most slavishly the whims of the student is called the most liberal. In politics this popular view of liberalism holds that democracy is measured only by the degree to which the majority rules unchecked—the will or, indeed, the whim of the majority. These are popular views. Actually, of course, constitutional democracy is no such thing, but instead, the will of the majority tempered by justice; and for liberal education the nature of justice is the chief concern. The Harvard Report takes up this confusion about the nature of democracy and liberty and holds that freedom means submission to certain truths. "These are truths which none can be free to ignore, if one is to have that wisdom through which life can become useful." This is education in liberalism, which "has a pattern of its own."

Clearly all four of these beliefs fundamental to the structure of the curriculum and its aims are neither unreasoned nor unlearned ones. The third belief, in the existence of a norm of human behavior, could not be entertained by anyone ignorant of man in the past as well as of contemporary man. Let us avoid the medieval dispute over *credo ut intelligam* and for the present observe the remarkable fact that a group of learned men agreed, in our time, on the evidence of human experience, that belief is involved at the start and throughout learning; and that contrary to the favored philosophies and literary and political opinions of the day they agreed upon that third proposition, a combination of critical judgment and faith: namely, that wide experience of mankind reveals in its thoughts and deeds a norm, the approximation to which is education itself.

All of these affirmations are notable, both in themselves and in the simple clarity with which they are linked together in the Harvard Report and applied to school and college practice. They would not be notable in some periods in history, but they are particularly notable now because most of the current reports, books, and essays on liberal education avoid or gloss over or deny them. These relegate belief to a separate compartment and usually affirm the impropriety or even disgrace of tainting matters of intellect with alien matters of mere belief. Running through these books and essays is the view that critical judgment can take the place of faith—or, at most, that faith is the business of some other institution, and intellect alone the business of the university.

Before considering what these affirmations imply, I shall digress to comment on the disappointing abandonment by the Harvard committee of religious belief as the means of unifying and integrating the higher learning. "Given the American scene, with its varieties of faith and even of unfaith," says the report, "we did not feel justified in proposing religious instruction as a part of the curriculum." "Whatever one's views," the report says elsewhere, "religion is not now for most colleges a practicable source of intellectual unity." Jacques Maritain, in his Terry Lectures, *Education at the Crossroads*, relies not only upon ethics, but on "agreement on ultimates" to make one out of the multifarious concerns of education. He is enabled to do this by his Roman Catholic faith. So also can Sir Richard Livingstone, describing the nature of present-day liberal education in the ancient Christian tradition of Oxford. Several non-Catholic American institutions, representative not so much of the whole American scene as of their own Christian foundations, could conceivably do the same: that is, their members could, as Protestant believers, develop on the basis of

Christian faith the structure of the higher learning. The Harvard committee has not done this, and in warning to such attempts as theirs Sir Richard Livingstone says, "Those who reject Christian beliefs, cannot count on keeping Christian morals."[6] The Harvard committee does not reject them but declines to make them at once the basis and the guide of the curriculum.

If the faculty at Harvard succeeds after many years of trial in providing a college course which is primarily concerned, to use the words of the committee, with "the apprehension of the norm—by approximation to it," it will indeed have made educational history. To put generations of students into a way of understanding and believing, as the committee believes, that the norm exists will be to change profoundly the fundamental thinking of the times. This is not to say that there are not competing accounts of what the norm is, and that learned men would ever be able to agree on a statement of it; but presumably there is enough they could find in common to lead scholars and teachers to agree on what parts of human experience are central and most worthy of study by every man. For a whole institution to set out to show forth the evidences that there is a norm in the hope that students generally will not only see them but believe that what they suggest does exist: this would constitute a very great accomplishment and the proper one for liberal education to undertake.

But when we talk of bringing students to believe something, we tread close to the chasms of dogmatism, propaganda, and the substitution of doctrine for free inquiry. Quite properly, and in the tradition of modern and American life, the books and essays by groups of scholars to which I have referred have explicitly described these dangers and tried to secure us against them. The problem is difficult; it confronts every college which declines to tell people what they *must* believe. But clearly we hope that they can and will believe something that will give them a common bond as men, and the Harvard committee goes rather far in stating what.

The terms of this problem are perhaps best set down in the *Charmides* of Plato:

> Monster! I said; you have been carrying me round in a circle, and all this time hiding from me the fact that the life according to knowledge is not that which makes men act rightly and be happy, not even if knowledge include all the sciences, but one science only, that of good and evil. For, let me ask you, Critias, whether, if you take away this, medicine will not equally give health, and shoemaking equally produce shoes, and the art of the weaver clothes? whether the art of the pilot will not equally save our lives at sea, and the art of the general in war?
>
> Quite so.
>
> And yet, my dear Critias, none of these things will be well or beneficially done, if the science of the good be wanting.

How temper all knowledge with the science of good and evil? The preceding chapters have attempted to give the answer, which in brief is this: let the early teaching of knowledge be primarily liberal. This means, let the end and aim of common education be the understanding of ourselves, our kind and what surrounds us.

When we consider that the science of good and evil, like all knowledge of man, is useful only if its postulates and elaborate testimony are believed, we see that the problems of belief cannot be consigned by all other departments to the department of philosophy alone. The philosopher would be faced with an impossible task if he were required to carry the whole burden of liberal education. He would have both to teach and to inculcate belief. The philosophers of the report on "Philosophy in American Education," moreover, quite properly decline the job. They cannot be responsible to "help youth 'believe something' " if the appeal that they do this "is an appeal to throw the weight of their discipline behind traditional faith." The creedal agreement of these particular philosophers stops with a common belief in the value of inquiry. Philosophy, they rightly hold, is not the generator, but the arbiter of experiences of value and the delight in it. "It is important," Edward Caird used to say, "that a belief should be true, and it is important that it should be reasoned, but it is more important that it be reasoned than that it be true." So, and quite properly, speaks the professional philosopher. Philosophy is the intellectual conscience, not the whole of conscience. Its purpose is to criticize and judge, not to promote belief.

How, then, convey a faith in liberal education? To use the definition of the Harvard committee, how propagate the faith that human experience reveals a norm? One way to propagate faith is by dogma; and that we renounce in the modern secular or Protestant university. The other is to familiarize people with evidence that is persuasive. The most vital persuasion of our life is not argument but fact, sometimes pointed and appraised fact, often fact presenting itself to us in the midst of strong feeling. The simplest facts offered by experience to character are supercharged: death, birth, the deeds and thoughts which give rise to love, treason, friendship, loyalty, worship. When the important human facts are all studied in order to find out what our nature is, the things studied carry their own persuasiveness. There is no reason why the deplorable state of higher learning implied in Professor Perry's utterance, quoted on Pages 101–2, should prevail. He said in effect that if the scientists, social scientists, historians, and literary scholars renounce the liberal treatment of their subjects the philosophers will have to do their best to provide the account of man and matter and their meaning. While it is true that much teaching in institutions labeled colleges of liberal arts and sciences is merely technical, the greatest historians at present endeavor to "reconstruct and interpret the life of man"; the greatest political scientists are constantly seeking to find and show forth "the meaning of society and the purposes of human institutions." If the new plans at Harvard succeed in injecting into the study of science, the social sciences, and the humanities the single and constant endeavor in the pursuit of these subject matters to apprehend the human norm by approximation to it, the conclusions of Professor Perry will not become necessary. The study of philosophy itself, obviously, is one of those which at present more than others contributes to an effort at apprehension of the norm. This part of its task should not be unique but shared by all the sciences and arts.

Belief will even then not precisely take care of itself. But the belief of teachers who affirm that there is a standard to seek and who themselves seek it is infectious. More important, the evidence on man, particularly in all the humanities—that is, the recorded evidence of what man has thought and done in his hours of greatest intensity, in hours of tragedy, heroism, prayer, and reasoned refusal—is itself persuasive. It has been said of the study of ancient Greece as defined by the school of *litterae humaniores* that the very study is a way of life. It is not the subject of preachment or admonition. The ideas, the histories, the tragedies, comedies, epics, the science and government of ancient Athens carry their own persuasiveness. The same is true of any humanistic study of modern life, such as the works and times of Milton or Jefferson, available to contemporary students largely without the benefit of ancient languages.

How convey the belief? By studying the evidences for it and the affirmations of it in all the complexity and subtlety of their best statements—statements implied by nature, statements made by man. One does not need to argue about the easy descent to Avernus to a student familiar with Iago; the student of the Continental Congress and the Constitutional Convention needs no sermon about the general availability to brave and thoughtful men of the concept of justice; those ignorant of physics may admonish you to expect order in nature: the student of physics senses the order and its limits also. The great affirmations of the human spirit in one way or another are called classics. They carry in themselves their own credentials. We have but to think of any of the most valued possessions of our minds in their context and implication to recall how eloquent, how very convincing they are: "His will is our peace," said Dante; "Let us bind up the nation's wounds," said Lincoln. What is important for teachers is a rather generally held belief that the standard or norm may be approached, and a determination to direct a considerable part of the undergraduate's energies to seeking it.

The faith of a student consists in this: that unpredictable though we are, given to failure and even to evil, there is something in us which has proved abiding; that though lower than the angels, we also are higher than the beasts; and that the elements of manhood discoverable in our own nature, for all its variety and contrariness, are rather admirable than the reverse. This is the common faith, and for each student reasoning and seeing, there is also the faith that manhood in its fullness is available to him.

13

"To Believe and Doubt Well"

THE FOREGOING chapter is an account of the faith which should be implicit in the aims of the whole system of schools and universities in America. The faith there described is a limited thing, founded on common experience, not derived from what is officially called religion. To go beyond its limits will invite misunderstanding in many quarters. To begin with, the positive affirmations just described, which are necessary to any fruitful use by the mind of science or humane knowledge, are far from general acceptance. It is important that they be understood by many a person now and by long experience wary of any talk about ethical belief. The wariness arises from two fears: of church polity and of religious dogma. In the modern American system of training the intellect, they say, let's not run the risk of either. There is the suspicion that reference to belief of any kind arises out of something extraneous to the working decisions of the day—from tradition, perhaps, or mere sentiment, or the authoritarian demands of church. And it is of vital importance that these fears be dispelled and that the simple human terms of belief "at the level of action" be recognized for what they are, so that the academic mind will willingly and freely renounce the sin of "non-committalism."

But, clearly, the inwardness of the problem demands further investigation into how, in the midst of free and responsible inquiry, belief in something outside ourselves may be nourished and maintained. In pursuing the matter through this chapter we must remember that we have passed beyond the bounds imposed by the public educational system. That may not deal with religion. It is especially necessary to bear this in mind because certain Roman Catholic leaders have recently demanded that public moneys be spent in schools controlled by them. American experience and old American wisdom are against this. Religious education is important to young Americans, but the dangers of paying for this by tax money or even of confusing the public mind by dispensing tax money in schools under religious control are evident.

Yet what of Vice-Chancellor Livingstone's warning: "Those who reject Christian beliefs cannot count on keeping Christian morals?" The institution of belief is a church; of scepticism, a university. Pascal said, "To deny, to believe, and to doubt well is to a man what running is to a horse." To believe and doubt well—the effort to promote this twofold motion of the mind in modern times falls roughly into two kinds. Let us eliminate from consideration for a moment instruction supported by the State. Then there are two types of university to be considered in terms of the effort to believe and doubt well: those controlled by the church, and those controlled by independent boards. Among universities, most of those truly controlled by a church are Roman Catholic, and in them formulated creeds have the last word, whenever there is conflict with the systematic scepticism of science or scholarship. In universities of Protestant or secular foundation now independent of churches or only loosely related to them, scepticism has the last word. Neither condition would have pleased Pascal.

To Protestants and other non-Catholics, the presiding beliefs in Catholic universities appear a confusion of two forces, one of them a clear and free faith in Christ and his teaching, the other, in Protestant eyes not religious at all, but mere polity. To many Catholics the casual genuflection to Christian belief in universities of Protestant foundation appears so weak as to be hardly sincere, and they sense what seems to me to be the fact, that in the critical contest of ideas which flourishes at several brilliant and powerful universities, Christian morals and Christian metaphysics and faith figure so little as to be negligible. Why do we lack in this country, in large part settled for Protestant Christian reasons, any great and distinguished university commonly regarded as representing Protestant Christianity so clearly and so well as half a dozen distinguished institutions represent the Roman Catholic faith? The reason is either that the Protestant Christian faith is weak or that scholarly Protestants are no longer interested in reasoning through, in modern times, a method to provide young men and women with an education designed to equip them to believe and doubt well.

The usual analysis of the relation of learning and religion in American non-Catholic universities makes an academic assumption. It is the view that Christianity can be encompassed in systematic argument. The contemporary academic discussion here becomes a prolongation of the medieval one concerning reason and faith, occupying itself with "arguments" about the existence of God or for or against religion. That dialectical exercise is fascinating, to be sure, but only loosely related to the human fact of our need for salvation, which is fully as irrational as it is rational. The true question concerns the thought, imagination, and actions of young men and women in early maturity, and the quality of their private lives. These, especially in the university years, are peculiarly important, for this is the period in which what they do and feel will be most closely associated with radical and genuine ideas.

The whole humane testimony concerning men's lives reveals two facts about our relation with divinity. One is that in deeds and decisions which matter to them most, men have almost always testified not only to their own attentiveness or inattentiveness to the will of the gods or God, but to their conviction that forces above or beneath them have taken a hand both in what they themselves did and in what happened to them. It is this strictly human experience within, attested so frequently in tragedy, which is responsible for our understanding of Nemesis; in similar fashion Christians have borne witness to the Heavenly Grace and Socrates to his daemon. The other is that our relation to divinity is known and felt in actions, as we live, and must be grasped by imagination as well as by reason: in short, it is a mystery. This being true, the practical problems for teaching and learning are: How to live fruitfully under the mystery while engaged in critical and scientific inquiry designed to push back the boundaries of the clear, sensible, and rationally understandable world? How to accept and maintain our participation in a mystery during the years of early maturity when our chief intellectual task is to eliminate mysteries from the territory of the knowable? How to live with the mystery, indeed, when surrounded by many learned persons who have literally no idea of the meaning of the book of Job; who imagine that there is no enduring mystery and that given time we can understand and master all?

In practice, religious belief furthers itself in ways radically different from the development of critical reason. This human fact is obscured by the illusion that courses describing religions comparatively are the grown-up and intellectual way of arguing oneself to the conclusion that this religion or that is the right one and should be adopted, or that religion should be eschewed as a hindrance and anodyne. Comparative religions may fruitfully be studied by teachers and students who truly know one of them at the start. But when after beginning his consideration of religion in virtual ignorance of all, a thoughtful person renounces religious belief of any kind because he has read Frazer's *The Golden Bough*, the triviality of much "study" of comparative religions appears. The pretence that university students are such thinking machines and that religion is so rational is as fantastic as the idea that by taking a course in philosophy, instead of by living, one adopts a philosophy of life. The confusion is also promoted in numerous colleges of Protestant foundation when the chapel doubles as the assembly hall and the student hears from the same platform political lectures, frivolous or serious entertainments, and prayers and sermons. It may be still further assisted if the student is invited or required to hear visiting preachers every Sunday, each representing a different sect, and if most of these preachers prepare for the visit to the academic halls "a sermon for college students," under the illusion that living in an "intellectual" atmosphere makes them different from any other poor mortals who, for all they may try to be good, flounder and faint.

The characteristic gesture of the university is not altogether doubt. As we have seen, the university involves extensive affirmation and commitment; and when the bachelor of arts lives up to his title, he can perform in the arts peculiar to liberal thought: that is, he can speak, write, and reason. The degree declares him able to do something, and action demands faith; you commit yourself, precisely as you do in any game, be it tennis or love. The ball placed there commits you to the return shot which may go to the open corner of your court. The avowal made on an evening in spring may commit you for life. But the mode of the university is largely critical thought. Its routine involves observation, hypothesis, and proof. The mode of church is worship. This should be the mode of the nourishment and growth of faith.

Worship takes many forms and is sometimes even formless. Corporate worship, humanly speaking a necessary part of worship, since we are social animals, requires some minimum of form, the simplest Christian one seeming to be the Quaker meeting. But that is no lecture. When lecture intrudes upon it, the meeting is spoiled. This and other forms of corporate Christian worship usually require to be housed, and the theatrical elements of many of the forms require certain shape, furniture, and even decoration of the building. The fact that the Christian church, both Protestant and Catholic, developed cathedrals, has distracted attention from the necessary function of worship in the small parish church, where in the midst of the drama of communion, for instance, the question whether one truly lives in love and charity with his neighbor is constantly raised by the presence in the next pew of the neighbor himself.

College students would benefit from an opportunity to sustain and instruct their faith equal to that accorded others in the community. This means first of all the opportunity to worship in a house set apart, designed for the purpose, and used for no other. It means also the opportunity for each to worship with his neighbor, whom he knows by name.

Whether modern Britain would have been able to produce a Protestant Christian university during the past century, when the modern American university came into being, if it had not started the century with its ancient federations of colleges at Cambridge, Oxford, and St. Andrews, I do not know. The contemporary fact is that there are such predominantly Protestant Christian institutions in Britain and that their scepticism is as brilliant and fruitful as any in the world. Britain is not America, our people and conditions being different. But there are elements in the British experience with church and university which we might profitably study.

The historical accident of the association of residential colleges in a single town and their gradual federation for mutual aid give the ancient British universities many advantages, along with the sometimes heavy burden of resistance to experiment and new theories of organization. In their treatment of faith and doubt the British universities have been much assisted by the housekeeping arrangements of the old colleges. This assistance from the beginning lay simply in the fact that each collegiate household had a chapel of its own and one member who was the chaplain. These households persist, and nowadays number from two to six hundred. Though worship in college chapels is usually brief and formal, most members of the congregation know the rich human and divine meanings in the forms—the forms of the service, the hymns and prayers, and the forms of architecture, window, and altar.

It is a pity that when the oldest American universities decided to regain the lost educational values of collegiate life by dividing themselves up into houses or colleges they did not add to the library, the dining room, the common rooms, and the athletic facilities of each college, a chapel. Perhaps, "given the American scene, with its varieties of faith and even unfaith," this could not have been done. It surely would have been damaging to build chapels in the houses and colleges primarily for architectural reasons or to satisfy an over-all theory which did not have lively personal conviction to put it into being. Considering the large number of Christian secondary schools, however, and the vital life of Protestant as well as Catholic churches in American communities, it seems to me possible that able chaplains with responsibility not for a whole university but for a small collegiate household within it, and with the help of like-minded instructors and students, might have given the residents of separate colleges and houses this benefit of collegiate life in a university along with the others. The difficulty may have lain in the first place in undue attention to what is described by the reporters as "the American scene." Or it may have lain in plain scepticism on the part of the authorities.

There remain, of course, the university churches, in which some of the ablest preaching of the decade may be heard, and some of the best-trained choirs. For the occasional student and professor who wants to worship alone, and for the few groups of pre-theological students and others keen about religion, there are the small and beautiful chapels, sometimes neatly tucked into the architecture of the university place of worship. Collegiate chapels for worship would be expensive to build and maintain. They would require attention not only by chaplains but by at least a few instructors. Until in some fashion, however, the student is put in the way of worship in addition to discourse, no matter how brilliant, he is not likely to be impressed with the importance of Christian belief.

One start of this consists in the discovery that goodness, right conduct and self-respect are prerequisites to understanding, a proposition out of favor in the higher learning. Like most of the central facts about ourselves, it cannot be proved in words, but it is proved in action. Probably no person believes it until he sees it in lively demonstration. Its very foreignness to argument illustrates the difference, for all the reasonableness of Christianity, between the realm of discourse proper to systematic knowledge and that proper to worship.

So close to each other are the modern leaders of the principal churches in Protestantism, it would not be truly difficult to build and use Protestant Christian chapels in considerable numbers in collegiate households, to provide as a basis for the brilliant sermons and splendid services of the university church the worship on which any valid religious discourse and drama must be based. One may even hope that the day will come when Catholic and Protestant Christians may with mutual respect and understanding hold services together. Judaism has so much in common with the Christianity which sprang from it that, particularly with respect to the ethics and metaphysics important to the university, it has with comfort enjoyed the welcome accorded by universities of Christian foundation. If there should be a large number of collegiate chapels in the immediate future, some should be Catholic, some Jewish, and some Protestant. As things now stand, Protestants seem to expect to promote tolerance among these three groups by neglecting, while notably the Catholics and a great many Jews cultivate and enrich, their own faith and worship. Surely mutual respect among churches will arise rather from a clearer and more constant inward sense of religion itself than from the abandonment of it either to intellectual debate or to merely humanitarian activity.

Institutions of private control enjoy many advantages not shared by the state universities, and one of them is the opportunity to cultivate both sides of Pascal's proposition. At present the universities chiefly alert to this opportunity are the Roman Catholic ones. Among Protestant colleges, there are notable examples of the incorporation of worship into collegiate life, though many a college with clearly stated Christian purpose would be assisted in its religious practice if it possessed in separate buildings a chapel and an assembly hall.

Churchmen should not imagine that the establishment of clergy in universities is bound to resolve the age-old warfare between doubt and belief. Some clergy are equipped to assist the effort to understand the conflict. Others are not. We are accustomed to the opinion that college chaplains and professors of Bible and religion should be open-minded and scholarly. But they should also be men of God. Churches of all kinds are heir to the same confusions evident in political and literary thought in America between the wars. Theology has had its share of sentimentalists, and of lazy-minded ritualists, who do not wish to be made aware, for instance, of the existence of any other than an atheistic humanism. Nominalism—the opinion that there is nothing really fixed, and that all we have is names—has its ecclesiastical as well as its academic and legal votaries. In referring to the new semantics in Chapter 2, I quoted in conjunction the opinions of the Chief Justice of the United States that there are no absolutes and of a learned bishop that God changes as our conceptions of him change.

In religion the difference between the relativism of men's limited understanding and the absoluteness of the *I am that I am* should be fairly easy to observe: "Now we see through a glass, darkly, but then, face to face"; "Jesus Christ the same yesterday, today and forever." In law, politics, and ethics, this distinction, while discoverable, is not so obvious. But even in religion, where it is evident, the contrast for many has been erased. Obscuration of the difference between the fallibility of human concepts on the one hand, and on the other the abidingness of the truth which presides over us, ever to be sought but never fully to be stated, should bear the whole blame for the moral confusion of universities—a confusion to which religious leaders have often contributed.

Sad to say, during the 1920's and 1930's the term *church college* began to connote nothing so much as poor scholarship, so many colleges supported by churches or maintaining a fairly close tie with their churches finding it difficult to accumulate the money necessary for modern scholarship and science and the best teachers. As an offset to the antiliberal effects of zealous sectarianism, some foundation funds were made available provided colleges could prove their independence of denominational control. The separation was necessary in view of the confusion by many churchmen, Protestant as well as Catholic, of polity with faith; and the experience of those two decades led many to regard the church colleges as a vestige of an America that is no more. When in the period of amalgamation, merger, and efficiency people decided that there were too many colleges, and when in the depression there were not enough qualified students with sufficient money to pay their way, people again said, "There are too many colleges in America." By this they meant too many weak colleges, and usually the weak colleges were the church colleges.

That opinion now appears to be ebbing slightly. The collectivism of the New Deal led many towards the end of the 1930's to see in the small independent colleges the bulwark of a certain kind of individualism. The considerable strengthening of Protestantism of recent years has led some to observe the value of the small church colleges for ethical reasons. The first critical and scholarly opinion to this effect that I have happened to see reported was expressed by the humanities conference at Princeton in 1947, where a company of scholars, artists, and critics came to the conclusion that for the sake of developing ethical knowledge and judgment in America there should be more, not fewer, "denominational colleges."

In non-Catholic American universities today one may enjoy a reputation for learning in letters, ethics, political theory, or history, without ever having seriously read theology, church history, or any critical discussion of one book of the Old or the New Testament. At least one student has been found struggling through Milton's *Paradise Lost* without any knowledge of the Bible at all, and that in spite of thirteen years of Sunday School. It may be noted that even the Sunday Schools for some time appeared to turn away from religious in favor of a merely social training. Indeed, in not a few university circles a scholar may enhance his reputation as a modern and emancipated soul by boasting ignorance of Christianity. It is not so in the ancient humane universities of Europe. There the divine studies stand side by side with the secular as parts of liberal thought. The theological ignorance of American humane learning has contributed to ethical ignorance and moral decline. This is not to say that in Europe or elsewhere all scholars somewhat familiar with Christian and Jewish religious literature and with ecclesiastical history read these parts of the human record with entire approval. Far from it. But the sense of ourselves, the picture of man, includes the mystery of the forces outside of himself—in, for instance, the principle of growth and decline—and, inside of himself, as conscience and love. The account of what we have imagined and believed, and why as a race we have inflicted and suffered martyrdom, is never complete without the studies that have to do with God and the mystery of existence and experience.

In America, theology effectively left the Protestant universities about a century ago, when self-contained professional seminaries were established either within the university or elsewhere. Making the study of theology professional no doubt improved the average pastoral performance of the clergy, but it worked injury both upon the forum of liberal ideas and upon theological thinking itself. The one gradually lost the presence in its discussions of men especially learned in one great part of human experience and in consequence began to avoid the hard intellectual work of considering it at all; the other—that is, theological thinking—gradually turned its attention more and more to the immediate training of active ministers and more and more lost both its feeling for and its grasp of the worldly concerns of secular critical minds.

In place of this, theological education has here and there shown a rather uncritical interest in two or three of the techniques which have grown out of secular learning. This has been notable in the approval by some theological schools of the sociological and psychological fads of the times. Their growing reliance upon the study of the physical basis of mental and spiritual being has produced the tragic paradox of fatalism in Protestant thought, which its promulgators do not even seem to recognize. The university at its best is first of all concerned to approach the norm for man. Theologians out of contact with this central human enterprise can complacently say, as some now do, that they are progressive because they have substituted Housing for the Old Testament.

The university would be enriched by the return of the theological faculty to full and active membership. The quality of the common education, which to a degree is influenced in its temper and aims by the traffic of scholarly ideas, would be improved. The improvement would come not because dogma and conformity to creeds had influenced common education. Far from it, for that describes neither the Protestant nor the liberal relation of faith to learning. The improvement would be effected because the purely human principles on which men may agree at the level of action would not be analyzed in ignorance. Knowing more fully the human experience and the human principles, men would know the intimations concerning ultimates which they contain. For while it is true that throughout the ages and at present there has been earnest disagreement about these ultimates, it is also true that belief in their existence is of paramount importance to all men.

14

The Third Dimension

So far these chapters have dealt with learning, on the theory that light may be cast upon the aims of education by a critical inquiry into self-education. Many times, however, what we seek in studies has been illustrated or accounted for by the reasons why we keep school and by examining what has been taught. The present chapter deals with teaching; but just as the preceding ones could not restrict themselves entirely to learning, so this chapter will be unable to speak of teaching as if for the teacher everything had already been learned. Colleges of education have been so engrossed in the professional obligations of their graduates that they have taken up most of the students' time in training them how-to-do-it. Thence arise most of our educational woes. The dedicated teacher when he really teaches is more absorbed, more moved by his subject, and this means more familiar with it, than the schools of education can imagine. This is alike true of the schoolteacher and the teacher in college.

What is the quality of understanding which distinguishes a good teacher from a poor one? In dealing with instruction and the imparting of experience this chapter will treat what is taught in its dimensions.

The first two dimensions outline the world for us, much as the x and y axes outline a curve on graph paper; they show the flat of the matter and suffice for a survey, a bird's-eye view or a symbol in design. The fourth dimension signifies something beyond the thing itself which you may hold in the hand. It qualifies it by time, color, its import or the general proposition for which it stands. Abstract painting is chiefly concerned with this dimension, endeavoring on the length and breadth of the canvas to represent some idea or mood, thought too refined or rarefied or elusive or drawn-off to be pictured. Did you ever notice how many abstract paintings remain in two dimensions? They have no body, no air behind the objects, no depth into the canvas. If you read the catalogue for the title or the explanation, you make a leap from the two dimensions outlined to your eye to the fourth dimension, conveyed perhaps by the painting, and if not thus, at least by the words. The third dimension is left out.

Stop a minute in daylight and look at an elm tree. The blonde world is there, all over the top and the outside of it, a glistening green yellow in the sun, so bright on some leaves that you see no color at all, only incandescence. Step by step, your eye may dwell upon the increasing shades to deep shadow: the olive of the outside leaves, illuminated not by sun but by sky reflection; the sea-green in the first shade; the blue-green deeper in; the black-green and the holes of blackness against the columns of the dividing trunk. How bright the rough gray bark, how dark the recess above the crotch; you can count fully half a dozen stages from the trunk in open light deeper and deeper into the slate and opaque shadow of the wood. Behind all is the brilliant sky, brighter and colder and clearer than anything on or in the tree itself, even than the mirrored sunshine of the top leaves. The darkness of the single trunk increases on its shadow side, deeper and deeper until the very edge where the trunk meets, in our vision, the distant lawn. Here the darkness is impeded by the light sweeping around the tree toward us, as if the light itself bent round the tree, and there the edge vibrates, now dark with trunk, now bright with air. See beyond the tree the blue-green striped shadow on the grass. Suddenly, with amazement, know that there it stands—an elm tree, upright, at right angles to the flat earth, spreading toward us and away from us out of darkness into light and backward towards the entirety of sky, fragments of which we see straight through the outer leaves, the inner leaves, the branches, trunk, and rearward foliage.

The third dimension, the dimension in which we see the thing as it stands, whole, solid, laved all about by air, there by itself, for its own sake: this is the dimension most neglected by education. The pedagogue, as rapidly as he can, reduces the things of this world and the people and ideas in it to their *x* and *y* axes and leaves them there. I am speaking of most of us who teach. We make things cast their shadow on a plane, and we outline the shadow, a two-dimensional silhouette. Thus we may reduce to number not only the elements and compounds which make up matter, but men. We literally "get their number." The number of a steel worker is different from the number of a farmer; both, if organized as laborer or grange member, have numbers which can be related to the number of a taxpayer or an employer. These are complex numbers, with an *x* element and a *y* element. We reckon in a person's yearly income, number of dependents, church affiliation, health record, war record, kind of hobby, weight and height—and there, sociologically speaking, we have him. Recently the scholarship committee at a great university was asked by the administration to construct a formula representing all the intellectual, moral, physical, and spiritual scores (note the word) describing a candidate. The plan was to buy a gadget from the International Business Machines Corporation that would single out from a thousand cards the worthiest human being!

Probably necessary in the twentieth century, but nevertheless a source of innocent merriment, the endeavor to describe men by measurable quantities, which calls itself social science, has become the characteristic way for an educated person to think. True, we study a great deal of natural science, where measurement in two dimensions properly belongs, and we still pretend to study the humanities; but these are largely now a matter of "social documents," the bright gems of our small human treasure having become sockets for the moving parts or drill-points for tools which serve a purpose, the purpose being a flat and final description of mankind—mankind in history and mankind in society. History, indeed, is no longer a way to think, but a two-dimensional measuring chart, grouped with the social sciences. Two of the most authoritative recent statements on the purpose of liberal studies have reduced to abstractions the knowledge of even our greatest possessions, of poems and plays, of concertos and statues. These things exist in our minds, say the learned men, only for the sake of something else. I refer to the belief that the mode of university learning should be the encyclopedia and the opinion that the high way to think should be chronological and systematic—that is, historical and philosophical. Chronology and philosophy—these are but abstractions. Necessary, valuable, but you can lay them down flat on a graph; you can draw them in without any third dimension at all.

Nowadays you will see this lust for reducing all things to abstract general propositions in every utterance of the sophomoric mind. It is altogether natural for the young writer to dwell upon the usualness of the things and people in his story: "a typical middle-class front porch"—that cherished word, *typical*. Schoolteacher, small businessman, tycoon, minister, labor leader. How these mannikins people the stories presented in theme class! To be blasé a sophomore should know all the categories. This, of course, is to progress only half way (and maybe not that much) in observation; you can at least pin an explicit and obvious adjective on a thing. This girl is a schoolteacher. You may not know or perceive that a period of terrific anguish has altered her within the last year, but at least you have noticed that she is a teacher and is beginning to talk like one.

According to the *Book of Boners*, a boy once wrote that Petrarch stood with one foot in the Middle Ages, while with the other he greeted the dawn of the Renaissance. We laugh at the boy, but the joke is probably on the teacher. No doubt the examinee got that half-stated fact from class, and what measly stuff it is, remembering what might have been said, if in only a few minutes, about the sonnets to Laura—or better, a translation of one of them—thus giving the boy a small taste of the thing itself instead of an utterly useless abstraction about it. To read the sonnet, to say the words—this is why we have Petrarch at all and why he is worth regarding.

I do not know whether it is the natural instinct of the growing mind to reduce a vivid, lively thing to a pale abstraction, void of mystery, unworthy of wonder, or whether young men when they begin to try to grow up talk insipid generalities in order to ape their elders. Heaven knows there are plenty of flat minds writing books and teaching in school, college, and graduate school. William James in his early twenties had confronted such deadness among the abstractionists. He was rescued by Agassiz, who taught him how to live "in the light of the world's concrete fullness." A youth discussing poetry with other students at an intercollegiate poetry contest said, "Oh, John Donne—we disposed of him in our seminar." I do not know how that boy's education came to work backward and uneducate him. He was toplofty about Michelangelo. At numerous universities obscure and great, I have known learned professors capable of destroying what natural humility and power of enjoyment a youth might bring with him. But perhaps the particular boy was suffering from a premature middle age of his own. In any case, he had read a great deal of Donne's poetry and prose, but something had closed his mind to mysteries there.

Progressive education proposed one important corrective to this sort of teaching. It observed that the chief aid to good teaching lies in the nature of childhood itself and that the finest minds, for all their severe discipline, have retained something childlike. A child has not learned to judge by appearances. He sees with surprise and entirely, letting nothing escape because he thinks he has seen it before. A small girl on the beach exclaimed, "Oh! the water comes upside down!" In Walter De la

Mare's story, Maria sees a fly for the first time—really sees it, the only fly there ever was, her fly. "For some reason, this particular fly was different; and Maria sat watching it with the closest attention. It seemed to be that just as Maria herself was one particular little girl, so this was one particular fly. A fly by itself. A fly living its own one life; confident, alert, alone in its own Fly World."[1] After the entirety of her moment of absorption, she tries and tries to tell her elders about it. "I have just seen a fly. It had wings like as you see oil on water, and a red face with straight silver eyes, and it wasn't buzzing or nothing, but it was scraping with its front legs over its wings, then rubbing them together like sticks, all round and round one another, like corkscrews. Then it took its head off and on, and then it began again—but I don't mean that at all. I mean, I sawn the fly—saw it, I mean."[2] She tries to tell them, but one by one they smile and say yes and run along now. They have long ago exhausted the fly as an object. But Maria knows it has been *her* fly. "For when Maria herself came to, it seemed she had been away for at least three centuries—as if, like the stranger in the rhyme, she had been with her candle all the way to Babylon; aye, and back again: as if she had gone away Maria, came back Maria-Fly; and now was just Maria again. But yet, when she came to, everything was a little different."[3] Finally, for a brief space, the gardener's boy seems to heed. He smiles a different kind of smile, which Maria takes for understanding. But he, alas, is only a half-wit, and when Maria asks him if he has seen his fly, his own fly, the poor boy comprehends even less than the others did.

Take almost any discourse of educated men, and count the jargon phrases in it, the trite locutions, the terms no longer attended for what they mean. The apparently natural process by which we lose the object and deal more and more with its image alone seems regrettably helped along by our common studies in school and college. These draw us farther and farther away from the vivid, direct sense of the world and its people and creatures on to a clumsy scaffolding of ideas. The higher learning is now smartly praised according to the degree of its abstraction. We think that by dealing wholly with images and ideas we may avoid meanness. The modern snob of the intellect is interested in particulars only if they will take him somewhere in his calculations. There are, in fact, two species of snob in *academia*. There is the snob of the first two dimensions, who despises anything but the dried descriptive facts appropriate to footnotes and the glossary; and there is the snob of the fourth dimension, who despises anything less than a system. One snob of the fourth dimension praises the university for teaching a theory of society; another, for teaching metaphysics; another, for teaching a method, be it a method of therapy for the mind, called psychiatry, or a method of teaching, called the science of education. At its worst, the higher education concentrates on pure relationship, and you will hear in the lifeless voices of its votaries an almost insane emphasis on prepositions and connectives rather than on nouns and verbs, which gives them away. To know relationships is said to constitute intelligence. Even at its best the higher learning tends to be a little ashamed of things valuable for their own sake—of the Hippocratic Oath, for example, unless completely located in its proper context of medical history. The sweeping proposition, the general statement, is more respected than durable things endowed with mystery and truly admirable.

To describe this state of our studies by the metaphor with which I began is to say that once having reduced things and ideas and experience to two dimensions, where they may be outlined largely by numbers, we leap to the fourth dimension and try to state their meaning. Here, as modern thinkers, we are fascinated. Philosophy is our joy—especially the philosophy of science. (Since we have already reduced, so far as we can, all things to science—if not natural science, then social science—we leap from the two-dimensional description we have outlined to a wonderful and elaborate system relating all things which exist by the fourth dimension.)

Indeed, every apology for education which I have lately seen cherishes the system it serves. Blessed system! I propose that the virtue of good teaching is that it is not especially systematic. In philosophical terms the fault of being systematic is forcefully summarized in Paul Elmer More's essay, *The Demon of the Absolute*. We really have few absolutes of any kind in our life. Whatever we can use as an absolute is not something we can argue for, but something which by experience we gradually come to believe in and even to trust.

And so, abstractions have tried to take the place of faith. But on all sides, men now confess that these bright and crystal relationships constructed in the intellect are tenuous indeed when life, tragedy, and the demand for courage put strain upon them. People deplore their loss of faith and wonder where, in their elaborate and careful reasoning, they happened to build on sand.

The way to faith is not argument but love. To see the world in affection, the things of the world as well as its people, is to begin to have feeling and conviction about it. Intuition of the world, the mighty intuition out of which faith is born, comes only to the man of trained and disciplined feelings. The right love of things shows the way. Notice in the following passage from *Death Comes for the Archbishop* how the simple objectivity of a few choice things in the desert sunshine seems to make the prayer.

Jean Marie Latour, the Vicar Apostolic of New Mexico, was lost in the measureless waste of hills. Willa Cather described him:

> When he opened his eyes again, his glance immediately fell upon one juniper which differed in shape from the other. It was not a thick-growing cone, but a naked, twisted trunk, perhaps ten feet high, and at the top it parted into two lateral, flat-lying branches, with a little crest of green in the centre, just above the cleavage. Living vegetation could not present more faithfully the form of the Cross.
>
> The traveller dismounted, drew from his pocket a much-worn book, and baring his head, knelt at the foot of the cruciform tree.

Under his buckskin riding-coat he wore a black vest and the cravat and collar of a churchman. . . . His manners, even when he was alone in the desert, were distinguished. He had a kind of courtesy toward himself, toward his beasts, toward the juniper tree before which he knelt, and the God whom he was addressing. His devotions lasted perhaps half an hour, and when he rose he looked refreshed. He began talking to his mare in halting Spanish, asking whether she agreed with him that it would be better to push on, weary as she was, in hope of finding the trail.[4]

True, the Cross is a symbol, a fact which perhaps gets in our way at the moment, but notice that Miss Cather says that Latour was courteous towards the juniper tree. He was also courteous towards his beasts, evidently in the way in which he was courteous towards God. Perhaps the degree of greatness in a pagan like Leonardo da Vinci should be measured by the degree of this type of courtesy or reverence.

To see things standing up by themselves, with their depth as well as their breadth and height, is usually to cherish them for what they are. One does not think of them first of all because of their connection with other things, either that they come after something or will produce such and such, but for themselves. Emily Webb in the play *Our Town* returns from death to live one day of her life, and she was advised to choose an unimportant day. She knows what the dead know, that things carry in themselves the joy we may find there if we see them for themselves. But the living won't pause. Her own mother won't look at her. In desperation she turns away.

EMILY. *(In a loud voice to the* STAGE MANAGER.) I can't. I can't go on. Oh! Oh! It goes so fast. We don't have time to look at one another.

(*She breaks down sobbing. At a gesture from the* STAGE MANAGER, MRS. WEBB *disappears.*) I didn't realize. So all that was going on and we never noticed. Take me back—up the hill—to my grave. But first: Wait! One more look. Good-by, Good-by, world. Good-by, Grover's Corners . . . Mama and Papa. Good-by to clocks ticking . . . and Mama's sunflowers. And food and coffee. And new-ironed dresses and hot baths . . . and sleeping and waking up. Oh, earth, you're too wonderful for anybody to realize you.

(She looks toward the STAGE MANAGER *and asks abruptly, through her tears.)* Do any human beings ever realize life while they live it?—every, every minute?[5]

Somehow or other all our work of learning and teaching is inclined to rob us of that warm delight or hustle us past that surprised pause or dull that sharp view or flatten out that vertical, stereoscopic look of the picture of the world which makes it possible for us to love it. The systems, the abstractions, the propositions of mature thinking often do violence to us as, first of all, human beings. Without systems we are not men, but it is possible for systems to turn our heads from the thing-in-itself until we seek images instead of life, as in the mirror.

This is a matter of good teaching and, directly, of self-respect, modesty, and religion. The stuff of school and college, the biology, history, mathematics, and French literature, can be taken as just worldly stuff; and according to his understanding of it the young student affords himself a large or a small chance to hold close the things of earthly experience in an affection for their existence and creation and the laws which govern them. So the teaching, if abstract, leading to a flat and statistical account of our life, becomes irreligious. If, on the other hand, the teacher can lead a student to see things with the kind of spiritual as well as physical exactitude which causes him to cherish them, to enlarge the family of his private mental and emotional possessions in learning, this combination of accuracy and humility in teaching will be religious instruction of the very best sort.

Two instructors on successive days take the laboratory class in biology. On both days the class dissects a frog to draw the alimentary tract. The first instructor, a graduate student, has studied hard and knows all the answers. She has many times seen everything there is to see about the frog's digestive organs, and to watch her set about a model dissection before the class you'd think she had been the special confidant of the Creator.

The older instructor knows how artful and delicate is the structure of the tissues she is cutting, and even though she has cut up a hundred frogs, she cannot fail by the attitude of her own mind towards the mystery she approaches to convey to the class unawares her profound respect for the strange and wonderful creature on the table, and the astonishing fiat by reason of which she is there.

True, human experience is related, related to itself and to nature and to divinity. That the learner must finally see relationship it would be sentimental to deny. John Livingston Lowes said that an educated man should be able to hear the march of the ages. That is a difficult thing to hear. You cannot hear it unless you begin by hearing one footfall, to hear clearly and in isolation one set of sounds—in Chaucer's England, Calvin's Geneva. Instead of trying to hear anything from the past, any footbeat or any voice, we appear, in our systematic cleverness, to be content to record the vibrations. As if one were unable to play the record on the phonograph but were satisfied to hold it in the hand and look at the concentric grooves.

What was done in Rome, what was said in Florence, how they hated in Venice—these things must be known by themselves and for their own sake long before and regardless of whether they are ever related. A young person should be able to take out for inspection and enjoyment his few nuggets of knowledge, vividly known and warmly apprehended. His joy in them should be separate and independent, like the joy of the French Canadian in Robert Frost's poem, "The Ax-helve,"— " 'See how she's cock her head!' "

General observations about the teacher are dangerous, for teaching is an art, not a science. But in the spirit of commenting on a poem or a painting, one may say about the teacher that the way he talks and whether he stands or sits and how he organizes his material and whether he uses an outline or asks for written work is of small importance, perhaps none. But if he can do one thing he will be a teacher in the full sense—if he can know what he is teaching so well that his feelings continuously accompany his apprehensions and critical conclusions about it. Then he will become, like all good teachers, one who conveys to his students the habit of looking at the ideas and objects of this earth as they were to the first man, Adam—in short, by conveying to his students his own love of the world he will lay down in their minds the basis of belief.

15

Education as a Social Science

THIS BOOK began with the statement that American education still promotes the kind of sentimentalism and disintegrated liberalism which many political and literary thinkers of the 1940's abandoned in the face of war. I have stated further that the aims of education still popular among educators are such that they continue fundamentally in the direction of educational thinking of the 1930's. The crux of this thinking is its substitution of society for the individual. As in the Thirties, so at the beginning of the Fifties, education is thought to be a social science rather than primarily a matter of the ethos: that is, the standard or norm of humanity.

Put more precisely, the basic issue in the dispute over the aims of education is drawn between ethics and collectivism. Education as a process involving two or more people, learner and teacher, is, of course, a social matter. It is as social as the ethos itself; it is a social art. But American treatment of education has by and large imagined it to be a science, and not even a science in the best sense, but an applied science or technique. Measurement has become as important to the applied science called education as to applied physics, called engineering. The issue which should be sharply drawn in the debate over the proper aims of education is the following: on the one hand stands the ethical and liberal view of education, which holds that the learner seeks human values which must be described and understood pre-eminently in terms of a single person, no matter how intensively one seeks these values by studying political philosophy, history, drama, and other experiences of a person in society. And in opposition stands the theory that education is a social technique, deriving its evidence and its principles from a collective conception of men as pre-eminently important not in themselves, but because organized, however loosely, in groups or masses. Education as a social technique is thus preoccupied with group behavior. It seeks not human values but political or economic or institutional ones, applicable to men because they are collected together. It is based on the sentimental belief that the individual can best be served by neglect of his character and by attention to the circumstances which surround him. By contrast, the ethical and liberal theory of education holds that he can best be served by intensive study of the nature of men and their character as persons, undertaken *before* a direct study of social problems, which, while of immense importance, is an advanced and less central study than the great humane one.

The four final chapters of this book will deal with a few statements of the aim of education and endeavor to show the difference in the application of the two ways of thought about school: the sociological and the ethical.

One of the most vigorous analyses of the aims of teaching and learning in America in recent years is the book by President Conant, *Education in a Divided World*. It is peculiarly arresting because it considers what should be taught in terms of the intellectual conflict which separates the liberal from the totalitarian nations; and the realism with which Mr. Conant strikes at the heart of the contest gives special relevance to his opinions about the school's and the university's share in the cold war. He states the spiritual fact about studies and the nation: "A set of common beliefs is essential for the health and vigor of a free society. And it is through education that these beliefs are developed in the young and carried forward in later life. This is the social aspect of general education, one might say."[1]

Dealing here with men's most precious and private convictions, Mr. Conant rightly says that there is a border line which public education may not pass, and that the metaphysical implications of these ethical matters soon turn into theological doctrine over which sectarians are divided. Nonetheless he observes that the center of what makes us a nation and separates us from all totalitarian dogma, including the Russian, is measured by how man faces his own problems—"by the success or failure of the inner conflict within his soul."[2] Our postulates, the liberal and American assumptions, he adds, quoting Arthur Koestler, are the "Christian and humane ethics," which are in conflict with the Soviet philosophy and are the basis of the American proposition. Mr. Conant says:

> Those who base their case on history, utilitarian ethics, and practical politics can be stanch defenders of the American tradition of civil liberties. But those who affirm that our passionate adherence to the doctrine of personal liberty is a consequence of our belief in the sacrosanct nature of the individual have a still stronger case.[3]

So clear and apt is all this reasoning about the ethical issue of the times and its relevance to education, that one is at a loss, on first reading this forceful book, to find how it arrives at some of its conclusions. For the account of man proposed is in an elaborate and complicated fashion a sentimental one, and the uses of learning recommended are not those likely to produce the excellent results desired. The difficulty begins with the assumption that the humane ethics referred to will be viable if treated as a *given.*

> The study of man in our American schools must therefore start with certain postulates. The first is the sacrosanct nature of the individual; the second, an individual's obligation to other individuals; the third is that our type of society requires a high degree of personal liberty and at the same time active and sympathetic

cooperation toward certain ends. These postulates should be placed in their historic setting. They should be developed as given elements of our culture.[4]

It is true that President Conant proposes that in late school years and college the "philosophical background" be explored, but his proposals for the exploration prove to be cultural history and the analysis of group behavior. This he proposes even though he has stated that at the center of the issue of the century lies the inner conflict of a man's soul.

Throughout his pages he refers to given goals, traditional aims, and "the universally recognized ethical ideal" as things supplied us in a package by history. But it is not to a bundle from the past that the young for long devote their lives, their goods, and their sacred honor. When the senior Henry Ford, interrupting a visit to the Morris-Cowley works, had been shown about New College, Oxford, he had apparently had his fill of medieval walls and windows. "Take me back to the twentieth century," he said. According to his lights, he was right. His own knowledge of history was evidently inadequate to make contemporary the lively humanity whose symbols and signs he beheld. It is so with our own beliefs and aims. We have them only in the twentieth century, when we live and may use them. Our study of them perforce employs old and ancient records, but our use of these must be as contemporary as the whole life of an imaginative mind. To be known and used, the inner conflict of a man's soul, regardless of time and place, must be understood in some small degree even by the young as a part of their own inner conflict. That this is available to the young, none will question who hears a discussion by early adolescents of any well-taught passage of history.

President Conant distinguishes between two views of education, calling the distinction a watershed illustrative of the central issue of general education. "For what purpose do we have a system of public education? If the answer is to develop effective citizens of a free democratic country, then we seem to be facing in one direction. If the answer is to develop the student's rational powers and immerse him in the stream of our cultural heritage, then we appear to be facing in the opposite direction."[5] This volume agrees with President Conant in favoring without reservation the former of these answers. But it must ask two questions: What are the implications of this purpose? and who nowadays seriously busies himself with immersing the young in the stream of the cultural heritage? In answer to the second it is clear that there are antiquarians left in the academic halls; but they are not many, nor do they represent any serious threat whatever to the lusty and active engagement by the young with the contemporary world. To worry over them is to hear the echo of faculty-club talk of half a century ago. It is also to deal with a sociological illusion about the ancient studies—that because they are old their age is what chiefly occupies the critical minds concerned with them.

It is true that there may be enough of the echo left to bid one drown it out, but the proper issue lies in the analysis of the former proposition: that the purpose of education is to develop effective citizens of a free democratic country.

In his chapter on "The Study of Man" Mr. Conant establishes another antithesis in the contest over the aims of school. "Should one use the phrase 'The Nature and Destiny of Man' or 'The Behavior of Man as a Social Animal'? Should one of the two main currents of general education be described as an attempt to answer the question: 'What is man that Thou art mindful of him?' Or should we rather say that the modern educational problem is to teach children how to grow up to live normal lives, which means 'acquiring the proper responses to the batteries of social stimuli which compose our social order'?"[6]

As I have noticed, Mr. Conant properly observes the necessity of avoiding the metaphysical and theological disputes to which these moral considerations of the aim of common education are related. The phrase *Destiny of Man* in current use invites theological controversy, though historically the understanding of man's destiny in the Greek tragedies is paralleled in the ethics of Judaism, Catholicism, and Protestantism. Current use here should determine the matter, however, and it would be proper to delete the phrase *Destiny of Man* from one half of Mr. Conant's proposition. Something similar, as Mr. Conant later points out, can be done with the gigantic inquiry taken from the Old Testament: "What is man that Thou art mindful of him?" "It is the assertion implied in this question, not the answer, that is basic in any faith."[7] So understood, the issue is clearly drawn. Shall American secular education deal at its center with the assertion implied in this question? Should it take its direction from the inquiry into the Nature of Man? Or should it deal primarily with "The Behavior of Man as a Social Animal" and set out to teach children to acquire "the proper responses to the batteries of social stimuli which compose our social order?"

It is surprising, after reading Mr. Conant's clear perception of the moral issues of our contest with the Russians to find him favoring the second set of proposals.

President Conant begins with the proposition, "To be well founded an educational philosophy must be part and parcel of a comprehensive social philosophy."[8] In his reasoning the philosophy which he favors, though related to a clear and liberal philosophy, is derived from social thinking, which is characteristically concerned with groups, measurement, and externals. This start leads him to an eccentric view of the humanities, which he regards as separate and distinct from the disciplines responsible for the "study of man." The humanities he defines as the art and literature of the past and present; humanists in his view are transmitters of this corpus of culture. Among the numerous and conflicting definitions of the humanities he recognizes that he must choose one, and the one which he takes is based on a romantic and sentimental idea of the arts. In this view the humanities do not include ethics, the art of judgment. His limited view of the humanities adequately describes the work of some editors and annotators, but hardly the vigorous and original minds known to history or contemporary literary and moral discussion. It fails to account for the ablest of those historically called Humanists, whose work was characterized by judgment and ethical acumen. Erasmus, for all his timidity, was engaged with the time; so was Sir Thomas More. When in his chapter on "The Humanities" Mr. Conant has finished his account of the editorial and cataloguing intellect and the mood of the neoclassical grammarian, what stands is perhaps the picture of an elegant instructor of Latin or Fine Arts at an exclusive and expensive school, or the group of youthful aesthetes sometimes found in the offices and cataloguing rooms of a few choice museums devoted to the rarer arts. What has been described is hardly the virile and capacious critical thinking and contest of the Rialto which have stimulated students of the leading historians and literary scholars, and gone with them into the field of action.

In his chapter entitled "The Study of Man," which he distinguishes from the humanities, Mr. Conant takes up the proper subject of the humanities. Nothing is lost by this individual use of language, provided one is willing to deal with the facts. The word *humanist* is already battered beyond recognition, and some other—say, *student-of-man*—will do. But the working use of the humane studies themselves is thrown radically off focus by sociological attention to trivialities. The chapter on "The Study of Man" properly abandons sociological externals and observes that what distinguishes us from the Russians is our belief in the Christian and humane ethics. It proceeds, then, to analyze this distinction in ethical and religious terms and to perceive that what is at issue is the nature in man "of the inner conflict within his soul."[9] The implications of this central fact are so great, indeed, that it becomes difficult for Mr. Conant to maintain his premise, that the subject under review is at center one of social behavior. It is rather a question of ethical behavior, the proper theme of all the humanities.

But to eliminate the humane studies from this central contest in the study of man is to leave a great lacuna quickly filled up in contemporary thought by such inadequate substitutes for history, letters, and philosophy as cultural anthropology. You cannot adequately describe and analyze the "inner conflict within [man's] soul" by means of the disciplines of largely external description and measurement; for this purpose it is imperative to make use of the exacting and central testimony concerning men: letters, history, and philosophy. Doing this will not bring you to conclude that letters are primarily useful as emotional release; it will not lead to the rhetorical question: "Why should the future truck driver, shoe salesman, bank teller, or assembly-line foreman read the English classics?"[10] The answer expected by the context is that there is no good reason. The Committee on the Objectives of a General Education in a Free Society asked the same question, and gave its answer based on experience of the reading of the English classics by future and present truck drivers, shoe salesmen, and the rest. The answer given by the committee is that the primary effect of the reading is not merely enjoyment and emotional release, but ethical perception. (The idea expressed by some that joy would make reading something less than ethical will occur only to Calvinists and other Scots!) The first opportunity afforded by literature, says the committee, "is direct access to the potentialities and norms of living. . . . All other aims in the teaching of literature are subordinate to this."[11]

President Conant has proposed a quite different aim in the teaching of literature. For the general student in school and underclass years of college he advises that the aim be an understanding of society. "The significance of the dramas, novels, and poems of the English-speaking people of the last three hundred years for the vast majority of our young people lies in their ability to help us understand the origins of our present civilization."[12] A similar purpose in studies is proposed by Dr. Algo Henderson in his volume *Vitalizing Liberal Education.*

Both educators weigh the alleged tastes and prejudices of the young, and in doing so they are consistent with the practical spirit of all their books and essays on education. President Conant said in his Sachs Lectures:

All concerned with the future of the humanities in the schools might well proclaim the fact that since we are living in a technical and scientific age, some attempt must be made to relate the present of this bewildering scene to the much more simple past. . . . To the academically slow-minded youth who wants to do something practical, the appeal of the printed word must be an appeal to a story of simple origins in order to illuminate an amazing picture. . . . Curiosity, I believe, is more widely distributed than innate love of literature. It is to curiosity that I should turn to bring out in the vast mass of our pupils the willingness to immerse themselves in our cultural heritage. . . . By appealing to the curiosity of *all* youth about the origins of an obviously complex and unintelligible technological society, we may evoke a willingness to learn about the past.[13]

And Dr. Henderson, in *Vitalizing Liberal Education*, says: "to improve society for all men. . . . Whether or not this is the ultimate purpose of life for all time, it is the one which stands the best chance of capturing the imaginations of the young people of today."[14]

To regard the rim of the argument before the hub, my experience does not lead me to think that curiosity is more widespread than something which makes possible a love of literature, even as we love life without being cajoled into loving it. I should agree, it is true, that in evangelical terms there is probably no good thing more alluring in the thoughts of most of the excellent young than the immediate improvement of society; but one well might ask whether our purpose as teachers is evangelical in this sense and whether to the extent that the teacher is a preacher, he should be beguiled into a doctrine because it is easy to preach effectively to certain audiences. I fail to see how one can teach well, except according to his idea, however hazy, halting, and tentative, of the ultimate purpose of life.

To inquire whether curiosity is more widely distributed than innate love of literature, one should go pretty far beyond the classroom and batteries of tests. Curiosity, I suppose, begins small. It must grow considerably before it becomes an innate love of science, but that is just what it grows into, and it is magnificent. You have seen it in the mere crib, recognizing it by the baby's response to something—toes, red, or a whistle—noticed for the first time and worth investigation. The love of literature begins small, and it, too, is amazing. You see it in response to something ordered, like a nursery rhyme, and you see that it is a desire to find form in experience. All experience being personal and all important experience touching us deep, from the start this desire involves affairs vital to our existence, our existence *now*.

To see the matter socially we have but to observe the ballads, the crowds at the theater or the movies, the myriad juke boxes and dance floors, the millions of radios. Are more children curious than eager for order superimposed upon experience? You would have to ask Dr. Gallup. My observation is that the young, academically slow-minded and academically speedy, can learn to read poetry and understand it and write poetry, some of it meritorious, and that the reason why few do this is that as a nation and as professors we do not think the matter important. So much for the incidental proposal that the humane study in General Education should be confined to a description of societies because the young can readily be made curious about it.

The study of the humanities themselves, President Conant says in *Education in a Divided World*, "must be approached from a revolutionary point of view."[15] In his opinion the chief consideration in determining the aim of studies in the later years of high school and beyond is vocational. General education, he agrees, should continue through what constitutes the second year of college for those equipped to proceed this far, and the aim of general education is citizenship, not vocation. But like the authors of *Education for* All *American Youth* he holds that the controlling consideration is the probable job of the student. Parenthetically, in criticizing the effect of this line of reasoning upon teaching and learning itself, a word of praise should be said for the administrative opinions expressed, especially those recommending a great expansion of post-high-school education as near home as possible, and much of it related directly to the city high-school systems. The nation needs a great increase in local junior colleges as well as of vocational institutes. One should further agree that the improvement in analysis of job needs by industry, and of job abilities, is a distinct gain. The criticism here set forth is not directed at the realistic establishment of high-school and post-high-school vocational training, or the intelligent employment advice which accompanies it. The point here at issue is the character of general education and of the subsequent study at the level of the present upper-class years of college.

Recently the sociological account of American colleges has stressed the obvious fact that in the old days nearly every student was preparing for a profession. One has but to read the petitions, letters, and charters of the founders. One petition for the charter of Brown University speaks of "a Succession of Men duly qualify'd for discharging the Offices of Life with usefulness & reputation."[16] *New Englands First Fruits* refers as follows to *Harvard Colledge:* "One of the next things we longed for, and looked after was to advance *Learning* and perpetuate it to Posterity; dreading to leave an illiterate Ministry to the Churches, when our present Ministers shall lie in the Dust."[17] To ministers soon were added teachers and lawyers, and college study usually constituted the only formal advanced study for these. They needed Greek, Latin, and history in their business. The social behaviorist therefore concludes that all liberal study was professional or pre-professional in the sense in which we understand those terms today. The fact that we have now greatly multiplied the number of professions leads some social thinkers to conclude that the proper development of the old colleges would be to devote college study to the pre-training of all the modern professions.

Mr. Conant, in considering social status in America, urges that all professions and semi-professions be regarded as polite. This would undoubtedly constitute a step forward in democracy. But it should not blind us to the intellectual requirements of the various professions themselves. The reason why in the chapter on Social Science of this volume the pre-professional training of a lawyer was taken up at all, was that the American Bar Association report on the subject was informed with the ethical opinion that the object of law is justice. This is also the object of liberal education, and, so understood, as Judge Vanderbilt's report rightly said, the pre-professional training of a lawyer and liberal education occupy common ground. The object of the ministry is the conversion of the soul; of teaching at its best, the conversion of the reason. This is why what we now know as liberal education was developed in the old American colleges as the proper study of the future minister, lawyer, and teacher. Examination of the courses in the old catalogues reveals a single-minded attention to human nature and physical nature and innocence of utilitarian training in how to practice or how to meet the special problems which the minister, the lawyer or the teacher would confront. How-to-do-it as a systematic study is a product of the instrumentalist era.

President Conant finds in their future vocation the reason for the upper-class study, by such students as continue them, of letters and the other humane disciplines. It will be useful to lawyers, doctors, and politicians—"a study of the liberal and humanistic traditions is of great value for those professional men who perform their main work through human contacts,"[18] he says in the Sachs Lectures, *Public Education and the Structure of American Society*. But why, he asks in *Education in a Divided World*, "should the future astronomer, protozoölogist, or research chemist"[19] study literature?

Surely the central usefulness of the humanities to professional men and all others is not instruction in how to win friends and influence people but rather experience in the elaborate and essential inquiry which occupies every mature and responsible mind: how in new circumstances and unforeseen conditions may justice be understood and achieved? Karl Jaspers, at the re-institution of the medical faculty at Heidelberg after the war, stated that what is most important for the doctor and medical scientist to seek and hold before himself is the "picture of man." It is of equal importance that the astronomer, the protozoölogist, and the research chemist do the same, first, because they are men, and second, because in this engineering civilization of ours these highly trained men are quite properly accorded extensive authority, and on the clarity of their own private perception of the picture depends the well-being of many of their fellow-citizens.

It is true that the limitations of time require extensive attention by professional students to exceedingly narrow and sometimes purely technical studies. Less time is left over for the mastery of basic and general ideas than one would wish. It is a serious mistake, however, to advise students that what study is devoted to an understanding of the law for man is a utilitarian one; because the expectation in the heart of the student colors more than any other one thing—even excellence or lack of it in the instructor—what he will make of his instruction. The purpose of letters, philosophy, and history is precisely the reverse of the professional use of the hints these subjects contain concerning how to handle people. It is disinterestedness. It is to establish in the heart of a naturally ambitious and energetic youth, despite the utilitarian atmosphere of his home community and this whole century, a habit most difficult to master—the habit of understanding and judging in terms of history, of reason, and of the liberalism whose study has a pattern of its own.

In strictly sociological terms the reduction of liberal education to make it vocational offers America a dangerous course.

Central European society in the Twenties was such that a university man would not soil his hands with labor. He was a university man! That in a way became his profession. He was a sort of intellectual, at least a white-collar man, and popular speech began to call him an intellectual. In Vienna, if you carried a book, they called you *Doktor*. Worried social thinkers wrote treatises on "the overproduction of intellectuals," a phrase which struck old-fashioned Americans and Scots as odd. One of the natives at Albert Schweitzer's hospital would not help him with some planks because he was educated. Dr. Schweitzer replied, "I always hoped to get an education myself, but have never had the time!"

The economist, Seymour Harris, recently analyzed this problem in an able volume entitled *How Shall We Pay for Education?* In it, the economics of education are rigorously examined, but there is no effort to reduce the ideas taught and the purposes of teaching to economics. One virtue of the book is its confinement of social science to the measurables clearly amenable to economic treatment. He deals with "the overproduction of intellectuals." In America the present teacher shortages and the depression in teachers' salaries, he says, are in large measure the result of the overproduction of white-collar workers in relation to "black"-collar workers, with the resulting greater increase in incomes of the latter. The market for college-trained personnel has been glutted. Teachers have not only not received salary increases commensurate with the increases in living costs; they also have failed to share in the general financial gains of the years 1939 to 1947. As a result, many have left teaching. Fortunately, Professor Harris carries the reasoning about overproduction far enough to observe that the economic distress caused by certain types of education in too great abundance refers specifically to vocations and professions, and that liberal education in itself is both an intrinsic and an economic good when dissociated from vocation. In this and the matter of standards he disagrees with the President's Commission on Higher Education.

The argument is that from the viewpoint of (1) facilities available for a sound college education, (2) employment opportunities for college trained men and women, commensurate with training and expectations, and (3) numbers capable of profiting from a good higher education, too many are going and are likely to go to college. Yet in order to train for citizenship and life, the more widely the colleges are thrown open the better.[20]

First among the solutions to the problem, Professor Harris places "greater dissociation of higher education and vocational or professional training."[21] Thus strictly economic and political reasoning supports the policy of restoring liberal education, which appears imperative in the light of the need for ethical understanding.

At the underclass or junior-college level, where the humane studies are said to be a part of "general education," Mr. Conant's sociological view of the end of studies produces comparable difficulties. In *Education in a Divided World* he describes two schools, ninety percent of the children in the former coming from families holding a union card or eligible to do so, and the second, "a school in a well-to-do residential suburb."[22] "Now to assume that the way the two schools teach literature and art should be the same," says Mr. Conant, "is like assuming that the diet of a lumberman in the north woods should be the same as that of a desk worker in a southern city!"[23] What is disturbing about this opinion is its overtone. Mr. Conant has said in the preceding paragraph that "General education . . . should be presented in terms of a wide spectrum of occupational goals."[24] My experience in labor schools and colleges, and in those with students whose family incomes are higher, underlines the common ability and interest as well as the common need of young people. I grant that the tempo of studies may be different for children of different abilities. Also, there are local requirements of vocabulary and other glossarial matters, but such is the illiteracy of the white-collar class in America, it is difficult to claim for them that they are all or even most of them better-read than many a manual worker.

The need for stories, reflection upon these, for human facts and a sceptical analysis of the record to determine where it is inadequate or false is the same for every man, as every man must have protein. The ability to judge these human matters with shrewdness seems distributed without reference to father's occupation. It is true that the boy from a house where books are read and talked about has an advantage in examinations over the boy who began to see books only at school; but this is a pedagogical problem, not one of the ability or even the ultimate interest and accomplishment of those who are invited to consider what we know best and with the greatest candor about ourselves. Any who doubts this indiscriminate distribution of literary interest and capability among all classes and conditions needs only cast his eye about the cinema audience when, as occurs infrequently, a truly durable story is told by Hollywood or the studios of Britain, France, or Russia.

The objections here voiced to the intrusion of sociological considerations upon the aims of teaching and learning itself refer to the degree to which housekeeping is permitted to obscure and even obliterate the reason why the house is kept. There are, to be sure, techniques of teaching stories to those handicapped in their ability to read which are not necessary for those who can easily be taught to read. But when one sets the whole purpose of schooling in terms of vocation, he begins to say that this and that vocation require no spelling and little use of words; so we shall slight the expensive and hard work of teaching how to read, and these future truck drivers may get their stories from the comics, the films, and the radio. To argue thus is unintentionally to deliver a wound; since the reasoning of most minds depends in large measure on words and on at least a little mastery over them. To reason thus is not only to cripple the unfortunate in the future use of their natural abilities—it is to prepare them for the most dangerous kind of demagogy. As citizens they need to know something examined about human nature and to be able with the assistance of some small training in reasoning to judge what is reported by the newspaper and television, or what happens at the office or garage.

The efficient-sounding devices invented in order to train boys rapidly in the Army and Navy how to handle machinery are thought adaptable to education. Some of them undoubtedly are, but when enthusiasts say, "One picture is worth a thousand words," a fallacy is introduced, particularly in the school work of those whose expected calling is not supposed to require words. To think hard about the issues on which he must vote, every citizen must think with words, but the gadgets of education are rapidly depriving him of any reliable practice in this.

True, there are some differences of technique in teaching literature and history at the union-card school and in the suburbs. But the differences are slight, and not one hundredth so important as the similarities. For the one who is addressed in both is everyman, whatever the academy may pretend.

To the layman the distinction here being drawn in the use and purpose of letters in the schools may sound over-refined and technical. The end proposed in Mr. Conant's volume is the same as that proposed here: that "a set of common beliefs is essential for the health and vigor of a free society"; and it is the proper job of the schools and colleges to see to this in order to provide a succession of understanding and courageous minds equipped to cope with the philosophy of the totalitarians which now divides the world. Why worry whether literature is a serious matter or a frivolous? What matter whether the ethical problems are those of society or concern first of all the nature of individual man?

The reason these ethical definitions are here pursued with what may appear to the onlooker an undue emphasis is that to construct American schools and universities with the purpose pre-eminently in view of teaching children to acquire "the proper responses to the batteries of social stimuli which compose our social order" means, as Mr. Conant rightly observes, something vastly different in practice from organizing the teaching and learning of schools in order to show forth to the very young and equip the older to inquire for themselves into the Nature of Man and the affirmation implied in the ancient question, What is Man?

To enter this caveat is particularly difficult in view of the sound and practical recommendations of *Education in a Divided World*. These deal with scholarships, equalization of opportunity, academic freedom, the need to study Russian thought and practice, and numerous other important matters of school and college administrative policy. But to treat the analysis of aims as merely a social problem is to lead too soon into the practical problems of vocation and to make merely mercenary many a study to which the student has a right, in the freedom of his own direct apprehension and judgment. If the analysis of aims of teaching and learning is a social science, it is almost inevitable that matters of ethical value become translated into programs of social expediency and that the ends of reflection in the minds of all men, the nonintellectual along with the hyperrational, become inferior and inadequate to the fierce contest of faith in which we are as a nation engaged.

The social aim which Mr. Conant proposes for schools is to keep American society fluid, so that people may move freely from one class or calling or status to another without undue attention to status. This is a laudable end, to be achieved largely by administrative arrangements extending the opportunity for schooling. The purpose may be assisted, but only incidentally, by studies themselves.

Mr. Conant also proposes an absolute alternative: one may direct his attention to "the fundamental relation of formal instruction to the social pattern of the community. If he likes to deal in absolutes, he will refuse this offer and insist, instead, on examining the various current remedies offered for our educational ills."[25] None will deny that particularly in administrative matters the relation of schools and universities to the community is of utmost importance, nor that studies themselves are involved with society. But the alternative to the "view that education is a social process" is not, as Mr. Conant assumes, a single one whose characteristic is that it deals in absolutes. True, there are educational principles based on absolutes, notably the doctrinaire Christian ones and the doctrinaire Communist ones. But the humane reasoning upon our best evidence about ourselves which, side-by-side with Christianity, provides the belief of liberalism, is not a matter of absolutes; and it is peculiarly important that schoolboys and mature men know enough of the human record to understand why it is not, and how, without mere acceptance of ideals handed down in the heritage of history, free men may renew year by year and generation by generation the reason of their faith.

The aim of common education applies to all men, whatever their ultimate profession, whatever the limit of their ability to progress in school. This common education of all is susceptible of direction by the ethical proposition which lies at the heart of democracy. This is not a mere ideal, a hope, an aim. It is an observed fact of human experience, the sufficiently understandable norm of manhood.

16

Adjusting to Life and Conditioning the Attitude

THE AIMS proposed in these pages are those motivating the work of literally thousands of excellent teachers at all levels of school and university. They teach science, social science, the humanities, and the three R's. For their fortunate students these aims are often effective, leading them to a maturing concept of the world, and increased ability to handle themselves and their experience with good judgment. They are effective, that is, to the limit where contrary aims on the part of their institutions interfere. For some this interference does not occur: the whole school, the whole college, or the operative bulk of it enjoys a fairly common purpose.

But the announced aim of the educational system in America is at odds with the intention of some of our best teaching. This disparity is not unusual in human institutions, the admiral sometimes remaining in ignorance of what really goes on in the engine room. One definition of a dean is that he is the man who stays home and tries to make the institution half as good as the president says it is! Taking the American system as a whole, there is of course no official spokesman, and many voices proclaim its intentions. The trouble with the disparity between the statement of aims and the best teaching lies in the fact that it is the statement which influences legislative and other financial support by presenting to the public mind the nature of what it is to keep school. This chapter deals with the statement usually made.

On the whole, what is said represents managerial policy, and this, at present, is the resultant of two major forces: the history of university teaching and the school instruction which reflects it on the one hand, and the philosophy popular for the past fifty years, on the other. A fundamental shift in the aim of the educational system is observed by examination of the colleges a century ago and at present.

In 1824, when Kenyon College was founded, nearly all such institutions had the same purpose, and the differences between them were determined only by differences in their resources. Colleges still differ widely in these, both human and financial; they now also differ in objective. The significance of this new variety among colleges is great indeed and important to understand. To begin with, there is the simple and basic distinction between colleges of the applied arts and those which are non-vocational, the former being an outgrowth, direct or indirect, of the agricultural and mechanical institutes, and engaging a large fraction of the students and professors in the country.

But non-vocational education itself has undergone a change in aim since 1824. One sees this immediately if he studies catalogues and attends classes at the so-called colleges of liberal arts and sciences, whether in state, municipal, or other universities, or standing by themselves as colleges. At the risk of oversimplifying, the change can be stated as follows: until about the middle of the nineteenth century, higher education endeavored to serve in intellectual terms the purposes of the Christian Church; in the twentieth, it serves, by and large, those of the State.

This is a hazardous reduction of a complex movement in the history of ideas; but, with a few qualifications and within limits, it will prove useful. In 1824, the Church was concerned with individual minds and hearts and souls; and the colleges were concerned with them too: with what they would think and decide and accomplish, and what account they could make of physical nature—that is, how each man could try to understand his own and the race's experience. The State in those days was concerned with justice for the individual and, to some extent, with the common welfare.

Since then, the interest of the State has shifted in the direction not only of common welfare, such as the building of roads and harbors, but the welfare of individuals and groups, exemplified by unemployment insurance, old-age pensions, and public health. The wisdom of this movement is hotly debated; for good or bad, it has occurred. Education is related to this change in the interest of the State both as cause and effect. The primary purpose of many universities and colleges now, like that of the State, is welfare and justice. As analyzed and taught by the universities in these days, this means both justice in the old sense and a new version of justice applied to groups—"social justice," a conception, paradoxically enough, which is sometimes at odds with justice for the individual.

In the committee reports and speeches on higher education today, one finds such words as democracy, citizenship, social responsibility, at points where similar documents a century ago spoke of Christianity, sacrifice, devotion. The prize-winning student most praised at commencement, then, was the youth in preparation for Christian foreign missions; now, the same youth has won a fellowship to take overseas training for the State Department. The ideal of the school and college committees at present revising the course of studies is an intelligent voter; then it was a life of service. In lay circles, this change might be thought beneficial, representing hard common sense. Examined closely, however, it will prove of small advantage, even to the workaday and housekeeping affairs of the commonwealth. The change is a change in purpose; its effect upon what will be studied is profound. Today, the new courses and the revision of the curriculum are designed to help the student find out what to think about the nature of society and the market; then, the purpose was to help him think about the nature of man. That old concern with individual souls is readily dismissed when the power we see obviously at work in America is not the Bible nor the Protestant Church nor moral ideas. Ballots and money represent power to us; and these are what our best minds and our most magnificent libraries are designed to study.

If, however, we translate the phrase "concern for individual souls" into modern terms, the old purpose of the college appears relevant indeed to these times. It was the study of the nature of man which produced our best conception of justice. The ancient Greeks achieved this without benefit of Christianity; for moderns, the idea has been available almost exclusively by way of Christian teaching, which has made justice more widely attainable in the world by adding to it the Christian idea of mercy.

A simple difference between colleges nowadays might be that between church and secular colleges, or between colleges of private control and public. These distinctions are meaningful; but they are slight compared with the distinction in moral philosophy which I am here drawing between those whose chief concerns are those of the modern State—welfare—and those whose chief concerns are human, that is to say, justice, which entails a somewhat detailed understanding of the nature of man.

If I emphasize the central importance of this study it is because the higher learning in our own lifetime has shifted so far from the center of truly liberal learning. In the non-vocational parts of the universities, most professors, students, endowments, laboratories, and libraries are now devoted to welfare, an important application of liberal study but not the foundation of it. I stress this perhaps obvious fact because contemporary thought has largely lost the implications of Micah's question: "What doth the Lord require of thee, but to do justly, and to love mercy, and to walk humbly with thy God?" He who would obey this commandment must begin with the long and exacting study of the individual, his nature, his potentialities, what makes him precious, and how he succeeds or fails to be a man; without this preliminary, the demonstrably necessary study of welfare becomes jejune, ephemeral, and fraught with danger.

The key question about any college is how large a fraction of its scholars, scientists, and teachers are committed to the central inquiry concerning man in the universe and what portion of these understand the peculiarly human terms of the problem. If the portion is large, the education pursued is likely to be liberal.

The philosophical influence most evident in the affirmation of our present aims of education has been the system of John Dewey and its educational application by his followers. In his *Logic* Professor Dewey states that means and ends are correlative, that the good, the beautiful, and the true are ideals; when they are taken as ends in themselves violence is done to the situation. What we actually do, he says, is take a former good and use it as a means to achieve some new end. Ends are important to logic, where they are known and understood only in the continuum of judgment as steppingstones in reasoning to logical conclusions, which in turn have existence only in use toward further objectives. This association of ends with means or treatment of ends only in process has led to the epigram among John Dewey's followers: There are no ends, only means. The proposition underlines the concern of the instrumentalist philosophy of education with processes and means and its slight concern with ends.

The honorable word *pragmatic* has been associated for a generation with the philosophy of John Dewey. But the pragmatic educational philosophy which has grown out of Dewey's philosophy was found wanting by the Committee on the Objectives of a General Education in a Free Society: "Yet, if not the philosophers of pragmatism, at least their disciples seem in practice, if one may put it so, not pragmatic enough. That is, there is always a tendency in this type of thought to omit as irrelevant the whole realm of belief and commitment by which, to all appearances, much of human activity seems in fact swayed."[1]

There are no ends, only means. In his system Dewey has both moved with the age and led it, like the lead log in the river. Ours has been the era of ways and means. "Results! Results! And damn the consequences!" Other nations and periods have become famous for *scientia*, for measure, for *goût*, for *gentillesse*. We have been famous for *know-how*. How-to-do-it and how-to-fix-it has been our study, and our success has amazed the world.

Americans have not been of one mind about the worth of this success, and in recent years the expressions of alarm, in the spirit of Kipling's "Recessional," have tended to a single proposition: Our success in the control of matter has outstripped our skill at social control. The reasons why the commencement orator now speaks of social control instead of self-control are elaborate, and to find their roots in modern history one must go to the romantic thought of Germany and France in the late eighteenth century and of those countries and Britain in the nineteenth. They stem from the romantic idea of the individual, that let alone by convention he is naturally good, and the consequent opinion about society, that if its arrangements are corrected, goodness will follow by nature. They stem from the illusion that gregariousness if left to express itself naturally will produce peaceable communities and from the romantic denial of the war in the cave.

The opinion that education is a department of social science and may be fruitfully projected only in terms of a social philosophy is a natural corollary of these theories. It is supported by two circumstances: that the personnel of schools and colleges are so numerous that properly to manage them is a social study in itself; and that many leading speakers and writers on the aims of education are themselves engaged with the pressing political and governmental problems of the day which, in the short run, at least, are altogether a matter of social philosophy.

Schools and universities are indeed social institutions. They cannot be well administered without a social philosophy. One has but to think of a few issues of management—representation on governing boards, prejudicial policies of admission, and the distribution of dollars necessary to pay for the education of the ablest—to perceive what a voluminous social science the administration of the educational system is. It would be for reasons of social philosophy, for example, that you favor or oppose the administrative device recommended to Congress for making scholarships and fellowships available to the talented with funds appropriated to a National Science Foundation.

Many important administrative reforms have been conceived and accomplished in the light of a social philosophy, and there is no denying that much more must be done, administratively, in these same social terms. These are group terms. Some of the rearrangements must be analyzed in the light of group needs. There are, for example, the minorities, notably the Negro minority, for whom as a group inadequate facilities for training doctors, dentists, and nurses are now afforded. To treat such matters fairly is an immediate problem of politics, economics, social institutions, and philosophy.

Know-how is altogether an affair of means, not ends. It is, of course, fascinating. So charming has it become, it has diverted much money and talent from the true ends of keeping school. Fascination with modern means brings it about that many a school in a prosperous small town has an impressive built-in two-way speaker system permitting the administrative officers to interrupt any class or listen to it, but an altogether unimpressive school library. One shock for foreign visitors is the efficient splendor of our school buildings. When a school or college enjoys a magnificent athletic plant, the reasonable assumption should be that its instructional and research budgets are commensurately handsome. Where they are not, means have been confused with ends.

But these human failings in our practice are not the subject of this volume, whose purpose is to assess the announced over-all intention of teaching and learning in America. Teaching and learning themselves are subtle; their relevance to the center of American life is best understood if administrative problems are kept in second place. Administrative policy has a way of becoming cantankerous and obstructing good instruction. It may be enlightened or not; *qua* administration it is just as important as housekeeping but no more important. It cannot supply out of its own problems the reason for keeping the house.

Unfortunately, as our system is organized, this is just what administrative policy may try to do. Worse, in the popular reason this is precisely what administrative considerations have done. The accepted argument runs as follows: A social philosophy is necessary to guide such decisions as who will be admitted and who will receive scholarships, or where new institutions will be built and whether they will be vocational institutes and of what kind and level. All these are social problems. Solving them with good sense leads to the conclusion that what and how to teach is a social problem, too. When teaching amounts largely to vocational training, it clearly is a social problem whether the need for nurses is greater than for switchboard operators. But popular thought extends the same type of analysis and philosophy to discovering the aims and content of liberal education. This leads to determination of the common education of everyone, what recently has been called "general education." The argument is plausible enough. The felicity of everyone is certainly affected by group welfare; deciding what everyone should be taught might therefore with good sense be guided by some kind of group philosophy.

Those who reason in this fashion urge schools to devote more energy even than at present to the study of contemporary problems. So a committee officially reporting to the American Youth Commission said that the following subjects should be studied and debated by high-school pupils: "Housing, conservation of natural and human resources, community planning, coöperatives, pressure groups and their methods of influencing legislation, the stock exchange, corporations, labor organizations, the industries of the nation, various forms of municipal government, governmental services such as those of the Departments of Agriculture, Commerce, and Labor, the origins and nature of money and systems of exchange, international relations, consumers' needs and investments"—all this for schoolboys. Yes, perhaps some of it—if there is time. *Education For* All *American Youth* makes similar demands, starting as it does with a social philosophy.

The Army, devoted altogether to means since the Secretary of State, the President, and Congress are there constantly to determine its ends, quite properly translated the study of English into Communication, when during the war it translated most American higher education into training. The word *Communication* has a good, down-to-earth practical sound, like telephones; and many a professional educator, taught that there are no ends, only means, now proposes that peacetime education retain that instrumentalist idea of the Army and substitute for the pre-war study of literature by the young, with its reading, writing, and reasoning, the merely utilitarian study of communication. The confusion here of means with ends becomes clear when one asks: "What will the young so taught have to communicate?"

The recent history of American education has paralleled that of American bread. By removing the hull of the wheat, bleaching to make the flour chalk-white, and by other chemical processes making the loaf soft enough for baby teeth and those of the aged, by chemical treatment to keep it damp within its wrapper, despite the pre-slicing which reduces the operations in the home kitchen—by elaborate treatment in the laboratory, American bread has been deprived of food values implicit in the old-fashioned stone-ground flour, and the yeast-raised, oven-baked, brownish, granular, and hard-crusted loaf. To make up for the complex chemical destruction of vitamins, minerals, and other salubrious elements in our bread, the millers and bakers have injected all sorts of fortifying drugs and powders, until, according to their avowals, the loaf is almost as good as if they hadn't tampered with it in the first place.

Learning in American schools and colleges became increasingly desiccated by attention more and more to the dissemination of social techniques and an abstracted account of man called "culture." The whole thing began to be a bore for the best students and the best teachers. The student himself did less and less; there was less and less performance in his education, more and more conditioning of his attitude, more and more attention to his reflexes and his reactions, more and more marking printed examination forms by the best guesses or quickest bright thoughts which happened into his mind while the tester held the stop-watch. To liven things up and make life more "meaningful" (as if there exists any more meaningful part of it than science well taught or stories and history well taught!) the teachers began to take over play. They made a study of this, forming it into an elaborate, supervised, technical business —synthetic, to be sure, but controlled, like the vitamins reinjected into bread. Games had coaches, the playground had teachers; the charming wild ingenuity of make-believe and duck-on-a-rock was eliminated from the lives of any but the underprivileged who might grow up on the edges of the educational system, on the back streets or remote farms. The chief synthetic injected back into the loaf is an enterprise which sounds sensible enough and like all managerial reforms of education has much, on the housekeeping side, to recommend it. This is called counseling.

One of the principal statements of the necessity of counseling at the center of all schooling is *Education for* All *American Youth*. The importance of this report and its sponsorship of counseling should not be underestimated, for in many states and cities it has become the single official program "reforming" the schools.

The responsibility of the counselor, says the report, is to all of the student's significant decisions in life:

During the years just ahead, most of these youth will make plans and decisions with far-reaching effects on their lives. They will have to decide what occupations they are going to enter; whether they will stay in the Farmville district or move away; what education they want and where to get it; when to go to work, where, and at what jobs; whether to marry soon or wait a few years; and so on. For each decision, plans must be formulated and carried out.[2]

The counselor's discussion of these matters with ninth- and tenth-grade students is supplemented by a course occupying a large part of study time.

When they enter the tenth grade, the 120 boys and girls of the class go to work directly on their educational and vocational plans. One of their major activities during the first term is the study of "The World at Work." This serves a number of purposes. It acquaints pupils with their own dependence on the labor of farmers, workers in factories and transportation, clerks, managers, homemakers, physicians, engineers, teachers, public officials, mechanics, carpenters, and many others. It yields a better understanding of the way in which the economic system is operated. It promotes appreciation of the necessity of labor in human society. It fosters respect for all useful work well done. And it helps pupils to become familiar with the facts about the chief occupational fields, among which their choices are likely to be made.[3]

The report states that "The study of 'The World at Work' is a project of the entire tenth-grade teaching staff, rather than of one teacher or department. Teachers of mathematics and science, for example, undertake to acquaint students with the nature and requirements of scientific and engineering occupations, as well as to show the uses of mathematics and science in other occupations; so also with teachers of English, health, agriculture, home economics, machine shop and business education."[4]

Hardly a man or woman but would covet for his own children in the management of their lives the sense of responsibility to the community and to the choice and performance of a job envisioned in the plans of *Education for* All *American Youth.* But the pedagogical fact about the understanding by the young of the science important to them and the letters and history important to them is this: the frame of mind with which they approach a study limits altogether its usefulness to their reasoning. If they are taught to think about important ideas in terms of the job for which they may prepare, their whole understanding of ideas will become mercenary and mean. Much is written about the difference between vocational and liberal education; it is hotly debated concerning a given subject, let us say, geography: is it liberal or not? The decision, like the decision whether some forms of life are animal or vegetable, can only rest upon a point of view. The reality lies in the expectation in the mind of teacher and learner as each approaches the principles and facts of geography. Does a student seek to find what use he can make of them only for his own advantage such as bread or station? The most brilliant of scientists would probably fail to make this student's study of geography anything but utilitarian.

I doubt if counseling and tenth-grade courses in "The World at Work," in which the entire teaching staff collaborates, do in fact foster "respect for all useful work well done." The effect is more likely to be the reverse, for devotion by adolescents of a major part of a semester to an elaborate discussion of their future jobs in the world cannot fail to steal time from the responsible accomplishment of imperative intellectual tasks which the tenth-grader is competent to finish well. Permitted to slight these tasks, he soon learns from school that intellectual work is unimportant, that what counts in the world is the job you do for pay, and let's not worry too much about mathematical or critical inaccuracy. If the good teacher of mathematics and science is required to devote a major part of time "to acquaint students with the nature and requirements of scientific and engineering occupations," how is he going to have time enough left over to undo the harm which he has been required to work upon his students as persons? He will of course let his students see, by the way, some of the industrial and occupational applications of his subject, but his chief business will be to lead them to see the facts and ideas of biology, chemistry, or mathematics, and their fascination, excitement, and direct usefulness to reasoning.

This task is not so easy for the teacher of the 1950's as it was for the teacher of two generations ago, for the idea of exploitation is much more general in American society now than then. Virtually everything the boy and girl hear from radio, magazine advertiser, and the murmur of the town admonishes them to get ahead, to do things which win friends and influence people, to make themselves up to look attractive, and in all ways to conform to the recent and paramount admiration in our midst of management and the manager. The teacher of English, geometry, and general science wants this boy or this girl to admire facts and ideas either for their own sake or for what he and she will do with them in their own minds. Only so instructed can he or she make intelligent use of these school studies when the all-important life decisions are to be made, which call for the judgment which is the result of trained mental and emotional faculties rather than a dependence on pamphlets and questionnaires.

Like most proposals that school should become pre-eminently a social service, *Education for* All *American Youth* entertains a sentimental view of letters and holds in low esteem the usefulness of ability to judge rigorously by use of words. The latter is revealed in its neglect of hard work with words at school. Its sentimental idea of letters is revealed in such opinions as the following about a twelfth-grade course, which is designed to be "a great and glorious adventure": "Throughout the year we expose our students to a wide variety of experiences of beauty—in music, poetry, drama, in other forms of literature, and in the visual arts. . . . I have said that we expose students to these experiences of beauty. That, we think, is all that we can do."[5]

For exposure to "beauty" in no less than three separate arts, each with a medium of its own, the sample schedule for the five years, tenth through fourteenth grades, allots one-twentieth of the student's time. The mastery of words in English and foreign languages is regarded as "preparation for occupation," and it must share time with science, mathematics, and social studies, to all three of which disciplines together the schedule allots but one-third of his time!

Education for adjustment is not dead. The United States Office of Education now devotes energy and public money to promoting in the public schools something called "The Life Adjustment Program." In *This Week* magazine for August 14, 1949, Jack Harrison Pollack calls it "the brightest educational hope of this generation." The editor advertises Mr. Pollack's article with the words on the cover: "Revolution in U. S. Education." Says the author:

> Here is a summary of what Life Adjustment intends to put on the curriculum along with the usual cultural and vocational courses:
>
> 1. Family-life training—learning as much about marriage as math, as much about children as Chaucer.
>
> 2. Consumer education—learning how to get your money's worth in store, home, insurance and other buying.
>
> 3. Good work habits—learning how to study, how to get along with fellow workers and other down-to-earth help. It includes school "work experience" either for credit or wages.
>
> 4. Creative use of leisure time—learning that recreation means more than just going places and spending money.
>
> 5. Citizenship—learning an individual's obligation to society, that government should be an instrument of the common good.
>
> In addition to this training for maturity, Life Adjustment also stresses youth's immediate needs. High schools are urged to give instruction in social relations, how to get a job, choose a career, live with parents, and above all, in knowing and understanding one's self.[6]

So thorough is the effect of the sociological treatment of school in the reasoning of educationists that the simple and central purpose of liberal studies themselves has been forgotten. The study of the law for man and the law for thing is nothing less than the study how in maturity and reasonableness to live well. But the sociological fact that certain parts of this study are required or preferred for college entrance leads those preoccupied with the statistics of education to observe that a certain minor fraction of secondary pupils proceed to college. For them, the college-preparatory course also becomes a kind of vocational study. Its "business" is to get students into college somewhere. So the educationist is left with two kinds of vocational training: that of the college-preparatory pupil and that of the pre-business or pre-industrial pupil. Sensing that something important has been eliminated, he proposes the Life Adjustment Program.

In many schools the vocational idea has spread so far that subjects like history are officially listed as "non-vocational." The critical subjects are now distinctly regarded as luxuries; in large sections of higher education the liberal student of science, the humanities, or society is dismissed as one marking time until, perhaps with professional counseling, he can make up his mind about a calling. Where apologies are offered for the central concerns of manhood, maturity and grown-up importance attaches largely to the work of those who soon will be drawing pay of their own. It is a great deal to expect in such schools that students of "non-vocational" subjects will ever grasp an idea hard enough to cut their palms. They are not likely ever to look at an object in the mind so intently that they forget their overshoes. The object of their schooling has become the proper one of driving all that out of them so that they will understand that to forget your overshoes is the worst crime in the world. They are to be taught the functions of modern society and how to function in it.

None should complain that the routine of American cities and towns is planned with skill and thoughtfulness. The complaint arises when routine is permitted to provide the reason for what and how we teach. Educational planning and the analysis of the aim of keeping school in America has been reduced to a question of arrangements, and in terms of management it is impressive. But to imagine that the objective of general education in a free society would be met by requiring teacher and taught at every turn to consider the possible arrangement of one's private affairs or even the "set-up" of community affairs is like confining conversation to recipes for pies.

If I am told by educationists that more and better than this is all right for the top tenth who can go to college but not for *all* American youth, I must ask: What has been offered *all* American youth? From direct experience with youth of almost all types and in almost all social conditions I know for a fact that the plain American boy and girl are capable of dealing actively with some of the ideas men live by. I do not mean mere "appreciation"; I do not mean "exposure"; I mean *use.* That they have a right to the teaching which will equip them to know and use some of these ideas, and that to acquire this knowledge and skill is the first task of *all* pupils seems self-evident. To withhold this teaching from the majority constitutes an unacknowledged insult and requires an initial decision concerning privilege and class which should be alien to America.

To improve schools by training counselors and attending to the practical problems of vocational and other guidance is a reasonable and wholesome task of educational management. What has been done by the planners is to set before themselves a cat. What is wrong with this cat? She needs a smile. The slide rules and graphs are consulted, and what is attached is a smile so magnificent that the creature turns into the one from Cheshire, all smile and no cat. This is what happens when the thinking responsible for finding out how-to-do-it undertakes the job of deciding where-to-go. The American educational system has learned too well the corrective taught by John Dewey—that in practice we concern ourselves with means, hardly ever with ends.

Counseling and adjustment to life are developments of the progressive education movement, a reform necessary at the time but so run to extremes that, as Bacon said of Gilbert, it now endeavors with the materials for the oars to manufacture the whole boat. Despite the intrusion of these reasonable auxiliary ideas into a dominating place, the thinking of the leaders has returned somewhat, during and since the war, from the pupil-centered school to the old American and Occidental purpose of education, the tribal purpose: to keep the tribe safe and make it prosper. In pursuing this purpose, these thinkers have added an important qualification. It arises from recent confidence that our ills are largely social and that by mobilization of field workers we may solve them; schools and colleges are thought to be not only the proper seminary for these field workers but an appropriate means of providing a climate of opinion favoring the view that by the mobilization of social techniques we may order our life.

During the war scientists were organized into teams to solve predetermined problems, and their success was magnificent. Numerous managerial problems of the nation appear susceptible of the same treatment, and the wartime techniques of mobilizing talent are proposed for these; as we marshalled science and engineering we shall mobilize social theory. Social planning suffers limitations not implicit in scientific planning, yet there are clearly social gains to be made, especially in fields involving scientific as well as sociological knowledge, such as public health, soil conservation, exploitation of resources of the sea. Here again the possibilities are so fascinating as to be heady. Education clearly plays a part, at least to the point of training the field workers for vast sorties against social evils and maladjustment, but such training hardly constitutes the chief contribution which society should expect from teaching and learning.

When this reasonable sociological purpose is applied to school and college, the argument is brought forward that as they deal with most young people their chief function should be to influence public opinion. That over a number of years they do slowly influence if not specific opinion at least public attitude is beyond doubt. When one thinks of the reform of the general conception in the minds of masses of people of the importance of sanitation, vaccination, improvement of farms, conservation, fair opportunity for Negroes and other minorities, to name but a few, the effect of humanitarian propaganda in school and college becomes clear. And it is not, I think, too much to say that as the British Labour movement arose largely out of the Nonconformist chapels and other Christian churches in Britain, the strictly social legislation of the New Deal arose out of the social and social-Christian teaching of the American churches, schools, and universities.

When one remarks that many educational thinkers regard schools and universities in their treatment of the mass of their students as primarily instruments for influencing public opinion, he should hasten to say that there is no evidence whatever that these institutions have been manipulated as dictators have manipulated others for similar uses. On the contrary, in America the scholarly and scientific core of universities has to a notable degree been left in the unfettered hands of the scholars and scientists. The few recent examples of meddling with the proper intellectual task of universities, such as the shameful events at the Universities of Texas and California and at Ohio State University, exhibit by their rarity and by the indignation they engender the fact that freedom of thought and investigation is common in those parts of universities singleheartedly devoted to thought and investigation.

Furthermore, in those sections, particularly of the state universities, where for a variety of reasons the energy of teaching is expended upon young people ill-equipped by training or inclination or both to cope with ideas, the effort to influence public opinion is of an innocent kind. The attitudes which these young people are conditioned to entertain are proposed almost wholly by members of the academic profession itself. The professors whose chief activity is to influence public attitude act out of conviction in favor of ideas in which they profoundly believe. They and their deans and presidents are realists, and they reason as follows: if these young people in our charge cannot be brought to think for themselves, at least we can try to condition them so that when they act or speak as if they had done some thinking, what they will do or what will come out of their mouths will appear respectable in the middle of the twentieth century. If possible, it will promote reforms of society in favor of more opportunity for all and especially for the underprivileged. The philosophy and critical analysis of what is actually good for everyone is debated in the public prints; and the professor, if he is conscientious, knows why he believes what he believes and why he tries to impart a particular "attitude" to his amiable but half-interested students.

But isn't it quaint that any serious proposal for social reform in America, once it has achieved a letterhead and an impressive list of advisory directors, tries to persuade schools and colleges to propagandize for its cause? "We should revise the textbooks!" "Every teacher in the land should convince his pupils, and they in turn will influence their parents." From incidental propaganda at assembly and in classes devoted to social problems the reform committees endeavor to establish courses, perhaps offering a little temptation in the way of financial aid. Most of the causes are good—temperance, driving automobiles safely, wild-life preservation. Currently there is an effort to increase the attention in college classes to the implications of atomic fission. The visitor from another planet might not question the worth of the causes. What ought to surprise him is that the simple and perennial task of teaching and learning—largely that of the teaching of the young—should be so confused with the political task of reform. We at home may comment that given the educational system as it stands, with the social demands now placed upon it, the performance of these enterprises of reform propaganda is a kind of half-loaf—better than nothing.

We are here concerned with the thinking of educational leaders about the purpose of teaching and learning. It is significant that while since the war the presiding purpose is the safety and prosperity of the nation, that purpose is qualified on the one hand by the notion that the individual must be entertained and on the other by the idea that human problems are subject to the strategic and organized treatment so successful in the technical part of military defense and the material part of prosperity. This latter conception further involves an opinion among educational leaders that one way to achieve the human results envisaged in the securing of peace is to regard what goes under the name of education for the majority of American young people as not education at all but conditioning, the end being the improvement of public opinion or attitude.

A cynical view indeed! The cynicism lies here: that the mass must be "conditioned," its "attitude" molded. Paradoxically all this is done in the name of the common man. The proposal for expanding this kind of education is supported by populist and egalitarian sentiments. But examined closely the proposal turns out to put a low estimate indeed upon the trustworthiness of the common man's own thinking. It is time to consult the shrewdness, the integrity, and the sound reasoning ability of the common man—the common man whose habitual rightness has led us to name after him that great corrective—common sense.

Clearly there is something wrong in the substitution of means for ends, but in analyzing the trouble for our own time we should not imagine that the educational task of teaching and developing the famous American know-how is either small or unimportant. On its success now depend not only the welfare of our own country and its military security but the food, health, and fortresses of a large part of the freedom-loving world. To train thousands of young technicians, some of them to a highly advanced level of graduate study, is an abiding obligation of the American system. But that the national safety will be immeasurably advanced if these same technicians are also permitted to learn and know in history and letters something of the ethos is part of the thesis of this book. Many an engineering school, sensing this problem, has added a few courses in the "humanities." Study of the catalogue announcement of many of these reveals, however, that they are not very mature courses nor are they accorded time adequate for truly mature study. A large portion of the courses is not strictly humane at all but merely descriptive of contemporary society. The few engineering schools which have extended the course to the Bachelor of Science in Engineering degree from four years to five are making a serious attempt to recognize in their students the double vocation: of an engineer and of a man. Better still are the curricular arrangements whereby a college graduate in the liberal arts and sciences may by postgraduate professional study obtain an engineering degree.

In summary of the current American practice and discussion of educational aims, it may be said that they are those of the modern state, largely welfare; the aims announced have substituted means for ends and are derived from social science. They may be summarized by the slogans: Education for Life Adjustment, and Conditioning the Attitude. They have dislodged the aim still effective in the best work of the best teachers: Conversion of the Reason. In implementation of these ends educational leaders have laid stress upon two elements of the management of the social enterprise represented by schools and universities: one of these is counseling and the other is vocational training. So thorough have the discussions of these two useful activities become, they have behaved like any camel once his nose has entered the tent. American educational thinking about the intent of teaching and learning is now largely managerial, despite the fact that our status as men and our national status in the world present to the teacher and learner problems which are largely ethical.

For American society to seek the aims of instructing young Americans strictly in social technology amounts to cultivating beauty in the beauty parlor while ignoring the inward experience which produces in men and women alike real beauty of countenance. Social aims for education are necessary for its arrangements, but when they guide teaching and learning, the result is necessarily meager—good, if the social philosophy is good, but still puny and inadequate beside the great ethical aims which have always motivated conversion of reason at its best.

Absorption in means has led many to sense, usually in maturity, the poverty of their plan, and frantically, at the eleventh hour, to add a paragraph somewhere in their thinking, concerning ends. The echo most easily heard in the times is a sentimental one. Today the word most commonly coupled with *moral* is *fervor*. The popular connotation of *spiritual* is related to the candle on an altar, the flame beneath a tripod, or a revival meeting. The admired head of a great engineering school recently said that the affairs of mankind should be guided by two things in addition to the splendid application of scientific knowledge to material problems for which his institution is justly famous. These two things, he said, are social technology and spiritual uplift. What we really need is not spiritual uplift at all but a critical understanding of spiritual fact.

Traditional American goals, American ideals, the American Dream—what should engage us first of all is not a goal, nor an ideal, nor a dream. It is an idea, something which exists, a fact about the natural world or our experience as men. It is to be hoped that we shall be brought face to face with the facts that freedom is first of all an affair of checks and balances in man's own private thought and action; that outward freedom safeguarded by checks and balances can be maintained—has been maintained by nations of men and women who in large numbers hold in common certain opinions about human nature; and that this idea has been made effective in the United States for over a century and a half.

There is indeed a dream that these facts will one day be recognized and applied for all. This is an objective towards which we work by means of law and our institutions. But it is downright risky to speak as frequently as we do about dreams and ideals, for to do so is to spread the illusion that the ethical understanding of the individual is a mere hope. Ideals are hopes, something longed for, and in popular usage the notion prevails that we *hope* that freedom of the individual may be true. There are plenty abroad and in our own land to seize upon this sentimental language of the "liberals" to announce that the hope is a false one. But the idea of freedom is a moral fact, perceived for centuries and exemplified now and then, here and there, among civilized peoples.

To talk about the American dream is to confuse this fact about our manhood with dreams of riches and comfort. To many, the American dream has become the picture advertising construction materials—a suburban "home" modestly landscaped, with a convertible in the garage. To others, the American dream connotes the hope of the immigrant for a farm of his own. These in their place are blessings, but to mix them up with the fact on which free government is based is to countenance the sugar-and-water philosophy which really holds at base that freedom is fine *for those who can be given it*, a kind and gentle humanitarian social security which has nothing to do with self-understanding, self-restraint, and self-mastery.

Sentimental talk about dreams has cast a hazy veil of fog across one of the greatest issues of political theory to arise since Magna Charta. It is defined by C. K. Allen in his *Law and Orders* as follows: "One conviction, or prepossession, is that the greater good consists in the maximum of individual liberty which is compatible with the common weal. The opposite conviction, or prepossession, is that the greater good is the common weal, of which the State is the supreme arbiter and dispenser, and that therefore individual liberty, though a good . . . must be secondary to the general welfare as planned and managed by the State."[7]

Wistful talk about the American dream has led to the dangerous confusion of economic guarantees with political ones, exemplified by the translation of the four historic American freedoms into a new and half-humanitarian set of four. Historically the four American freedoms are all political. Those affirmed by the First Amendment are freedom of worship, of speech, of publication, and of assembly. Since President Roosevelt's message to Congress in January 1941, on the State of the Union, the Four Freedoms have become freedom of worship and speech plus freedom *from* want and fear. No one likes want and fear of insecurity, but it is vital to our understanding of freedom itself that we never forget that if freedom of speech, worship, publication, and assembly are to be maintained, it may one day become necessary to abandon or qualify the recent American dream of guaranteed social security.

Preoccupation with social techniques and terminology and the consequent romantic reference to the ideas at the center of liberalism, has the following effect upon school work. On the one hand, these American dreams and hopes being treated as a "given" of history, little time is expended upon them; they are assumed. On the other, extensive descriptions of the social arrangements of the day interfere with devoting the precious hours of school and college to the critical knowledge and understanding of freedom itself, the ethical core of American life. Little time is left for the childhood and youthful mastery of letters and numbers essential to that critical study. The effect of devoting education to small if worthy social ends is to rely almost altogether, when it comes to commitment to the American idea, upon slogans. The chief and first obligation of education for all Americans would be some critical and active and inward understanding of what the slogans mean, by the beginnings, at least, of a study of our nature as men.

We cannot remind ourselves too often that schools are for teaching and learning. There are other institutions fit to serve other functions. Society may be served by schools if they perform tasks proper to them. These may not be clearly understood if one's thinking is confined to the philosophy of groups. The reason for this is that the society properly served by education is better understood as a community of persons than as an aggregate of individuals or groups with measurable characteristics and behavior. To see how the American community may be served we must inquire into the nature of community. It is not produced by natural gregariousness at all, but by passions and opinions held in common, by *le sens commun*, by the convention: that is, by the coming together of the best minds. Community is a moral matter, not first of all political or economic or even ethnic.

This fact was illustrated by a speech of Count Carlo Sforza, now Foreign Minister of Italy, to a class in Kenyon College. He had come that morning simply to read some *terza rimas*, and naturally he read them from Dante. Before reading he held the book before the class and said in substance: What makes a country? What would you say makes my country? Certainly not race; the origins of the Italian people are various and obscure. But wherever you walk in the street, north or south, you will hear words and phrases from this book, sometimes spoken by people who do not know they are quoting, sometimes spoken in complete stanzas. It is this one book more than any other one thing which unifies us. It is so with you. If ever an Englishman pretends that you have little, ask him what he has to compare with some of Lincoln's speeches and your Declaration and Constitution. These words and ideas make you a nation.

Those words and ideas signify what makes community. To find the fit aim for education in this mighty nation we must inquire what truly is common, until we lay down the beginning of the ways to the common apprehension of our common manhood—that is, the norm of human conduct. The Commission on Liberal Education says:

> In a period of technological prodigies and economic complexity, the crucial problem of education is to sustain and develop the individual. If social and economic welfare are realized, we are told, the individual can take care of himself. It is at least equally true that if an adequate number of individuals are unusually elevated, society can take care of itself. Education must be concerned both with man and with society. Its purpose must be to create a community of persons, not a mere aggregation of people.[8]

The community of persons is an ethical achievement; it is to be accomplished by increasing the number of those who renounce the anarchic individualism of which Igor Stravinsky spoke and master those virtues which mature an individual into a person. It may be achieved by attention to ends, in order that the things we care for most be not displaced by those we care for least. As the Committee on the Objectives of a General Education in a Free Society put it: "The apprehension of the norm–by approximation to it–is education itself, which is thus its own aim."

17

The "Social Role" of Education

At the end of the war the President of the United States appointed a commission to report on higher education "in terms of its objectives, methods and facilities: and in the light of the social role it has to play." Unfortunately the commission did not seize the chance to examine the objectives. Instead it projected the old sentimentality into a plan for multiplying the weaknesses we have. In the first place it proposed that the American university and college system become great in size. To achieve this end the commission advised us, despite the relaxation of recent years, to lower standards. It urged that preparation for college become even less specific than it is, and that we reduce still further what emphasis is now put upon "verbal skills" and "intellectual interests." All this the commission proposed for sociological reasons, not pausing to ask what would be the grim social consequences to America of further casualness in the university.

The commission also proposed to substitute "general education" for liberal education. There are now current two definitions of general education, each designed to describe a reform recommended within a great university. The University of Minnesota, required to concern itself with numerous young people of small promise or ambition or interest, or all three, who by law could not be removed from the company of promising and serious scholars, developed general education for them. This provides something interesting to do for those not equal to more. It includes many lectures about society, and offers, according to the catalogue, a course in the recreational facilities of the community. Given the laws of the state, the General College at Minnesota has proved useful, for besides solving a political problem for the university, it provides at least some intellectual stimulus to all its members. So at Minnesota general education is something which can profitably be offered to those who initially are not interested in learning. At Harvard the term has a different connotation. It means the common education thought by the Harvard committee on a General Education in a Free Society to be necessary to all thoughtful men, whatever their ultimate specialty. The President's Commission has chosen the Minnesota word, but—unlike that distinguished university—has proposed it as the norm for all undergraduates.

General education, according to the commission, should redefine "liberal education in terms of life's problems as men face them, to give it human orientation and social direction."[9] Concerned with "social techniques" and "attitudes," the commission urges that we teach by generalization rather than particulars. In commenting on this, Dean ten Hoor observed that to teach by generalization is the way to authoritarianism. The commission reiterates its disapproval of the view that some subjects are more nearly central than others; it prefers the student's own tastes at the moment of being a student to the critical judgment of mankind concerning the intellectual usefulness of the various disciplines. "The student and his rounded development will be at the centre of instructional activities, and subject matter at the periphery." At Kenyon College we hold the reverse to be true: that a young man makes a step in development if for the time being he forgets himself in beginning to master a few of the central disciplines of the mind.

The preference of the commission for a popular and unexacting idea of general education indicates its limited view of the "social role" of universities. I do not suggest that there is no social usefulness in the low-level popular education recommended. The National Youth Administration college program, for example, was regarded by many as a device to keep the young off the streets in a period of mass unemployment, and if in truth this was its only effect, it had a real if limited value. A similar usefulness of education is found by many in the fact that enrollment in tax-supported universities goes up when there is unemployment. Another real but limited social gain is envisaged in the commission's recommendation that greater masses of young people be lectured at to improve their attitude towards UNESCO and the United Nations. This proposal has the practical sound of telling people under excellent auspices what they ought to think. The concern of the Commission for adult education is laudable; so is its indignation at discrimination against Americans because of race or creed.

The chief weakness of the commission's report is its failure to grasp the nature and importance of high standards. The late Dean Emeritus of the Graduate School at Brown University, Dr. R. G. D. Richardson, the mathematician, said of this report, "If I had to give a title to some sections of the first volume, I would call them 'The Apotheosis of Mediocrity.' " The social reason why university education should not be of this order could be easily illustrated in religion or morals. An example from politics is to be found in the philosopher already mentioned on Page 10. In 1930, when American intellectuals saw in Russia a Utopia on earth, I heard him say that our chief interest in Russia should be that she was a potential military power. How bizarre his opinion seemed to the academic world of the time. Notice that he did not condemn Russia; he spoke of what Americans ought to take into consideration about it. In the mind of the scholar who made the remark, a deep and accurate familiarity with history, philosophy, letters and religion contributed to his judgment. It represents the kind of reasoning which we have a right to expect of higher education when we consider its social role. The detachment, the precise and wide knowledge, the acumen, and the intellectual boldness which prompted that remark in a time when fad demanded a precisely opposite "attitude" towards Russia represent the kind of ability which a university can make possible.

The President's Commission might have started its analysis of the *means* by which the functions of higher education in our democracy can best be performed by quoting Admiral Nimitz's famous letter on arithmetic. He wrote it at the beginning of the war, when our steel mills and automobile factories had proved adequate to mobilization. Our schools, in spite of gigantic enrollments and impressive plants, in certain respects had failed us. A deplorable proportion of otherwise qualified candidates for officer training in the Navy could not do fractions. The Army and Navy observed something similar about the inability to express a slightly complex idea with simplicity and speed, and the Commission might well have consulted the report on reading and writing prepared by the School and College Conference. When the Army foresaw the need for many interpreters in the European theater, it discovered how badly we teach languages in America. Facts about this, and how best to meet reasonable objectives for American schools and universities, have been studied by some of the ablest teachers in the country, and their reports might make a useful beginning in a re-examination of "the adequacy of curricula, particularly in the field of international affairs and social understanding."

If a study of objectives, functions, methods, and facilities had begun in some such fashion as this, it would no doubt have led on to the social and political problems considered by the President's commission, but in temper and standard the study would have been different from the one which was made. The wastage of the talented which the commission records would have come under review. Many of the best, though perhaps not so many as the commission states, do not attend college for lack of money. If the commission had recommended devices whereby an equal number of the least promising be put out to make room for the more promising, it would have dealt realistically with our limited resources of trained men and women to do the teaching. President Truman expressed concern in his appointing letter for all *able* young people. In the opinion of many scientists and scholars the net result of the commission's recommendations would be to reduce the opportunity for the able by further cluttering up the academic world with incompetents. According to a committee of the Association of American Colleges, "a student has the right to as good an education as he can be given and as he is capable of receiving; anything less than that is not only undemocratic but dangerous to the whole concept of higher education and intelligent citizenship."

That schools and universities need money is now a popular theme. Many schools and universities are extravagant in their poverty. The extravagance of the educational system in the United States appears when we spend money and talent for half-instruction; when we present something to young people which they do not quite learn; when we let students dodge the hard work of writing essays and solving problems which require their own original use of mathematics, language, and ideas; when we let ourselves avoid the expensive chore of marking essay examination questions; in short, when for whatever reason we accept substitutes for good performance by the student. A small indication of this extravagance has been seen at the School and College Conference held at Kenyon. After two days of discussion by superintendents, principals, and members of the Kenyon and other faculties, a group of college seniors and juniors meets with the school officials; no faculty members are present. The students usually ask most of the questions. A frequent one, addressed to the heads of some of the best high schools in the territory, has been: "Why did you waste our time?"

Perhaps we could afford the wastage before as a nation we assumed world obligations. At the center of the problem of the social role of schools and colleges lies the question whether we can afford it still. Our country has accepted the fact that world leadership entails military and financial outlay. Will the academic world wake up to the fact that it means intellectual strenuousness as well? I do not refer simply to political and social information about the world. I refer to what it takes to govern. To espouse democratic government demands intellectual and moral sinew as well as armies and good feeling.

Britain and America have followed opposite theories in the development of education: the British to refine and intensify, confining the facilities for higher study to a few; we to broaden the opportunity. For our several tasks in the world these two different courses were doubtless wise. If we agree, however, that many of the British tasks in the world have now fallen to us, we could with profit observe British education. In order to remain a democracy and still to guarantee the freedom of the seas, the British found it necessary to do a rigorous—some would say a too rigorous—job of keeping school. Surely we shall exert world leadership in our own and not the British way, but if we, with their help, are to succeed where in the past we all failed, it will be partly by virtue of trained intellect.

In Britain the pre-war university population was around 60,000, and a national commission recommended that by the 1950's it go up to 100,000. More recently, the 100,000 figure was revised to below 90,000 lest the quality of a university education be depressed! In Ohio, with a fraction of Britain's population, the university enrollment is now over 100,000. Britain is not America, but surely the British experience means something to us. One thing it means is that if we are to analyze well the problems of Orient, Near East, the American continents, and the islands of the sea, we need to refine and enrich our human knowledge—all the knowledge which we convey to ourselves in words, and the related knowledge conveyed by numbers. Thus in intellectual terms the social role of higher education would involve first of all the best achievable mastery of the humane knowledge necessary for liberal and democratic government at home and abroad.

This should stand at the center of the objectives of higher education; every device and plan, for the schools as well as the universities, should be made in the light of it. The other half of the social role of schools refers to mass education in political and social matters, and this remains a gigantic problem. Faced with this problem some professional educators long ago decided that the way to deal with it was to develop "attitudes" rather than to cope with the hard job of increasing the number who can, for instance, read critically.

The President's Commission reflects this view popular among professional educators. Suppose instead that the social objective for popular education were to bring a large number of people to the point where they can read accurately the editorials of the day. If this could be done on a fairly mature level by a substantial proportion of high-school graduates, one could abandon the dangerous business of "attitudes," for the people would have been provided with a means whereby they could form judgments of their own. This would be a democratic move in education, similar to that in Scotland and the Scandinavian countries. Then in truth the social role of education would be fulfilled in popular terms.

But how is this to be done? Secondary education needs money, it will need much more if it is to accomplish this task. Suppose we should build up truly excellent secondary schools with adequately paid and sufficiently large staffs. Higher education would benefit. Suppose also that national scholarships were available in competition for the most talented and accomplished, and that the thousands of these not now in college for financial reasons should take the place in the seats of the higher learning of those lacking intellectual and verbal skill—shifting them into types of training more suited to their talents, and in which they themselves would be happier and more successful. This would indeed be higher education for American democracy.

18

Education for Greatness

IN PLACE of the "disintegrated liberalism" for which American education was in part responsible between the wars must be substituted genuine liberalism, the training for which "has a pattern of its own." This is the ethical liberalism which arises from the effort to approximate the norm of human conduct, employing in the process candor, scepticism, and commitment, and recognizing always that the standard of manhood can never be delimited nor stated in absolutes. It relies upon faith that the norm exists, that by its fruits men may know it, and that by analysis and comparison they may agree upon important elements of it.

That this liberalism entails a critical and factual understanding of the sanctity of the individual and his inward responsibility is, while subject to critical debate, hardly disputed except by authoritarians. That it is a proper object of education is proved wherever rigorous teaching of the sciences, social sciences, and of the study of man proceeds.

Mankind has witnessed so many monstrous versions of greatness that in this egalitarian day one apologizes for the word. Would greatness for Americans mean a repetition of the boast that the sun never sets, this time on *our* empire? Would greatness for Americans mean an Army of all generals with no privates?

History always deals harshly with those who had power, for the best men in the best ages have been no more than human. Thus it is fashionable to denounce the mistakes of those who maintained the peace of the world in the century following the Congress of Vienna. Yet given the times and their felt necessities, we may now accord a meed of praise to the men who presided over the nineteenth century. For what it was worth, they established the freedom of the seas. What little there was of it, they afforded some opportunities for self-development in the dark continents. It is the fate of Americans now to take a leading part in making and securing the conditions of what freedom the world may acquire in this century. We pray that our decisions will be more intelligent than those of the nineteenth. Will our stature as men attain to the fullness of those who then did their best for world order? One long look at Asia today and a candid look at ourselves reveals the enormous demand for spiritual greatness at home. The greatness needed is the ancient largeness of the magnanimous man. Much of the responsibility for this lies with schools, colleges, and universities. The eyes of the world are upon us.

No nation on earth has ever succeeded in leading the world without yielding to the temptation to dominate and without ultimately becoming absorbed throughout its every thought and decision by considerations of empire. For periods, some of them long, there has been peace and good management, but not for all peoples, and imperial management has rarely permitted the managers—that is, the folks at home—to enjoy the liberty which Americans now prize. How is this responsibility of ours in the world to be met? The manhood required is of a peculiarly knowing and intelligent kind, in history called magnanimous. In the words of Lewis Mumford's essay on "The Corruption of Liberalism": "What is demanded is a recrystallization of the positive values of life, and an understanding of the basic issues of good and evil, of power and form, of force and grace, in the actual world." This entails, he said, "a social conversion, deep-seated, organic, religious in its essence, so that no part of personal or political existence will be untouched by it: a conversion that will transcend the arid pragmatism that has served as a substitute for religion."[1] That the ethical basis of this understanding is the necessary task of secular education has been proved in America in the past and can be redemonstrated in modern terms.

The foregoing pages have outlined two views of general education now common in America, the one proposed as a useful and kindly substitute for serious studies themselves and designed for students unable or unwilling to undertake liberal education. The other is proposed for every man; it is to be made available to each according to his ability to take and use. Such the common education of all American young people should be. Such in the Scandanavian countries and in Scotland it has been for generations, irrespective of the final profession or calling of the student.

The object here proposed for the common education of all is the beginning of the understanding of our nature as men, to the end that all will possess some reason of the American belief about the individual. The Adjustment to Life program and other devices substituting for this an image of American society and determining education by vocations are offered by their proponents as an improvement on teaching "Tennyson and compound verbs." Let Tennyson and compound verbs be taken here as exemplary of the mastery of how to read and to understand ideas set forth in words. A greater poet might have been named, and a device more necessary to critical thinking than compound verbs; but let these two stand. To teach a boy and a girl how to read with accuracy and to alert him knowingly to sense and weigh what he reads is more conducive to peace than to discuss with him a few generalizations about society which social thinkers have prepared for him in advance—and will be likely to change within a decade.

Objectors will say that the students we now have in school will not "go for" this human "stuff," that they will drop out if you teach them "Locksley Hall." Let us remember that "Locksley Hall" is not the only possibility! And they do not drop out when some teachers teach even such a minor poem as "Locksley Hall."

I am answered: Oh, yes, those teachers are the exception. Do you know the kind of material we get for teachers these days? I answer that the colleges get excellent material for teachers. But examine what the teachers' colleges teach them! A young person of native ability and talent is asked to teach literature after the laws of the state have required her to waste her time for four years of college studying anything but literature—studying, instead, the mere techniques of how to teach it!

The reforms here proposed will have no effect whatever on the teaching of many good teachers in school and college, except that their work will be supported and praised. But if implemented, the reforms will have profound effect on the aims and curricula and climate of intention and opinion in most of the teacher-training institutions. Well-taught, the able young teachers can make letters and reasoning live for adolescents. But the reforms here proposed would require first of all a return to the center by the educational leadership, so that the public—which means parents and editors and the man in the street—would begin to understand that the cause why the schools demand more of the taxpayers' money is that the reason always needs conversion; that by good instruction and self-instruction it is slowly converted; and that this miracle, evident in every Thirty-fourth Street which boasts a public school, is a daily occurrence, but one which can be invited only when school and community provide the right conditions—these being, on the material side, ample pay for enough teachers.

Our dispute with the Kremlin underlines the fact that American education should choose: condition the attitude or convert the reason. If the latter is taken as the aim, several results will follow, of which I shall name four. The first is a change in the expectation lodged in the hearts of numerous officers of schools, numerous parents and students, of what schools and colleges properly may accomplish. If what is expected is the beginning of an understanding of the Law for Man and the Law for Thing, clearly the techniques of this understanding will be seriously respected—letters and numbers. That in itself would represent a major change in the announced aims of many parts of the educational system. In the middle of the twentieth century in America the change would probably not mean a revival of Greek and Latin as the nineteenth century knew it, but it would mean a serious study of language and literature for ethical purposes and for reasoning purposes, and a re-appraisal of the relation of this study to the new interest in aesthetics, which would be found, I believe, to fall comfortably within the great humane study of poetry or representative fiction.

A second change would be evident in the philosophy and program of the teacher-training institutions. In an able essay published in the *Universities Review*, Dr. Oliver C. Carmichael rightly observed that many of the young people most promising as teachers will continue to show little interest in study at the teachers' colleges unless these change their educational philosophy. In general the substitution of the techniques of teaching for knowledge itself of what is to be taught has probably discouraged more imaginative and honest minds from commitment to the American school system than lack of financial compensation.

Adoption of these aims for education would in the third place require that the strictly technical, philological, and escapist studies of the arts and letters be understood for what they are, rather recent peripheral movements in the great humane study and not central to it. These deflections of scholarly talent have their place. It will be important for education that their proper place be known and that the main energies of literary and historical scholarship and teaching be devoted to the matters of high seriousness which alone can produce the necessary maturity.

It will be important, finally, to distinguish between the immediate social problems which confront mankind and the related but more fundamental problem, particularly in the education of the young student, of knowing what really are the elements and qualities of human nature. At the recent half-century celebration at the Massachusetts Institute of Technology one of the panels discussed the antithesis so commonly mentioned in commencement addresses between the success of engineering techniques and the failure of social ones. Mr. Churchill in commenting on the discussion pointed out that the key to this problem lies in understanding the nature of the individual:

One of the questions which we are debating here is defined as "The Failure of Social and Political Institutions to Keep Pace with Material and Technical Change." Scientists should never underrate the deep-seated qualities of human nature and how, repressed in one direction, they will certainly break out in another. The *genus homo*—if I may display my Latin—is a tough creature who has traveled here by a very long road. His nature has been shaped and his virtues ingrained by many millions of years of struggle, fear, and pain, and his spirit has, from the earliest dawn of history, shown itself upon occasion capable of mounting to the sublime, far above material conditions or mortal terrors. He still remains as Pope described him 200 years ago:

> Placed on this isthmus of a middle state,
> A being darkly wise and rudely great;
>
> . . . .
>
> Created half to rise, and half to fall—;
> Great Lord of all things, yet a prey to all—;
> Sole judge of truth, in endless error hurl'd;
> The glory, Jest, and riddle of the world![2]

The concern of the teacher is not first of all "The Failure of Social and Political Institutions," but the fact that learning and systematic reason so often underrate the deep-seated qualities of human nature. Another wartime leader, General Omar Bradley, put the proposition even more sharply than did Mr. Churchill. "Ours is a world of nuclear giants and ethical infants," said Bradley; "with the monstrous weapons man already has, humanity is in danger of being trapped in this world by its moral adolescents." It is altogether possible that despite the fanfare of post-war reform the American educational system will continue to promote moral adolescence. That is the first danger of the present, the danger most pertinent to society and politics and most appropriate to be dealt with by education. For the proper object of school and college is moral maturity.

Would cities support the kind of education which would follow if the ends here proposed should become the presiding ones? We shall not know in modern times until we try. Two facts bid us make the attempt. One is the common possession by all men of fiction and history, and their spontaneous use of these in progressively re-forming for themselves the picture of manhood by which their ethical decisions are measured. The other is the stake for which, in our judgment concerning the aim of keeping school, we must play. For what hangs upon our decision is nothing less than the maintenance and renewal from generation to generation of our understanding why we can make no peace with tyranny.

At the beginning of the period of contemporary liberalism, roughly at the beginning of the nineteenth century, it was well understood among liberal thinkers that free opportunity was opportunity for greatness. Men were thought capable of greatness within themselves, whatever might be the limits of their own physical powers to do a job or acquire status in society. This greatness was expected. Being expected of everyman, it emerged in many. In terms of magnanimity—that is, of the perception and understanding and generous actions of which a freely and imaginatively instructed person is capable—this liberal expectation should be revived. The Supreme Court of the United States has handed down the statement that "nothing is more certain in modern society than the principle that there are no absolutes." It cannot be too often repeated that nothing is more certain in modern society than that the continuance of the republic is based on the quality of the individual and his education as a person, and that liberty is based upon a belief in and understanding of the moral law.

THE END

NOTES

NOTES

NOTES TO CHAPTER II

1. Robert A. Dahl. *Congress and Foreign Policy*. New York, Harcourt, Brace, 1950, p. 84.
2. Lewis Mumford. "The Corruption of Liberalism." *New Republic*, 102: 568-73, April 29, 1940.
3. Max Lerner. "The Left: End and Beginning." *Nation*, 150: 166, February 10, 1940.
4. Mumford. *Op. cit.*
5. Archibald MacLeish. "The Irresponsibles." *Nation*, 150: 618-23, May 18, 1940.
6. *Ibid.*
7. *Ibid.*
8. *Ibid.*
9. "A Reply to Mr. Evans." *Saturday Review of Literature*, 32: 22, July 2, 1949.

NOTES TO CHAPTER III

1. *Education for* All *American Youth*. Washington, D. C., The Educational Policies Commission of the National Education Association, 1944, p. 142.
2. *General Education in a Free Society*. Harvard University. Committee on the Objectives of General Education in a Free Society. Cambridge, Harvard University Press, 1945, p. 251.
3. *Ibid.*, p. 40.
4. *Ibid.*, p. 40.
5. *Ibid.*, p. 96.
6. *Ibid.*, p. 93.

NOTES TO CHAPTER IV

1. Alexander Pope. *Essay on Man*. Epistle II.
2. Sir John Davies. "The Vanity of Human Learning." Stanzas 25 and 45.

3. Letter of Donald Fay Robinson. *Saturday Review of Literature*, July 16, 1949.

4. Arthur T. Vanderbilt. *A Report on Prelegal Education;* presented . . . to the House of Delegates of the American Bar Association on September 13, 1944, and to the Association of American Colleges on January 11, 1945. Chicago, n.d., p. 27.

5. *Ibid.*, pp. 26-27.

NOTES TO CHAPTERS V-VI

1. *Harper's Magazine*. June 1943.

2. Algo D. Henderson. "College and the Century of the Common Man." *The American Scholar*, 12:468-69, Autumn 1943.

3. Winston Churchill. *Their Finest Hour* ("The Second World War," Vol. II). Boston, Houghton Mifflin, 1949, p. 118.

4. Sir Charles Oman. *The Sixteenth Century*. New York, Dutton, 1937, p. 62.

5. *Ibid.*, p. 68.

6. Oliver Wendell Holmes. *John Lothrop Motley, a Memoir.* Boston, Houghton Mifflin, 1889, p. 210.

7. Mumford. "The Corruption of Liberalism," *op. cit.*

8. *Works of John Lothrop Motley*. New York, Harper & Bros., 1900, VI, 7-8.

9. Maxwell Anderson. *Off Broadway, Essays about the Theatre.* New York, Wm. Sloane, 1947, p. 63.

10. *Ibid.*, p. 65.

NOTES TO CHAPTERS VII-VIII

1. Mark Van Doren. *Liberal Education.* New York, Henry Holt, 1943, pp. 22-23.

2. Igor Stravinsky. *Poetics of Music in the form of Six Lessons*, translated by Arthur Knodel and Ingolf Dahl. Cambridge, Harvard University Press, 1947, pp. 74-75.

3. Jean Anouilh. "Antigone," in *Nouvelles pièces noires.* Paris, La Table Ronde, 1949, pp. 165-66.

4. "Report of the Commission on Liberal Education." *Association of American Colleges Bulletin*, 33: 693, December 1947.

5. Ralph Barton Perry. "A Definition of the Humanities," in *The Meaning of the Humanities.* Princeton, Princeton University Press, 1938, pp. 40-41.

NOTES TO CHAPTER IX

1. Vanderbilt, *op. cit.*, pp. 31-32.
2. Oliver Wendell Holmes, Jr. "The Path of the Law" (1897) in *Collected Legal Papers.* New York, Harcourt, Brace, 1920, p. 187.
3. Oliver Wendell Holmes, Jr. *The Common Law.* Boston, Little, Brown, 1938, p. 1.
4. Vanderbilt, *op. cit.*, p. 41.
5. *Ibid.*
6. *Ibid.*, p. 38.
7. *Ibid.*
8. *Ibid.*, p. 39.
9. American Council of Learned Societies. *Liberal Education Re-examined: Its Role in a Democracy;* by a specially appointed committee: Theodore H. Greene, Chairman; Charles C. Fries, Henry M. Wriston, William Dighton. New York, Harper & Bros., 1943, p. 60.
10. "Report of the Commission on Liberal Education," pp. 695-96.
11. Vanderbilt, *op. cit.*, p. 41.
12. *Ibid.*, p. 42.
13. F. S. Oliver. *The Endless Adventure.* Boston, Houghton Mifflin, 1931, I, 99.
14. Murray Seasongood. *Local Government in the United States.* Cambridge, Harvard University Press, 1934, p. 145.
15. *Ibid.*, p. 144.
16. Edward Pendleton Herring. *The Politics of Democracy.* New York, W. W. Norton & Co., 1940, p. 34.
17. *Ibid.*, p. 33.

NOTES TO CHAPTERS X-XII

1. Massachusetts Institute of Technology. Report of the President, Karl T. Compton. ca. 1949.
2. Sir Thomas Browne. *Religio Medici.*
3. S. N. Behrman. *The Pirate.* Act I, Scene III. This passage is quoted from actor's text. The published text (New York, Random House, 1943, p. 77) differs from this, but the actor's text is used here.
4. *Liberal Education Re-Examined: Its Role in a Democracy.*

5. Brand Blanshard, *et al. Philosophy in American Education, Its Task and Opportunities.* New York, Harper & Bros., 1945.
6. Sir Richard Livingstone. *Education for a World Adrift*, p. 25. In *On Education*, containing two books previously published separately, *The Future in Education* and *Education for a World Adrift.* New York, Macmillan, 1944.

NOTES TO CHAPTER XIV

1. Walter de la Mare. *Broomsticks.* New York, Alfred A. Knopf, 1925, p. 306.
2. *Ibid.*, p. 315.
3. *Ibid.*, p. 306.
4. Willa Cather. *Death Comes for the Archbishop.* Boston, Houghton Mifflin, 1938, pp. 20-22.
5. Thornton Wilder. *Our Town.* New York, Coward McCann, Inc., 1938, pp. 124-25.

NOTES TO CHAPTER XV

1. James Bryant Conant. *Education in a Divided World.* Cambridge, Harvard University Press, 1948, p. 108.
2. *Ibid.*, p. 105.
3. *Ibid.*, p. 103.
4. *Ibid.*, pp. 105-6.
5. *Ibid.*, pp. 74-75.
6. *Ibid.*, p. 93.
7. *Ibid.*, p. 105.
8. *Ibid.*, p. 230.
9. *Ibid.*, p. 105.
10. *Ibid.*, p. 89.
11. *General Education in a Free Society*, p. 107.
12. James Bryant Conant. *Public Education and the Structure of American Society.* Julius and Rosa Sachs Endowment Fund Lectures. New York, Teachers College, Columbia University, 1946, p. 28.
13. *Ibid.*, pp. 28-29.
14. Algo D. Henderson. *Vitalizing Liberal Education.* New York, Harper & Bros., 1944, p. 45.
15. Conant. *Education in a Divided World*, p. 88.
16. Walter C. Bronson. *The History of Brown University.* Providence, Brown University, 1914, p. 500.

17. *New Englands First Fruits.* London, 1643. Reprinted in Samuel Eliot Morison. *The Founding of Harvard College.* Cambridge, Harvard University Press, 1935.
18. Conant. *Public Education*, p. 27.
19. Conant. *Education in a Divided World*, pp. 89-90.
20. Seymour E. Harris. *How Shall We Pay for Education?* New York, Harper & Bros., 1948, p. 17.
21. *Ibid.*, p. 18.
2.2 Conant, *op. cit.*, p. 85.
23. *Ibid.*, p. 86.
24. *Ibid.*, p. 85.
25. *Ibid.*, p. 113.

NOTES TO CHAPTERS XVI-XVII

1. *General Education in a Free Society.*
2. *Education for* All *American Youth*, p. 40.
3. *Ibid.*, pp. 43-44.
4. *Ibid.*, p. 44.
5. *Ibid.*, pp. 135-36.
6. Jack Harrison Pollack. "Revolution in United States Education." *This Week Magazine*, August 14, 1949.
7. Carleton Kemp Allen. *Law and Orders.* London, Stevens & Sons, Ltd., 1947, p. 280.
8. "Report of Commission on Liberal Education," *op. cit.*
9. The President's Commission on Higher Education. *Higher Education for American Democracy.* Washington, D. C., United States Government Printing Office, 1947 and 1948, I, 49 *passim.*

NOTES TO CHAPTER XVIII

1. Lewis Mumford. "The Corruption of Liberalism."
2. Winston Churchill. *New York Times,* April 1, 1949, p. 10.

INDEX OF NAMES

INDEX OF NAMES